WE KNOW ALL ABOUT YOU

WE KNOW ALL
ABOUT YOU

The Story of Surveillance in Britain and
America

RHODRI JEFFREYS-JONES

Reg

with thanks & best wishes

Rhodri

OXFORD
UNIVERSITY PRESS

OXFORD

UNIVERSITY PRESS

Great Clarendon Street, Oxford, OX2 6DP,
United Kingdom

Oxford University Press is a department of the University of Oxford.
It furthers the University's objective of excellence in research, scholarship,
and education by publishing worldwide. Oxford is a registered trade mark of
Oxford University Press in the UK and in certain other countries

Published in the United States of America by Oxford University Press
198 Madison Avenue, New York, NY 10016, United States of America

British Library Cataloguing in Publication Data

Data available

Library of Congress Control Number: 2016955206

ISBN 978–0–19–874966–0

Printed in Great Britain by
Clays Ltd, St Ives plc

CONTENTS

CONTENTS

LIST OF ILLUSTRATIONS

ACKNOWLEDGEMENTS

I would like to acknowledge the help of a number of individuals who helped me prepare this book for publication: Paul Addison, David Anderson, Richard B. Bernstein, Alun Burge, Duncan Campbell, Doug Charles, Bob Cherny, Frank Cogliano, Malcolm Craig, Jane Dawson, Harry Dickinson, Owen Dudley Edwards, Sylvia Ellis, Neil Evans, Frances Goldin, Alex Goodall, Annette Gordon-Reed, Fabian Hilfrich, Louise Jackson, Jay Kleinberg, John A. Logan, Chris Moran, Kathy Olmsted, David Omand, Lucy Parker, Damien Van Puyvelde, Charles Raab, Rob Singh, David Stafford, Pat Storey, and Reg Whitaker.

These men and women showed exceptional collegiality in advising me on research and in supplying critiques of my work in draft. Many corrections and improvements came from my private readers, and frank advice caused me to delete various ill-conceived passages.

The idea for the book arose in conversation with Matthew Cotton at OUP, and he has been a most supportive editor.

To all the foregoing, I am deeply grateful.

If I have retained my sanity throughout these proceedings, it is thanks to the distractions of matrimony, and for that I am grateful, as ever, to my wife Mary.

Introduction

'It's for you.' I left my room in search of the phone. Back in 1964, English boarding houses were primitive and there were no extensions, let alone Wi-Fi. Picking up the receiver four floors down, I heard my father's voice.

'The Bishop of Bangor called.' My father and the bish were pals.

'He has received a strange request from the security service.' The Americans had lodged a query about my visa application to be allowed to study in the United States. There was some troublesome information about me. Would the bishop kindly supply a report that would help decide the matter one way or the other?

I knew what this was about. As a schoolboy five years previously, I had attended a church conference in Bangor and fallen under the spell of Father Trevor Huddleston, a supporter of the South African communist Nelson Mandela. Responding to an invitation from BBC Radio Wales, I had delivered a Welsh-language talk in support of Mandela. I was quite impressed that the Americans must have translated it.

'So what shall I tell the bishop?', asked my father.

'If I phone you back tomorrow, Dad, can I reverse the charges?' The next day, I dictated a glowing character reference to the old man. He relayed it to the bishop. I assume that the bish passed it on to his original interlocutor, and that it found its way to the American Embassy. Anyway, the visa arrived.

I had further experiences with watchers in that decade. At Harvard, as a postgraduate fellow who advised an undergraduate committee on the selection of visiting lecturers, I had responded to the complaint that they had dull speakers. To enliven the programme, I suggested the historian Herbert Aptheker. A member of the American Communist Party, Aptheker had outraged the political establishment by visiting North Vietnam, a country engaged in military hostilities against American forces (the invitation almost got my undergraduate counterpart expelled from the university). The day of the talk arrived, and we headed to Boston's Logan Airport to collect our guest. Driving along Storrow Drive on the way back to the campus, I noticed we were being followed. 'Oh', said Aptheker, 'that's Fred, my FBI tail. He's a regular guy. We baby-sit for each other.'

Another experience occurred many years later, on 19 October 2015. On that day, I wanted to access the consumer magazine *Which?* and searched for it through Google. That private organization facilitates the lion's share of online searches, and what I am about to say is doubtless a common experience. Instead of putting me through to my chosen destination, Google asked me first to agree to its terms and conditions, a requirement I had not previously been aware of. Its privacy 'reminder' stated that Google collected data about its users, drawing on online search information about restaurants visited, videos watched, and so forth, and that it processed the information to find out, for example, where users were located. It used the information to improve services—and to deliver ads. In other words, if you use Google you are under a sophisticated form of private surveillance.

My goal in this book is to tell the story of surveillance in two countries that have been intimately linked in digital as in other matters, the United States and the United Kingdom. My focus will be on the understudied phenomenon of private surveillance, as well as on public surveillance in the two countries. I point to unsavoury aspects of the history of the surveillance state and underline the potential for further harm; I also emphasize that private surveillance has been detrimental to US and UK citizens' rights in the past, and represents a real danger today.

In the book I am at pains to show that private surveillance does confer benefits. Take, for example, the video facilities built into mobile phones. Quick-witted citizens have recorded racist chants in football games in the United Kingdom and France, and exposed the behaviour of trigger-happy policemen in the USA. One sociologist has noted how 'every individual can be a potential electronic eye on the misbehaviour of organizations and the abuse of power'.[1]

Nevertheless, the growing dangers of private surveillance are real and tend to be overlooked or subordinated to fears of state surveillance. For example, George Orwell addressed the danger of the security state in his 1940s novel *Nineteen Eighty-Four*, but ignored private snooping. Sixty years later, an article in the *Islington Tribune* focused on a peculiarity of the area around 27b Canonbury Square, Orwell's London address at the time of *Nineteen Eighty-Four*'s publication. Within 200 yards of his old flat, there were over thirty CCTV cameras—all of them private. (See Illustration 1.) A more recent novelist, John le Carré, has shown awareness of the private

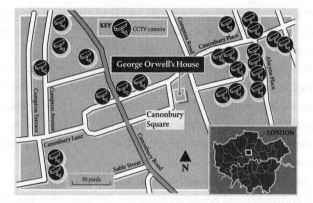

ILLUSTRATION 1. Private CCTV around Orwell's address. The presence of such prolific CCTV within 200 yards of George Orwell's final house in Canonbury Square, London, prompted the *Daily Mail*'s Bob Graham to remark (31 March 2007) that 1984 had 'finally arrived'. But the *Islington Tribune* (6 April 2007) found that 'far from being instruments of the state, the cameras—more than 30 of them—belong to private companies and well-to-do residents'.

dimension of surveillance. In his spy thriller *A Delicate Truth*, a Le Carré character rails against American 'carpetbaggers' who 'rush towards corporatization' in today's 'Deep State'. By and large, however, private surveillance is a neglected subject.[2]

A harmful and largely ignored dimension of the corporatization of intrusiveness has been the anti-labour blacklist. In the United Kingdom in particular, certain employers and their private agents kept entire workforces under surveillance. Did they visit the bathroom too often? Did they harp on about dangerous working conditions? Above all, did they engage in trade union activity? As indicated in the following pages, the more unscrupulous employers dismissed and blacklisted offenders. The practice encouraged fear and compliance amongst millions of ordinary working people long before the middle classes awoke to the perils of having their Facebook conversations monitored.

The histories of blacklisting and labour espionage in the United Kingdom and USA are often intertwined, and so are the stories of state surveillance. Anglo-American cooperation in code-breaking was a feature of the two World Wars and of the Cold War. It continues in the war against terrorism and is a cornerstone of the surveillance state.

'McCarthyism' was another strand in the story of surveillance. It had both public and private dimensions. Although it has long been regarded as an approximate label in the United States, everyone knows what it implies, and most believe it to have been an especially American problem. It did have distinctively American features, such as the Hollywood blacklist. It has long been asked, however, whether there may have been a 'silent McCarthyism' in the United Kingdom. Subsequent pages give an answer in the affirmative.

The book will review not just surveillance, but also the debate about it. The Fourth Amendment to the United States Constitution protects the 'right of the people to be secure in their persons, houses, papers, and effects, against unreasonable searches and seizures' and is accepted as a guarantee of privacy in the face of unwarranted electronic or other intrusion. This US constitutional right and its equivalent in other countries has nevertheless run into a pragmatic obstacle: the need to ensure public order and national defence. There has been a long debate about how and when the enforcement of Fourth Amendment rights may be appropriate or otherwise.

Take, for example, the criticisms of the War on Terror launched by President George W. Bush and supported by Prime Minister

Tony Blair and his successors. The enhancement of surveillance to the detriment of privacy was a salient component of the Bush–Blair campaign. But serious questions arose about their assumptions. In November 2014 the Global Terrorism Index recorded a growth in the number of fatalities caused by terrorism worldwide—from 3,361 in 2000 to 17,958 in 2013.[3] Did this mean that surveillance was a failure, with Fourth Amendment-style rights sacrificed in vain, or was there something wrong with other components of the War on Terror, or would the fatalities have been even higher without surveillance?

The story of surveillance cries out to be told, and demands treatment of both its private and its public dimensions. This book suggests the need for a reassessment both of the story to date and of its lessons for us today.

1

A Survey of Surveillance

There is no doubting the antiquity of the spying profession. The Bible and the Koran mention spies. Alfred the Great had his undercover agents. Sir Francis Walsingham directed intelligence operations for Elizabeth I. Conscious of the tradition, the Elizabethan playwright William Shakespeare cast Henry V as devious: 'The King hath note of all that they intend, By interception which they dream not of.'

The leaders of our modern age show no sign of abandoning these time-honoured practices. The American diplomat Henry Stimson once remarked that real gentlemen do not pry into each other's correspondence, but former CIA director Allen Dulles put him right: 'When the fate of a nation and the lives of its soldiers are at stake, gentlemen do read each other's mail.' Soon after Dulles's observation, the Democrats' outrage at President Richard Nixon's bugging of their Watergate headquarters prompted Mao Zedong to raise his Red eyebrow: 'But we all bug our opponents, don't we, and everybody knows about it?'[1]

Interest in spying has become universal. Thanks to fiction and the media, aficionados are now familiar with the elements of spying's 'tradecraft' ranging from trash trawling to white noise. The spy story is mainstream—and escapist, for espionage is a far-away activity that happens to other people and not to the average reader or viewer. Mr and Ms Everyperson can curl up in bed and enjoy it in safety.

Surveillance is another matter. Surveillance in the modern understanding of the word is spying on a *mass* scale. Pre-emptive and pervasive, it can invade any office, any home. The story of how it developed has never been fully told but it should be considered, as it carries the instructive force of a parable.

There have been antecedents to the modern phenomenon of surveillance. In major religions, after all, God is presumed to be all seeing. Mortals have periodically tried to emulate the example. The Torah's Book of Numbers relates how in the interest of social order the Israelites organized a census following their flight into Palestine from Egypt. Compilers of the Normans' Domesday Book of 1086 pried into the lives and property of individuals throughout the conquered land of England. The French historian Emmanuel Le Roy Ladurie explained how the Inquisition examined in the minutest detail the lives of all the people of one village, Montaillou, in an effort to understand and suppress the thirteenth-century Albigensian heresy.

Surveillance of a non-governmental kind has always existed in one form or another. Mothers spied on their pubescent daughters long before the age of literacy and the purloined diary. Until the nineteenth century, when larger and more solidly built houses became commonplace, servants routinely listened through walls and it was difficult to have sex in private. According to privacy historian David Flaherty, Puritanism in early America 'encouraged mutual surveillance'. Informing on one's neighbour was a religious duty and those who did not inform shared in the transgressor's guilt. Henry Adams wrote of the pre-Revolutionary American clergy that their power 'was originally minute and inquisitory, equivalent to a police authority'.

In spite of these early examples, surveillance as we commonly discuss it today is mainly a post-1770s phenomenon. It was the product of an inquisitive age. Europeans in the late eighteenth century exulted in a new spirit of inquiry, the Enlightenment. That spirit soon metamorphosed into something else. France's introduction of passports facilitated the movements of those who wished to broaden their knowledge through travel, but was also a means of inquiring into and keeping tabs on their activities. Napoleon's Europe-wide intelligence system was, according to his supporters, an instrument of liberation from royalist tyrannies, but its victims thought otherwise. Crossing the Channel, the Westminster Police Act and Alien Act of 1792 and 1793, respectively, led to domestic political espionage by the government of William Pitt the Younger and, according to historian Elizabeth Sparrow, 'a complete system of surveillance' that helped to save the United Kingdom from revolution. The Alien Office records might have revealed some dubious expenditures, had they not been destroyed. The system did not survive Pitt's death in 1806, but in the aftermath of the Napoleonic wars a renewed espionage vogue led to the penetration of the Chartist movement in England and Wales, and its equivalent, the Radical movement, in Scotland.[2]

However, the Enlightenment spirit of inquiry had other consequences: the desire to know what was going on in government, to probe into what lay behind some of its secret practices, and to curb those practices. In other words, it promoted anti-surveillance. The Scandinavian nations launched some initiatives. But a new nation, the United States, would play the leading role. If one is looking for turning points in the history of anti-surveillance, one of these occurred in the USA at the start of the 1790s. This was American resistance to the general search warrant.

Not least among the reasons for America's rebellion against the Mother Country had been the Crown's abuse of such warrants. For the authorities to search a person's house for good cause can be perfectly reasonable. But it is less reasonable if they search as part of an indiscriminate dragnet inquiry, entering people's houses without any evidential pointers to criminal behaviour. Such speculative raids can be politically motivated, vindictive, or an attempt to browbeat potential dissenters. The real motives behind such searches are usually kept secret or obscured by the issuance of vague justifications.

Europeans had long objected to the dangers inherent in the general search warrant. There was Roman legislation on the point. The framers of Magna Carta and of English common law tried to restrain the use of the unrestricted warrant. On the eve of the American Revolution, the radical Englishman John Wilkes prevailed in the case *Entick v Carrington* (1762) after the Crown had tried to silence him by raiding the houses of his friends. With their country in a state of upheaval, many Americans agreed with the principle that there should be a demonstration of probable cause before the Crown invaded a person's privacy. In 1780 John Adams incorporated a proscription of general warrants into Article XIV of the Massachusetts Declaration of Rights.

In their Revolution, Americans had purged their nation of royalism. With the exceptions of slaves and women they became sovereign citizens instead of mere subjects. Anti-federalists in the newly formed United States still feared that oppressive government might return, and took further steps to enshrine their principles in immutable law. They dominated the politics of several states, and had it in their power to prevent ratification of the United States Constitution drawn up in 1787. As a condition of their support for the Constitution, they insisted on the adoption of the first ten amendments, known also as the American Bill of Rights. Under the watchful eye of Thomas Jefferson who had drafted the Declaration of Independence, James Madison wrote the free speech and other clauses that would become so critical to the preservation of liberty.

Ratified in 1791 along with the other nine amendments and the main text of the Constitution, the fourth of these amendments declared: 'The right of the people to be secure in their persons, houses, papers, and effects, against unreasonable searches and seizures, shall not be violated, and no Warrants shall issue, but upon probable cause, supported by Oath or affirmation, and particularly describing the place to be searched, and the persons or things to be seized.'

The Fourth Amendment is still a live constitutional issue because it failed to kill off the general search warrant. It remained evident in the twentieth and twenty-first centuries that authorities on both sides of the Atlantic resented any such curb placed on their powers. For example, in 1911, Home Secretary Winston Churchill responded to fears of German espionage by extending the Home Office Warrant system, giving the domestic security service MI5 greater powers to conduct general searches. In the United States, the investigative tool known as the National Security Letter came into being in the administration of President Jimmy Carter (1977–81). An administrative subpoena, such a letter bypasses the courts to compel the delivery of information that might help defend national security. After 9/11, National Security Letters were widely used in the pursuit of terrorism suspects. They authorized surveillance of the internet, a practice that the American Civil Liberties Union and many other Americans found to be an affront to Fourth Amendment rights.

These examples show that the adoption of the Fourth Amendment did not settle the surveillance debate. But it did ignite it. It was a historical landmark because, for the first time, it enshrined the right to privacy in the written constitution of a nation state. It is of further significance because the nation state in question was a republican democracy. From now on, those in power would have to contend with the principle that privacy rights extended by constitutional decree to all citizens, and thus would have to heed the views of the voting citizens who held them to account on election days.

The Fourth Amendment sprang from colonial circumstances but also offered a way of curbing excesses that lay in the future, for the form of mass spying that we call surveillance had not yet become a major feature of American society. The amendment had come not a moment too soon, for such surveillance lay just around the corner.

Surveillance arrived on the world stage earlier than the emergence of police states such as the Soviet Union (with its KGB) and Germany (Gestapo, Stasi). The sociologist David Lyon notes that in Europe's nation states the growth of military organization, of urbanization, and of capitalism all contributed to the development of surveillance.[3]

The United States, however, took the lead. Contrary to the assumptions of those who have concentrated on the role of the organized state, it was the distinctively American combination of weak government and strong business that underpinned the rise of surveillance. That implies an urban setting, yet an early example of widespread private surveillance occurred on the slave plantations of rural America. Plantation managers, aptly known as 'overseers', were on the lookout for slave rebellions of one kind or another. The prospect of general uprisings was frightening, and individual slaves' attempts to escape to freedom were, if successful, costly to their owners. Slave patrols complemented the work of the overseers. They operated in Barbados and in the North American colonies. A group of private white individuals, either volunteers or paid for by slaveholders, would police their local area looking for slaves who were travelling without permission, and hunt for those trying to escape their plantation. The consequences for recaptured slaves would be horrendous, ranging from death to mutilation.

This did not make the American South a police state. Government was too decentralized, and those who undertook the task of placing persons of African descent under close scrutiny were private individuals. Slaves who were told to travel on their masters' business, for example to a local market, would carry passes they could show the patrolmen to prove that they were on 'legitimate' business. Private entrepreneurs, the slave owners, issued the passes. Together with France's passport, these privately issued slave passes were precursors of the modern ID card.

Though the slave passes were privately issued, there was some enabling legislation. Both before and after the revolution, South Carolina set a legislative framework for the system of passes, or of identifying tags to be worn by slaves. In the nineteenth century the southern states and some northern states like Illinois passed 'Black Codes' restricting the movement of African Americans, thus subjecting them to surveillance. On the national level, abolitionists dubbed the Fugitive Slave legislation of 1850 the 'Bloodhound Law' to highlight the way in which slaves trying to escape to freedom were tracked down. The Civil War followed by slave emancipation in the 1860s marked the beginning of the end of a type of surveillance that was privately organized in the main, but had nevertheless attracted some government support.

The slave owners and slave hunters of the South were not organized in a nationwide manner. The world's first major surveillance operation of this kind arose from another of America's nineteenth-century business needs. It had to do with urban business and the problem of creditworthiness. To avail yourself of the opportunity of selling to customers spread across the nation, you had to know whether they were good for the money. The continental dimensions of America meant you were not personally acquainted with many of the people you wanted to deal with. The solution was surveillance on a grand scale.

Lewis Tappan started the process. He is, on the face of it, an unlikely claimant to the distinction of being one of the fathers of our modern surveillance society and of practices that are so often denounced in moral terms. For Tappan was a fervent Congregationalist and is best known as an abolitionist. In 1833, he joined William Lloyd Garrison and others to form the American Anti-Slavery Society. Later, he was a prime mover in the movement to free the kidnapped Africans who seized the *Amistad*, the ship on which they were enslaved, only to find themselves at the centre of an American property wrangle (the US Supreme Court decided in the Africans' favour in 1841).

Tappan was a dry goods merchant who perceived the need for reliable credit assessment. In 1841, he established the Mercantile

Agency in New York City with a view to selling credit assessments to other businessmen. Following changes in ownership, this became R. G. Dun and Company. In the meantime, in Cincinnati, Ohio, J. M. Bradstreet and Company had set up in competition. The two companies were to dominate the credit rating industry and would merge in 1933.

Tappan's agents made local inquiries into merchants' credit-worthiness, often equating it with moral characteristics. Under instruction from their boss, they would look for signs of sexual licence, slothfulness, and drunkenness as well as, of course, dishonesty. In building the profiles of potential clients, they paid heed to factors like ethnicity, age, and business history. The credit reporters also checked tax assessments, lawsuits, bankruptcy proceedings, and financial statements.

Procedures became more professional and organized over the years. In 1859 just before it became R. G. Dun, the Mercantile Agency published its first reference book. Available to subscribers, this assessed the creditworthiness of merchants nationwide. By 1880, Dun's book listed almost 800,000 businessmen. Both Dun and Bradstreet began to rely on professional agents instead of amateur informers; Dun had 10,000 of these by the century's end, spread over almost 100 branches.

By this time, Dun was benefiting from new technology. It had ordered its first 100 typewriters in 1874, and began to use carbon paper. The dissemination of multiple copies meant improved coordination of surveillance. Such technical advances connected with the rise of business were to have continuing effects on the means and extent of surveillance. The invention of the folding Kodak pocket camera put a new means of surveillance at the disposal of millions by 1900. Secret recording equipment was also available by the early twentieth century and an unbroken highway stretched forwards to today's cockroach-borne surveillance microchip.

From its earliest days, the Mercantile Agency came under attack. This was partly for personal reasons. Anti-slavery was a radical cause with passionate opponents, and Tappan was a hated figure in some quarters. But the agency also gave offence in its own right. In 1854, a New York businessman attacked credit reporting as 'an organized system of espionage, which, centered in New York, extends its ramifications to every city, village, and school district in the Union'.

Inaccuracy was one problem. If you received a low credit rating it could damage your business, and if that estimate were inaccurate, it was salt rubbed into the wound. In the amateur days of credit reporting, estimates sometimes drew on gossip, rumour, and personal bias. In the case *Beardsley v Tappan*, first tried in 1851, The Mercantile Agency had to pay $10,000 in damages, though in later cases the Supreme Court ruled that there was a presumption of confidentiality in credit reporting, so the law of libel did not apply. Complaints about inaccuracy continued, and in a number of states there was a demand for legislation making credit raters liable for the consequences of misrepresentation. In a counterattack that reflected the spirit of the age and frustrated the efforts of the reforming lawmakers, Dun and Bradstreet sympathizers denounced proposals for 'meddlesome legislation'.[4]

The business of credit reporting survived and spread to other countries. Geographically smaller than the United States, their need was less acute. Nevertheless a century later, British firms like Callcredit and Equifax gathered data on businesses, sometimes using private detectives. Their critics charged that they were indiscriminate in their use of the confidential data they gathered, passing it on to third parties. As in the case of the USA, though, they became an accepted part of the private business structure. Between them these British companies reputedly held more private information on people than any other entity outside government.[5] The abolitionist Lewis Tappan had set in train a private system that prepared the way for the acceptance of modern surveillance practices.

In the nineteenth century, no governmental activity remotely approached the scale of credit surveillance. However, in America developments at the federal level did take place, developments that were the seeds from which twentieth-century surveillance agencies grew. By and large, federal espionage had to do with foreign policy. In 1790, Congress supplied President George Washington with a 'contingency fund'. It gave him money to pay for spies, and the privilege of not having to account for how he spent it. By 1793 the sum amounted to a million dollars, or 12 per cent of the national budget. Washington and his successors used the money to pay for spies and covert operations, for example in connection with the acquisition of Florida, but there was no attempt at widespread domestic surveillance. A hundred years later, Congress would adopt the Hoar Amendment, expressing disquiet at the secret means used to acquire Hawaii and negating the validity of any agreements reached by 'executive agents'—even foreign espionage ventures went down badly with a nation that distinctly preferred the private to the public realm and was naturally suspicious of the latter.

Meantime, skeletal federal intelligence organisms had come into being. The Office of Naval Intelligence (formed in 1882) and the Military Information (later, Intelligence) Division (1885) would not engage in domestic surveillance until the twentieth century. There was, however, a temporary exception to all this federal inactivity. Formed in President Abraham Lincoln's last cabinet meeting in 1865, the Secret Service in the following decade swung into action against a serious terrorist menace, the Ku Klux Klan. The Service's leader, the 6 foot 10 inches tall Hiram Whitley, had previously been a slave catcher, and his knowledge of the South and its ways helped him to arrange the penetration and crushing of the Klan. When the southern states finally re-entered the Union, they reacted against the Secret Service and used their restored power to curtail its further activities—racism was behind their attitude, but also the states rights doctrine, which paralleled and reinforced businessmen's antipathy to federal government. The Secret Service survived and borrowed the technologies of business, such as the typewriter and carbon paper. It would be an antecedent of the FBI that, in the next century, conducted a very different kind of surveillance, but in the post-1870s nineteenth century its domestic operations were limited.

The Hoar Amendment and the curtailment of Secret Service activities were evidence of strong feelings provoked by federal clandestine activity. There was also evidence of emerging concern about private threats to privacy. In 1890, the *Harvard Law Review* published what would become an influential article on 'The Right to Privacy', authored by the Boston lawyer Samuel D. Warren and his friend, the future Supreme Court justice Louis D. Brandeis. They were upset at the intrusions of press photographers at private functions such as weddings: 'Instantaneous photographs and newspaper enterprise have invaded the sacred precincts of private life.' They set about collating case law, especially in England, evaluating also a privacy law passed in France in 1868. Their assessment of legal opinions concluded that privacy was not sacrosanct, for example in cases where disclosure was in the public interest, but that in the right circumstances one could justifiably sue for damages and in a few cases obtain a restraining injunction.[6]

The United Kingdom had both a stronger tradition of state activity including police organization, and a reputation for spying expertise. This was of potential significance on both sides of the Atlantic, as the Anglo-American special relationship of the twentieth century would be so influential. But UK intelligence was skeletal for most of the nineteenth century. Parliament established the Secret Service Vote in 1797 just a few years after the American precedent. During the crisis of the Napoleonic Wars it provided substantial sums, but (with the exception of the Alien Office that spied on domestic radicals until 1806) did not supply them to a dedicated government agency. Then in the years preceding the 1832 Reform Act, numerous police spies operated domestically in an attempt to frustrate the franchise movement.

After that, there was a decline in activity. By the 1880s, the Secret Vote appropriation had sunk to a nadir. By this time, as in the United States, the seeds of future organizations had been planted: the Intelligence Branch in the War Office (1873), and, a decade later, the Irish Special Branch within Scotland Yard to combat a bombing campaign by violent Irish Nationalists. The Fenians, as they were known, acknowledged the new organization by blowing up its headquarters, but the Special Branch continued on its path. It would broaden its activities, and accordingly drop the word 'Irish' from its title. Also in 1883, the Naval Intelligence Department came into being. Acorns, however, do not amount to an oak tree. The day when the United Kingdom would become the most heavily surveilled nation in the democratic world lay some distance in the future.

Nineteenth-century surveillance was actually predominantly an American, and a private, affair. In addition to credit investigators, there were private detectives who, by the early twentieth century, constituted a substantial industry. Like the Dun corporation, detective agencies made use of technology. *The Literary Digest* of 15 June 1912 reported William J. Burns' detective agency's use of the dictograph: 'In walls, under sofa and chair, in chandelier, behind a desk, beside a window, it has hidden—the unseen listener to secret conversations.' In Britain, Charles Dickens had popularized the work of police detectives in his 1850s journal *Household Words*, and later in the century Arthur Conan Doyle immortalized his fictional private eye Sherlock Holmes, but it was in America that the private detective industry became a major institution.

The rise of the US private detective industry had little to do with the rosy pictures of crime fighting portrayed in the agencies' public relations efforts. As we shall see in Chapter 2, the private detective's main source of income was labour work. Spying on working people has been a dominant feature in the history of surveillance.

Two features of labour espionage invite attention. The first is that the detective agencies were loyal not to their employers, but to the dollar. They could be unreliable. This does not negate the overall conclusion that they were oppressive to American workers, but it is an early indication of how private contractors concentrate on the bottom line. The second feature is the nature of the protest against the practice. Though vehement and prominent from time to time, the protest against labour espionage was muted compared with the later uprising of the middle classes when their own ox was gored. This helps to explain why historians have tended to ignore the role of surveillance as an instrument of social control directed against less privileged sectors of the population.

Beginning in the early years of the twentieth century, employers directed a further form of surveillance at America's wage earners. Frederick W. Taylor was its most famous initiator. A management consultant who came to be identified with the drive towards 'efficiency' in the Progressive era which came to be known as 'Taylorism', Taylor had always been a quantifier. As a boy, he counted the steps he took each day and analysed each of his actions to make it more efficient. Rebelling against his professional parents, he worked in a steel mill. There and in other factories, he watched the workers, concluding that they typically 'soldiered', slowing down their actions at the workplace. Taylor's time and motion studies involved measuring the optimum time it took to perform a task—fuelling a furnace, turning out a yard of cloth, visiting the bathroom. In the interest of productivity, he reorganized the work process. To achieve a promised income level, employees now had to perform their tasks at a required speed.

In 1911, Taylor published his influential book *The Principles of Scientific Management*. In the same year, he placed the Watertown Arsenal in Massachusetts under observation, and concluded the workers should be producing a gun not every fifty-three minutes, but every twenty-four. Confronted with his methods and Taylorism's demand for a speed-up, the Watertown workers went on strike. There was a congressional inquiry, and, in a temporary setback, Taylorism and stopwatch surveillance were banned from government factories. Taylorism gave way to other forms of management, but the surveillance of employees had come to stay. Some two-thirds of corporations reported in 2001 that they exercised some form of surveillance over their workers.[7]

The close supervision of employees continued to give offence. Charlie Chaplin's 1936 movie *Modern Times* was an indictment of the supervised speed-up that had the 'Little Tramp' struggling to cope with accelerating factory machinery. In the mid-1970s women went on strike at the Puretex Knitting Company in Toronto when they were filmed visiting the bathroom. In some US hospitals today, nurses are electronically tagged to ensure that they move faster from bed to bed and tend more patients per shift, a deeply unpopular practice.

On the other hand, surveillance at the workplace can have benign consequences, a circumstance that helped to mute protest against it. There is, for example, the monitoring of employees' computers to make sure they are doing their jobs and not watching porn (a widespread problem). The bugging of truck drivers' cabs is another worker management tool that has inspired mixed responses, for it can have the effect of improving road safety. There have been fierce debates in the United Kingdom and the European Union over this issue.

Workers are sometimes inconsistent in their attitude towards surveillance. For example, while American working mothers may find employers' monitoring of their screens intrusive, they happily use their work computers to access the CCTV monitors in their toddlers' playschools to make sure their kids are OK—and that the playschool workers are doing their jobs and refraining from abuse. Other workers buy into the productivity argument. In 2014 the *New York Times* reported data from China that suggested higher productivity came from workers who were free from surveillance.

However, the *New York Times* also quoted Dallas restaurant manager Jim Sullivan on the issue: 'I was always aware and assumed that you're being watched at work…When people know they are being watched, I believe that productivity improves.' Workplace surveillance remained ubiquitous in part because there was a lack of consistent opposition to it.[8]

Americans living in the early years of the twentieth century witnessed not only private surveillance of business and labour, but also some federal initiatives. Following the assassination of President William McKinley by a deranged man who thought he was an anarchist, Congress in 1903 passed a law denying anarchists access to America. It was the first piece of immigration legislation aimed at political belief. It fell to the Department of Justice to watch for suspicious anarchist activity, and thus was born what would later be called the Attorney General's List of Subversive Organizations, which continued in the Cold War to be a weapon in the armoury of federal surveillance.

In 1908, the Justice Department acquired a new agency, the Bureau of Investigation. What came to be known as the FBI began with the specific task of chasing down identified suspects, but gradually acquired a broader responsibility and included counter-intelligence as well as, controversially, a watching brief on radicals regardless of whether or not they were criminals. Wartime hysteria after 1917 and anti-Red sentiment on account of the Bolshevik seizure of power in Russia two years later were the backdrop for the FBI's participation in 'dragnet' inquiries. As the word implies, there was indiscriminate surveillance leading to indiscriminate arrests; some of them were without the benefit of an arrest warrant.

Within the bureau, a General Intelligence Division headed by the young lawyer J. Edgar Hoover had files on more than 200,000 individuals by 1919. Moreover, surveillance voluntarism had reared its head. Formed early in 1917, by late 1918 the American Protective League (APL) had 350,000 members. It was a vigilante organization whose volunteers kept tabs on aliens, on dissenters like the socialist Industrial Workers of the World, and, once the United States was in the war, on draft 'dodgers'. Its members trawled the poolrooms and bus stops of America arresting men of fighting age who could not produce that latest form of identity proof, one of the 24,000,000 draft cards issued under the Selective Service System. Though a private organization, the APL aimed to help federal and state-level public agencies engaged in surveillance work.

Federal surveillance had other dimensions, too. At the back of one initiative of longer-term significance was Albert Sidney Burleson, Postmaster General throughout the Woodrow Wilson administration (1913–21). Burleson was an innovative public official who pioneered the US airmail service. But he was also a controversial figure—he racially segregated the Post Office, kept federal wage levels low, and oversaw the censorship of wartime mail. He courted yet more controversy when, by bringing the private companies under public control, he potentially made letters and telephonic and telegraphic communications available to government code-breaking and counter-intelligence officials. As a Texan politician influenced by Populism, Burleson saw public control as 'greatly to the interest of the public' in times of peace as well as war.

The Mann-Elkins Act of 1910 had made it illegal for the telephone, telegraph, and cable companies to disclose the content of the communications for which they were responsible. Burleson, more concerned with the efficient management of business than with espionage or surveillance, apparently went along with that principle. The State Department intelligence official L. Lanier Winslow complained 'the telegraph companies...are afraid to make any move without orders from Burleson, largely owing to a [1918] law which that gentleman had passed making it a penitentiary offense to divulge to anyone the contents of messages'. Under the leadership of poker-player-turned cryptographer Herbert O. Yardley, America was in process of setting up a permanent interception and code-breaking facility that would become known as the American Black Chamber and was the precursor of the National Security Agency (NSA). It was frustrating for Yardley and his backers that civil servants were blocking their access to messages they wanted to read. What they misjudged was the outlook of the private companies, who preferred to have no truck with government control of any kind, whether it involved strategic economic planning or the purloining of communications.

In the summer of 1919 the president of the United States Independent Telephone Association expressed his members' alarm at the government's takeover of the 'supervision, possession, control and operation of all telephone, telegraph, cable and radio systems through the United States'. His industry's viewpoint prevailed, and control and ownership reverted to the private companies. Given Burleson's ban on the interdiction of messages under the system of government control, privatization at first seemed like an advantage to the interceptors, but in practice the telegraph companies would be reluctant to cooperate with the American Black Chamber. Burleson had set a double precedent: government intervention in the communications business and a bar on interceptions. The former would be more in evidence than the latter in the years to come, but the tradition of private

resistance to federal intercept programmes would remain a coun-
tervailing force.[9]

The Red Scare of 1919–20 encouraged those who hoped that
there would still be a need for federal surveillance in peacetime.
However, the majority of Americans reached the conclusion that
the communists were not, after all, such a great threat to the internal security of the United States. The astute J. Edgar Hoover
ditched the anti-Red bandwagon as he cultivated the image of a
man who was qualified to take on the directorship of the FBI.

Against this background, however, another private initiative
took shape. The person responsible for it was Colonel Ralph Van
Deman (pronounced Demon), who had been a senior military
intelligence officer in the war. Unlike the majority of his contemporary colleagues and countrymen, Van Deman was determined
to fight what he portrayed as the domestic communist menace.
When the federal government reneged on its duty (as he saw it),
Van Deman took matters into his own, private hands. Basing his
operations in California, he compiled indices of labour union
activists and other radicals. His panoptic gaze reached beyond his
adoptive state—he told his friends in military intelligence that he
had records on troublemakers 'throughout the country'. When he
circulated his data to potential employers, they served as a blacklist. If you were on that blacklist, you did not get a job.[10]

Britain, in the meantime, had also tired of the government activism and expenditure associated with the World War. In the course
of that war, the Home Office, War Office, Ministry of Labour, and
other departments had decided on 'systematic surveillance of the
working class' with a view to anticipating and preventing strike
action.[11] Basil Thomson, an Etonian in charge of a special office at
the Metropolitan Police, had focused on dissent in strategic

industrial cities like Glasgow, Barrow, and Cardiff, and by the end of the war had 700 employees on his official payroll. His bureau became the newest incarnation of Special Branch in 1919.

With the advent of peace, the government did not entirely abandon the surveillance practices of the recent crisis-ridden years. The revised Official Secrets Act of 1920 required all cable companies to hand over copies of messages upon production of a government warrant and, under the direction of Alistair Denniston, the Government Code and Cypher School (GC & CS, the precursor of Government Communications Headquarters [GCHQ]) retained the wartime capacity to intercept cable and wireless communications, even if on a reduced budget. The nation's first Labour government led by Prime Minister Ramsay McDonald (January–November 1924) retained the Home Office search warrant system introduced by the Liberal Home Secretary Winston Churchill. Yet, for the time being, everything was on a reduced scale.

Admiral Reginald 'Blinker' Hall stepped into the breach. The former head of GC & CS's precursor, Room 40 in the Admiralty, the man with an eye twitch had impressed as a wartime code-breaker. Alarmed by Russian Bolshevism and by what he regarded as the untimely demobilization of UK intelligence, in 1919/1920 he set up his own organization, known from 1926 as the Economic League. Like Van Deman's enterprise but on a nationwide scale, the Economic League operated against the domestic left and against trade unions. Using informers and other undercover methods, it compiled a blacklist that it could sell to employers. This kind of blacklisting weakened the labour movement. That weakening is authoritatively held to have contributed in the long run to the polarization of wealth in British society that is today regarded as one of the United Kingdom's economic weaknesses.[12] Yet, aimed as it was against working people and not the articulate middle classes, blacklisting has not figured in the traditional litany of surveillance excesses.

Blacklisting was beginning to make surveillance a dirty word, but other private activities gave it a more positive sheen. In 1937, a private venture called Mass Observation was launched in the United Kingdom and over the next decade would provide a picture of how ordinary people lived—its data continue to the present day to be a boon to the social historian. The enterprise paid its way by undertaking commercial market research, and in the war it worked for Home Intelligence, a division of the Ministry of Information, undertaking an assessment of civilian morale. Its creation and successful operation are a further indication of how what is regarded as benign surveillance can be acceptable to the general public.

However, in the 1930s there was also a turning of the tide against the less salubrious types of private surveillance associated with Van Deman, Blinker Hall, and others. In 1937 first the Communist Party's *Daily Worker* and then the conservative *Times* exposed the activities of the Economic League, sparking debate in the House of Commons. In the following year Leo Huberman published his American exposé, *The Labor Spy Racket*, a book about the widespread hostile surveillance of American workers that further publicized the already sensational findings of a Senate inquiry into civil liberties headed by Robert M. La Follette, Jr (Progressive-WI). Against this background and faced with New Deal legislation that aimed to empower organized labour, the Pinkerton Detective Agency declared, not for the first time, that it was giving up supplying employers with undercover infiltrators.

Government surveillance, in contrast, began an expansion that has continued to the present day. This was in spite of what should have been dire messages from Europe, where the Gestapo, and its Soviet equivalent the NKVD, were engaged in a campaign of terror. Circumstances at home conspired to make people tolerant of their own government's surveillance initiatives. There was an unwillingness to believe that the United States could descend to the totalitarian depths of the European dictatorships. Because the Great Depression called for special measures that were tolerated at the time, and then because of international tension and 'fifth column' fears, Americans were prepared to accept a higher level of government activity such as surveillance. President Franklin D. Roosevelt laid the foundations of the modern democratic surveillance state even before Pearl Harbor precipitated America's entry into the Second World War.

At the end of that war, government surveillance did not subside to the degree that it had done in the 1920s. The Cold War saw to that. Republican Red-baiting and the Harry Truman administration's clampdown on the left triggered 'McCarthyism', the still widely used misnomer for the Great Fear of the later 1940s and the 1950s. Just over a decade later, the outbreak of another hot war, the Vietnam conflict, stimulated COINTELPRO and a cluster of other domestic surveillance activities that the federal government justified on the ground that communists in Moscow or Beijing or Hanoi were guiding the actions of anti-war protestors and black radicals. Nor did all this end with the termination of the Cold War. The emergence of self-styled Islamic terrorism and especially the 9/11 outrage of 2001 inspired the George W. Bush administration's War on Terror. This latest synthetic war gave rise to a renewed wave of intrusiveness with its novel technological panoply of social media surveillance.

Yet after 1945, the United Kingdom and USA also entered into an era of opposition to government surveillance. With his novel *Nineteen Eighty-Four* (1949), George Orwell aimed a nail into the heart of the surveillance state. He added new expressions to the language of satire: 'Big Brother is watching you', 'Ministry of Truth', 'Freedom is slavery'. Orwell's 'Newspeak' was a special language into which, he wryly remarked, it was impossible to translate Jefferson's Declaration of Independence.[13]

Debate has raged over What Orwell Really Meant. Was he attacking the Nazis or the communists? Was he really thinking of his alma mater, Eton College, a private institution? Whatever he thought about Eton, he overlooked the private sector in his critique of surveillance, and concentrated on the all-seeing state.

Yet even as Orwell penned *Nineteen Eighty-Four* in the remoteness of a Scottish island retreat, what one might call 'Vansittartism' was seeping into the core of English life (after the senior British diplomat Sir Robert, later Lord, Vansittart, 1881–1957, who we will meet again more than once in these pages). 'Vansittartism' had begun as anti-German sentiment in the Second World War, but could now be characterized as a private, silent, and thus more insidious, UK equivalent of McCarthyism that involved the blacklisting of BBC employees and the hounding of Church of England vicars. Meantime the Economic League had survived the parliamentary scrutiny of the 1930s and was entering a period of expansion.

If an exclusive concentration on statism was Orwell's weakness, his critique of the surveillance state was nevertheless salutary. Others would follow his critical lead in America as well as in Britain. In 1952, the *Washington Post* journalist Alan Barth published his book *The Loyalty of Free Men*, attacking the Attorney

General's List of Subversive Organizations. The Truman administration had deployed the list as an instrument of national security that created, to use Orwellian diction, 'non-persons'. In the following decade, *Ramparts* magazine revealed how the CIA had used the National Students Association for surveillance purposes. Then a whistle-blowing article by army officer Christopher Pyle prompted, in 1971, a series of congressional hearings into military domestic surveillance. More was to follow. Led by Idaho's Frank Church, Senate investigations in the mid-1970s blew the lid off several government surveillance programmes.

America in the 1970s adopted legislation aimed at curbing the excesses of government surveillance, for example the Freedom of Information Act (giving citizens the right to know and see what files were being kept on them), the Government in the Sunshine Act, and the Foreign Intelligence Surveillance Act of 1978 (FISA), which in specified circumstances enabled warrantless counter-intelligence and counter-terrorism surveillance, but protected the privacy of American citizens.

Across the world, government surveillance was coming under renewed scrutiny. In 1975, the French philosopher Michel Foucault published his influential book on the history of the prison regime, *Surveiller et Punir* (which appeared in English as *Discipline and Punish*). It gave rise to the question, why are we obsessed with surveillance? In the following year, the Scottish journalist Duncan Campbell exposed the existence and practices of GCHQ in Cheltenham. Margaret Atwood's novel *The Handmaid's Tale* appeared one year after Orwell's futuristic date of 1984 and was a Canadian contribution to a growing stream of concern. It added a new venue (apparently Cambridge, Massachusetts), new vocabulary (Computalk,

Birthmobile), and a new ideology (feminism) to what was essentially an Orwellian and state-focused vision.[14]

If the United Kingdom had lagged behind its American partner in the process of exposure and reform, in one area, the exposure of workplace surveillance, it provided a lead. *The Guardian's* re-exposure of the Economic League in 1952 had come to naught, but a Granada TV programme of 1988 started a process of political pressurization that led to the League's disbandment in 1993. With the collapse of communism in Europe and the dissolution of state surveillance organizations like the Stasi, for a while the prospects for privacy looked rosy.

However, by the beginning of the twenty-first century the political mood had changed. There was a renewed emphasis on national security and surveillance at a cost to the right to privacy. The causes of the change are open to debate, but three factors did play an important part. Beginning with the Ronald Reagan–Margaret Thatcher era, there had been a general turn to the right in politics—and while US conservatives had at one time been critical of the CIA and the intelligence establishment, they were by now firmly behind the intelligence institutions and their surveillance practices. Secondly, the rise of a self-styled 'Islamic' terrorist threat performed the part that international communism had once played. Arising from this was the third factor, 9/11. There is a debate about whether that event in 2001 was a turning point in the history of surveillance, with some well-informed commentators arguing that the anti-privacy trend set in back in the 1980s. But even these critics agree that 9/11 accelerated the intensification of surveillance.[15]

The US Director of National Intelligence released figures indicating the scale of FISA (Foreign Intelligence Surveillance Act) surveillance in 2013. There had been 1,767 FISA orders based on probable cause, affecting 1,144 targets. But in response to a single FISA order not requiring probable cause to be shown, a further 89,138 targets had been affected. Also with regard to 2013, the US Post Office revealed that it had acceded to almost 50,000 requests by government security agencies secretly to monitor the mail of Americans. The *New York Times* estimated that more than forty government agencies used undercover agents to pry secretly into the private lives of American citizens.[16]

In the United Kingdom, too, there was evidence of enhanced surveillance. There, GCHQ cooperated with its US counterpart the NSA. And stories began to emerge of the escapades of undercover policemen who penetrated perfectly legitimate protest and activist groups, even forming sexual relationships with their members.

On both sides of the Atlantic, private enterprises continued to be involved. The Office of the Director of National Intelligence indicated in 2007 that more than 37,000 private contractors worked for the federal government on covert operations and security matters.[17] Privatization was also the mantra in the United Kingdom, both for the Tony Blair Labour government (1997–2007) and for the coalition and Conservative governments that followed. In the United Kingdom, a private institution, the press, abused surveillance techniques to invade personal privacy. Journalists at the *News of the World* and other newspapers in the Rupert Murdoch stable, while notoriously at fault, were not the only transgressors. In September 2014, for example, the courts directed the editor of the *Daily Mirror* to pay compensation to victims of phone hacking.

All this resulted in a spate of revelations. So widespread had surveillance become in the United States and United Kingdom and beyond that it was virtually impossible to keep every secret—too many people knew too much. There was a wide audience for stories of malpractices, and a considerable momentum behind the demand for more protection of civil liberties. The social bases of protest had broadened to include people in every walk of life, including the professional classes who were not only articulate, but also had access to the media and potentially to the levers of power. It was a far cry from the story of labour espionage, the subject of the next chapter.

2

The Private Eye Invades Our Privacy

The American private detective agency posed a more controversial threat to citizens' privacy than that other nineteenth-century creation, the credit rating firm. Both before and after the rise of feminism changed attitudes to divorce, private detectives invited contempt when they preyed on men and women who were experiencing distress in their marital relations. Their impact on the workplace was even greater, and there they were to leave a legacy of bitterness that lasts to the present day.

A new phase in the history of surveillance began with The Eye That Never Sleeps, the self-description of the Pinkerton National Detective Agency. It was a tale that had its beginning 4,000 miles to the east, in Glasgow, Scotland.

In 1819 Allan Pinkerton was born in the Gorbals district of that city. As a young man he became an activist in the Radical movement, the Scottish equivalent of the Chartists in England. His comrades won a partial victory with the 1832 Reform Act's broadening of the male franchise. But progress continued to be slow, and the Scottish Radicals like their southern counterparts were infested with government spies. Pinkerton later hinted that he and his young wife left Scotland because he was only one step ahead of his pursuers. The police may well have been closing in on him, although it is also possible that he had betrayed his comrades and feared their retribution. Be that as it may, in 1842 he found himself in the New World. After an interlude in which he chased down horse thieves in Canada, he settled in Chicago.

The America in which Allan Pinkerton found himself was undergoing commercial transformation. Changes in the private sector outpaced the development of government, partly because the United States was a young 'frontier' society, and partly because of the great sectional crisis confronting the nation that weakened politics and ended in civil war. Like other western cities, Chicago had an underdeveloped police department, and few facilities for penetrating the criminal class.

Perceiving a business opportunity, in 1850 Pinkerton founded the detective agency that soon bore his name. The Pinkerton Agency—known after the Civil War as the Pinkerton National Detective Agency—undertook surveillance on a larger scale than its European counterparts, whether private or public. Pinkerton surveillance was primarily directed at organized labour. Anti-union work was a prime source of income for the agency, and the early history of organized surveillance for this reason overlaps with the history of American labour. In a letter to the *Glasgow Sentinel* in 1869 Pinkerton expressed sympathy with labour unions. But this is misleading. The letter was a throwback to his Scottish radical days. Like other radicals, when he arrived in America he became a conservative in a very short space of time. He saw two things: universal franchise, meaning he could now uphold instead of challenging the establishment, and opportunity. A poacher turned gamekeeper, he championed the American system, or at least his version of it.

In his 1873 pamphlet *General Principles of Pinkerton's National Detective Agency*, the founder explained that his creation was 'an individual and private enterprise, and is not in any way connected with...Governmental authority'. In a further publication in 1878, he warned: 'Every trades-union has for its vital principle, whatever is professed, the concentration of brute force to gain certain ends. Then the deadly spirit of Communism steals in...' His agency upheld the principles of private property and the employer's right to manage. In spite of public and congressional criticism and a number of promises not to engage in such work, the Pinkertons continued to penetrate and operate against unions for decades. The US Senate's La Follette civil liberties inquiry of the 1930s took a close look at labour espionage. It noted that the Pinkerton Agency by this time had offices in thirty-five cities, and in the United Automobile Workers alone had placed fifty-two spies.[1]

Pinkerton and his successors added a formidable weapon to an already bulging employers' arsenal aimed at the surveillance and control of American workers. As we shall see at the end of the chapter, though, it is a story with a curious twist.

For the moment, it is worth taking a closer look at the work of one of Pinkerton's agents, or 'operatives' as they were known. James McParlan came from one of Great Britain's frontier areas, Ireland. (See Illustration 2.) Ambiguities abounded from the start in the make-up of this controversial figure. At different times he claimed to have been born in 1839 and 1844. Midway through his life he added the letter 'd' to his name, becoming McParland. From a Catholic family, he grew up in County Armagh and went to a

ILLUSTRATION 2. James McParland (1843–1919), image from the 1890s. As a service to employers and on behalf of the Pinkerton National Detective Agency, he organized the infiltration of American labour unions from the 1870s to the early years of the twentieth century.

Presbyterian school, giving him the capacity to 'pass' both ways. He had the further professional attribute of being a 'cold soak'— he could drink other men under the table while keeping his ears open and his wits about him.

McParlan emigrated to the USA and engaged in a series of manual jobs, then worked for the Chicago private detective agency W. S. Beaubien. In 1872, he met Allan Pinkerton. Although Pinkerton had a temperance background and was a disciplinarian, he overlooked McParlan's bibulous habits because he realized that his new acquaintance understood the troubles afflicting his native patch in Ireland. And that qualified him for the job that Pinkerton had in mind for him.

The job arose from the labour and ethnic conflicts then rife in the anthracite coalfields of western Pennsylvania, especially Schuylkill County. In 1868, the region's miners formed their first viable labour union, the Workingmen's Benevolent Association. Led by English immigrants from Lancashire, it sought to improve members' wages and working conditions in a peaceful manner. However, parallel with this and with overlapping membership, a secret organization called the Molly Maguires, whose roots went back to McParlan's part of Ireland, fought for the rights of Irish miners using physical force. They set out to terrorize mine supervisors, officials, and owners of Welsh, English, and other Protestant descent. Sixteen assassinations of such persons are attributable to the Pennsylvanian Mollies.

The mine owners' leader, Franklin Gowen, turned to the private sector for assistance: 'Municipal detectives, employed by the police authorities of cities, who operate only for rewards, are the last persons to whom you could trust an enterprise such as this.' Gowen knew that public opinion was turning in favour of the labour movement, and police detectives might not automatically take the side of employers—sheriffs, after all, were elected and workers had more votes than employers. So Gowan asked Pinkerton to help. Pinkerton acceded to Gowan's request to place the Workingmen's Benevolent Association under surveillance, and infiltrated four private operatives into the union.

But there was a further plan. This was to penetrate the Mollies and bring their leaders to justice, a move intended to destroy not only the Molly Maguires, but also the legitimate labour union in the coalfield. McParlan accepted the dangerous task of penetrating the secret organization. He did so and was ruthless, for example failing to save the life of the Welshman John P. Jones, a superintendent at the Lehigh and Wilkes-Barre Coal Company, by warning him that he was about to be assassinated. But success crowned his efforts. Twenty Mollies were brought to justice and hanged.

Historians have earnestly debated the Molly Maguire episode, with assertions in later years that McParlan was a mercenary agent provocateur pitted against a heroic working-class movement. But from McParlan's perspective, the operation was a huge success. Drawing on McParlan's court testimony, Allan Pinkerton and others wrote books making the Ulsterman a hero who delivered America from a pernicious outbreak of terrorism. McParlan would acquire legendary status. He featured alongside Sherlock Holmes in Arthur Conan Doyle's Molly Maguires thriller *The Valley of Fear* (1915). Less sympathetically, he is assumed to have been The Old Man in Dashiell Hammett's Continental Op stories: 'The Old Man...was also known as Pontius Pilate' and 'Agency wits said he could spit icicles in July.'[2]

McParlan's performance against the Mollies having impressed the agency, he became chief of its Western division, with headquarters in Denver. The Pinkertons expanded under his leadership. By the early years of the twentieth century they had offices in eight western cities, employing nearly 200 operatives in that region. These western Pinkerton men continued what had started back East, and contributed to the development and shape of surveillance in American society.

The West might seem a strange location for union-busting private eyes. The explanation is that the West, like western Pennsylvania earlier, was embarking on a period of industrial development and turmoil that created an opportunity for anti-labour surveillance. Indeed, the word 'wild' in Wild West might be said to have applied more to the turbulent mining camps than to the deeds of gun-toting cattle men so favoured by Hollywood.

The problem with mining communities like Cripple Creek, Colorado, and Coeur d'Alene, Idaho (and indeed similar places back East) was that they were isolated monocultures. Because of the random nature of mineral location, a mine was likely to be isolated from the nearest city. A mining community was often monocultural in the sense of having just the one industry upon which everyone depended. There were no independent grocers, carpenters, textile workers, doctors, lawyers, architects, and so forth. The local store was the company store. The company owned local housing. The miners' union would run the local hall. The local man of God would likely favour one side or the other, and only the brothels bridged the social divide. There was no group of independent worthies to intervene and prevent a dispute from becoming extreme and bitter.

This socio-economic monoculture characterized the Rocky Mountain West. In addition the region spawned a breed of individualists. Panners for gold who might have driven their own stake into the ground to establish a claim did not easily bend the knee to bosses who sought to impose uniform working practices. This was the background to the militancy of the Western Federation of Miners (WFM), and to the employers' demand for industrial surveillance to augment order, control, and profits.

Formed in 1893, the WFM organized mainly metalliferous miners, extractors of gold, silver, lead, and copper from the spectacular hills and mountains that towered over their primitive settlements. The miners' battles with employers and mine owners' associations gave US industrial relations the reputation of being violent. A myth in comparative international terms, the reputation was nevertheless enough to frighten capitalists and politicians. Even if they were not frightened, it gave them an opportunity to ring alarm bells. For once the alarm had been sounded, it provided an opportunity to use draconian methods against the miners.

The methods included bribery—at one point, the entire state legislature of Colorado accepted money in return for voting down a law that would limit the length of the working day to eight hours. Employers also used physical force. In the course of a dispute in Coeur d'Alene in 1899, Governor Frank Steunenberg resorted to that practice. As the state militia was in Cuba on account of the Spanish-American War, he called in federal soldiers. In a turn of events that proved unfortunate for race relations, some of these were African Americans. Steunenberg, derided in the establishment press for preferring florid shirts and never wearing a tie, had links to the Populist movement and had in the past received support from the WFM, but now he was regarded as a traitor, especially as he accepted money from the Mine Owners' Association. His federal troops rounded up 1,000 union men and incarcerated them in a 'bull pen' or makeshift outdoor prison. It should be noted that the miners had not been above reproach. Protesting the dismissal of seventeen union members, they had blown up the $250,000 mill at the Bunker Hill Mine.

Another ploy used by employers was the penetration and disruption of the unions. The 'Eyes That Never Slept' promised to look, listen, and destroy. An incident in Colorado City offers an example of how this tactic was supposed to work. Ore smelters employed there by the United States Reduction and Refining Company worked a twelve-hour shift. A Colorado referendum having mandated an eight-hour day and the state legislature having failed to implement it, the WFM threatened industrial action in 1902 to achieve their goal. From the company's point of view, that meant three shifts, as smelters have to operate on a twenty-four-hour basis, and without a cut to wages that would have incurred substantial costs. They turned to the Pinkertons, who inserted A. C. Crane into the local union branch. The unsuspecting union men elected him its secretary, and he returned the favour by supplying their names to the management so that they could be blacklisted. The company did fire the union men, but on this occasion the Pinkertons and their employers lost out. The WFM called a strike, achieved the reinstatement of the union members, and won recognition in two out of three mills. Crane was exposed, beaten up, and railroaded out of town.

In another operation that year, McParlan personally supervised the insertion of A. W. Gratias into the Cripple Creek branch of the WFM. Again, the Pinkerton operative got himself elected branch secretary. At the time of a work stoppage in sympathy with the smelter workers of Denver, Gratias dished out generous strike pay with the aim of emptying union funds. When the WFM secretary-treasurer William D. 'Big Bill' Haywood objected, he tried to cause a schism in the union by turning the men against Haywood. This particular scheme collapsed, but the constant insertion of agents into the union for surveillance and disruption purposes did threaten WFM stability. These stories illustrate the point that surveillance is not a static and inconsequential process. When undertaken, it is characteristically for a purpose.

We turn now to the gruesome fate of Governor Steunenberg. By way of preface, it is fitting to take note of an event that took place in Chicago in June 1905. In that month, Haywood took a leading role in the formation of the Industrial Workers of the World (IWW or 'Wobblies'). In contrast to the Socialist Party of America formed four years earlier and led by Eugene V. Debs, the

IWW rejected parliamentary democracy. Its adherents had witnessed too much corporate political bribery and too many incidents of state force used against strikers, not to mention the activities of private detectives, to have any faith in the American political system. The IWW took shape against the background of the revolution then gathering pace in Russia (it would be repressed over the coming months). The Wobblies were committed to revolution and, though American born, seemed to be living proof that European class struggle was about to arrive in America.

On the evening of December 30, 1905, Frances Steunenberg gazed out of the window of her family's home at 1602 Dearborn, Caldwell, Idaho. The snow was a foot thick and still falling. She was close to her father, and hoped he would soon be home. There was a flash and an earth-shuddering bang. Had the stove blown up? Was it an earthquake? When the family rushed outside they saw the cause. Frances witnessed what no daughter should ever behold.

She saw the remains of her father. These were mainly from his left side. Other bits of the former governor were scattered over a wide area, and were still being found days later. Three doctors answered the summons for help, but Frank Steunenberg died a few hours later. In moving the latch on his garden gate, the villain of Coeur d'Alene had triggered a bomb. Soon, the authorities arrested Harry Orchard and charged him with placing the explosives. Orchard was a member of the WFM.

The mine owners sensed an opportunity to destroy the WFM and discredit the IWW. James McParlan now fought off a rival bid from Wilson Swain of the Thiel Detective Service Company, and took charge of operations. After many hours of grilling, Orchard confessed to the Pinkerton detective that he had murdered Governor Steunenberg on the instructions of an inner circle of conspirators headed by Bill Haywood, Charles Moyer (president of the WFM), and George Pettibone (a WFM activist). McParlan organized the detention of the three men in Denver and rushed them by non-stop train to Idaho—he said it was an arrest; the union said it was kidnap. The men went on trial in Boise.

The trial lasted a year and a half. There was immense bitterness on the union side. WFM official John M. O'Neil expressed regret that the gate at 1602 Dearborn had been 'completely wrecked'. Haywood issued the following opinion on a postcard-pamphlet: 'That you may know how small a detective is, you can take a hair and punch the pith out of it and in the hollow hair you can put the hearts and souls of 40,000 detectives and they will still rattle.'

Given its class-conflict overtones, the case had political significance. In an unguarded moment, President Theodore Roosevelt referred to the trial. He intended his speech to be a roasting of the railroad magnate whose anti-social behaviour had incurred his displeasure: Edward H. Harriman was 'at least as undesirable a citizen as Debs, or Moyer, or Haywood'. But, intentions notwithstanding, the highest official in the land had vilified Moyer and Haywood and risked influencing an ongoing trial. In protest, there was an outbreak of civil-libertarian buttoneering. Protestors wore badges declaring 'I am an undesirable citizen.'[3]

American radicals braced themselves for a guilty verdict, and no doubt dusted off their finest speeches about unfair labour trials. Yet this trial was not so unfair. William H. Borah, elected to the US Senate in January 1907 and destined for a glittering career in politics, led the prosecution. Defence counsel was a former corporation lawyer who had turned his hand to labour cases in the 1890s—he had failed to keep Eugene Debs out of prison after Debs had led the national railroad strike of 1894. But if Clarence

Darrow was relatively unknown before the Boise trial, after it he was on his way to being regarded as the nation's greatest criminal lawyer. In cross-examination, he tore Orchard's evidence to shreds. Rising above legal niceties, he declared that the WFM was fighting a just cause. The verdict in July 1907 was not guilty. It was a blow to the credibility of McParlan and the Pinkerton Agency.

Potentially, there was change in the air, with public opinion turning against private detective agencies and their methods. There was a spreading comprehension that private detectives who tracked down fraudsters and bank robbers—a highly publicized activity—undertook the work only at the request of clients who had the means to pay them. In other words, private detectives were a perquisite of the rich, making them a target for popular enmity.

They were also unpopular for the 'armed guard' facet of the labour work. By armed guard, people at the time meant what we would today call security guards, and these guards often had a strikebreaking function. This happened in the case of the Homestead, Pennsylvania lockout of 1892. Andrew Carnegie through his local manager Henry Clay Frick ordered his state-of-the-art steelworks on the banks of the Monongahela River to shut down, locking out the workers with the object of rehiring them later on lower wages. The Homestead works became 'Fort Frick', surrounded with a high fence with sniper towers and boiling water cannons. The workers responded by throwing a picket line around the plant to deter the introduction of non-union labour. Then, in a prearranged move, 300 Pinkertons armed with Winchester rifles crammed into two barges and in the middle of the night approached by river with the intention of storming the steel mill. There was an armed conflict as they attempted to make landfall. Twelve died, and the Pinkerton men lost the fight.

After an intervention by the state militia Carnegie prevailed in the Homestead lockout and imposed his wage cut. Yet while Carnegie and his political backers won, they also lost. Both the House of Representatives and the Senate investigated the affair. Defeated in the election of 1892, the pro-business Republican President Benjamin Harrison blamed his demise on Homestead. Hitherto an American hero for being a free enterprise, self-made man, Carnegie became, overnight, a villain. So upset was he at this transformation in his public reputation, that he sold his steel business and went into philanthropy.

Times were beginning to change in America. There was popular sympathy for organized labour, and resentment at the monopoly power of big business. Though the Sherman Anti-Trust Act of 1890 was proving difficult to enforce in the face of a hostile legal profession, politicians were still in a reforming mood. In 1893, Congress passed the Anti-Pinkerton Act, banning the employment in government service of 'an individual employed by the Pinkerton Detective Agency, or similar organization'. The law did not restrain private employers from having such recourse, and aimed at curbing physical force not surveillance, but it marked a low point in the reputation of the private eye.[4]

In 1898, the detective profession entered into a recovery trajectory, but in the public not private sphere. The war with Spain in that year affected opinion. Under the leadership of John E. Wilkie, the Secret Service broke up a Spanish spy ring, centred on Montreal, that had identified East Coast civilian targets for naval bombardment. The old animosities between North and South began to give way to a new American nationalism in the war to liberate Cuba and the Philippines, and the southern hostility to public detectives waned, giving rise to the possibility of an expansion of governmental surveillance even if the subject remained controversial.

Attitudinal change was thus underway by the presidency of Theodore Roosevelt (1901–9). The new White House incumbent deplored any remaining tendencies to criticize detective work. In fact, he had long been a devotee of detection. As a New York State legislator in the 1880s, he had helped vote down measures that would have placed restrictions on the activities of the Pinkerton Agency. Now as president, he planned to create a federal bureau of investigation—this was the precursor of the present-day FBI.

A conservationist, Roosevelt wanted the arrest and prosecution of corrupt businessmen and politicians who conspired to acquire publicly owned timberland in the West. Agents on loan to the Justice Department from the Treasury Department's Secret Service were already securing evidence, evidence that led to the indictment of several businessmen and politicians, including the rising political star William Borah (Borah escaped conviction, but others were not so fortunate).

The president and his Attorney General, Charles Bonaparte, argued that opportunistic reliance on Treasury agents was not good enough. Nor could they rely on the private sector. The anti-Pinkerton law had seen to that—Bonaparte reminded one congressman that 'we do not employ detective agencies at all'. Roosevelt and Bonaparte argued that the answer lay in a new federal detective force.

Bonaparte's opponents anticipated modern concerns about the surveillance state. Congressmen took issue with the way in which the existing Secret Service went about its business. Congressional hearings revealed that sexual surveillance was occurring—federal agents had kept watch on a naval officer who was having an affair with a well-connected society lady in the nation's capital.

Congressmen charged that the Secret Service chief, John Wilkie, was an empire-builder who tried to increase his power by engaging in political surveillance.

Opposition was so strong on Capitol Hill that Roosevelt gave up on obtaining legislation. On 26 July 1908, he used an executive order to set up a bureau of investigation, the precursor of the FBI. He had timed it to coincide with a congressional adjournment in order to avoid trouble, but in December 1908 he confronted his critics in an address to Congress. Like many a less reputable politician but on this occasion with some evidence in his favour, he equated opposition with criminality. The truth was, he asserted, that 'Congressmen themselves did not want to be investigated.' The ban on federal investigation 'could be a benefit only to the criminal class'.

Roosevelt may have won the day in that his new investigative bureau came into being, but he failed to stem the torrent of dissent. The *Wall Street Journal* articulated the business community's fears over the 'expansion of secret and sinister power'. Congressmen raged against the advent of a 'political secret service'. Senator Joseph P. Foraker of Ohio claimed he had been put under surveillance for challenging Roosevelt's policy on racial matters, and that the administration was in breach of the Anti-Pinkerton Act. Congressman Swagar could recall 'no instance where a government perished because of the absence of a secret-service force'. There now coexisted twin phenomena, surveillance both governmental and private, and strong opposition to the practice.[5]

Two further aspects of private worker-surveillance demand attention here. The first is the multiplication in the number of detective agencies offering labour services that rivalled those of the Pinkertons. For example, the Joy Detective Agency advertised in the May 1905 issue of the National Association of Manufacturers' journal *American Industries*, stating: 'We are prepared to place secret operatives who are skilled mechanics in any shop, mill or factory, to discover whether any organizing is being done.' Two months later, the Manufacturers Information Bureau offered similar services. It had offices in Cleveland, St Louis, and San Francisco, and had just opened new branches in Denver, Seattle, and Chattanooga.[6]

Overall estimates of the extent of such surveillance varied in size and reliability. Federal investigators on the eve of the First World War came up with a carefully documented estimate of the number of agencies practicing labour espionage: 275. In the 1920s, the left-wing writer Jean Spielman estimated that between them the Pinkerton, Thiel, and William J. Burns agencies ran 135,000 secret operatives. Sidney Howard thought that most major employers used spies to keep tabs on their workers. In his book *The Labor Spy Racket* (1937), Leo Huberman reckoned there was a spy in every union local. It does seem to be the case that the long arm of private surveillance extended into the lives of millions of workers.[7]

Private detectives had a gift for capturing the headlines, a gift that some of them transferred into the public realm when they undertook government service. The Pinkerton Agency's main rival, William J. Burns, is a case in point—he was to become one of the FBI's early directors. Burns had learned the rudiments of detection when serving with the US Secret Service in the war with Spain in 1898. Turning to private practice, he cultivated a Holmesian image. He even induced Sir Arthur Conan Doyle to pose for a family photograph, with a hand on the shoulders of each of Burns' two sons.

Burns enhanced his fame through his role in a famous labour case. This arose from the dispute between the Bridgemen's Union (officially the International Association of Bridge and Structural Ironworkers) and members of the National Erectors' Association. The dispute affected the cutting-edge industry of steel girder construction—that is, the building of skyscrapers and bridges. In some ways the dispute was a rerun of the Mollies episode. The Irish Catholic-led Bridgemen's Union for several years ran what came to be known as the National Dynamite Campaign. The campaign reignited old enmities running back to the Scottish colonization of Ulster in the seventeenth century, as it targeted an employing cadre that contained Scottish Protestant owners and engineers. If the employers did not recognize the union, 'unexplained' explosions would damage the structures they were erecting. The programme of intimidation culminated in 1910 with the dynamiting of the premises of a newspaper that campaigned for 'open shop' (union-free) workplaces. The destruction of the *Los Angeles Times* Building killed twenty employees.

Burns, as his name suggests, was of Scottish descent, and he led the investigation into the explosion. It was successful, and the leaders of the Bridgemen's Union went to prison. Burns' tracking down of the dynamiters had a disproportionate impact for two reasons. First, Burns, ever the entrepreneur, misrepresented the conservative, Catholic (if criminal) leaders of the Bridgemen's Union as Red revolutionaries. He wrote of an 'inner circle' waging a 'masked war'.[8] Secondly, the nation's leaders either believed Burns' distortion, or pretended to believe it for reasons of political advantage.

The *Los Angeles Times* explosion was the immediate trigger for the setting up of a US Commission on Industrial Relations. Claims that the nation was on the brink of a class war underpinned the decision by the administrations of Presidents William Taft (1909–13) and Woodrow Wilson (1913–21) to go ahead with what would be one of the largest-ever government probes. Daniel O'Regan, an investigator for the commission, researched the normally secretive role of private detective agencies. Though he complained that the agencies were obsessively secretive he did accumulate some data, and what we know about the history of labour espionage is largely thanks to his reports even if, due to political pressures, they gathered dust in a small number of archives and never appeared in print.

The class-war panic had other repercussions, too. Talk of 'inner circles' reignited American fears of an 'enemy within'. With the outbreak of the First World War, there was widespread surveillance and persecution of citizens with German sympathies, anti-war views, and left-wing opinions. The privately organized but not-for-profit American Protective League reported to federal law enforcement agencies on the political views of citizens in local communities. Then, following the Bolshevik triumph in Russia in 1917, the communists became the new internal enemy. Under J. Edgar Hoover at the head of the Justice Department's Alien Enemy Bureau, an illiberal chapter in the history of American surveillance began. Alleged and actual Reds were hunted down with some of them, Bill Haywood included, deported to the Soviet Union. William J. Burns, who served as director of the FBI between 1921 and 1924, was one of a number of private detectives who contributed to the mentality behind these events. He summed up his entrepreneurial approach in a comment to the House Appropriations Committee in 1922: 'Radical activities have increased wonderfully.'

Here, we come to the curious twist in our story. The private detectives Allan Pinkerton, James McParlan, and William J. Burns all represented themselves as class warriors and faithful servants of capitalism. Their stance was characteristic of the private-eye industry as a whole. But were they wholly loyal to America's employers and businessmen? To the private detective, spying on workers was a business matter, and wider surveillance meant big business and larger profits. Yet these goals if successfully pursued were self-defeating. For if unions were eradicated, a vital source of income would disappear.

There is evidence that private detectives put profit above class. An official of Pennsylvania Steel complained in 1910 that 'their expenses run up enormously and they only give you enough to lead you on'. Five years later, Burns hinted darkly at some of the deficiencies of his competitors: 'I render daily reports, and on these reports place the amount of money expended each day, which no other detective agency does'. If detectives worked for businessmen, it was because businessmen had the money to pay them. At least some of them would have been prepared to serve the other side. Doyle's Detective Service Company of Seattle and Boyle's Secret Service Agency of Monmouth, Illinois, both run by veterans of the US Secret Service, each offered to work for Samuel Gompers, the president of the American Federation of Labor.[9]

When a business opportunity arose, private detectives did not allow loyalty to the employing class to stand in their way. In fact, spying on one private business on behalf of another—industrial espionage—was the source of a significant income stream. In 1932, for example, government investigators discovered that the headquarters of the Farmers' Producers Association in Toledo, Ohio, had been bugged on behalf of speculators wishing to gain an unfair advantage in buying milk futures. Just after the opening of the new US Supreme Court Building in 1935 with its bronze reliefs depicting the signing of Magna Carta, the Federal Communications

Commission acted on a tip-off and discovered private bugging equipment designed to obtain prior knowledge of commercially sensitive judgments—to the unfair disadvantage of the eavesdroppers' competitors.

The rise of divorce presented private detectives with a new opportunity. Detectives sometimes liked to assert their integrity by saying that they steered clear of this kind of work. The fictional Philip Marlowe denied that he did 'all kinds of detective work'. He undertook 'only the fairly honest kinds...For one thing I don't do divorce business.' Evidence on private-eye divorce work is difficult to track down—even offered client anonymity, agencies refuse to cooperate with research. Such evidence as exists does, however, confirm what Marlowe implied, that detectives undertook divorce cases.

Private detectives' bedroom work invaded personal privacy on an escalating scale. The opportunities for it increased in the 1920s following the liberalization of divorce laws in the Progressive period. With still further liberalization of divorce law, it gradually became possible to obtain divorce without proving adultery. Drawing chalk lines on tyres to ascertain who had moved where in the middle of the night now became less necessary. Yet in the second half of the twentieth century there were still states that allowed divorce only on the ground of adultery, and additionally there remained those aggrieved spouses who were determined to prove adultery, if only for psychological and moral reasons. For with the rise of divorce came a rise in expectations of marriage, fidelity included. The divorce historian Mary Ryan has argued that 'heterosexual and marital attachments assumed an especially prominent place in popular culture' in the twentieth century (expectations of gay marriage are as yet an unknown quantity). The Manhattan

Yellow Pages in 1979 listed 170 private investigators, with several display advertisements offering 'matrimonial' services. In a language variation, the Los Angeles Yellow Pages listed 239 agencies, with displays offering 'domestic' specialisms.[10]

Originally inspired in some measure by the weakness of law enforcement in the American West, scores of detective agencies—including some of the largest—offered labour spying services. Their repertoire then expanded to include divorce work. The eyes that never slept watched by day when the citizen was at work, and at night at the behest of suspecting spouses.

3

The Blacklist

Tom Watkins was 22 years old in 1910 when Winston Churchill, then Home Secretary in a Liberal government, sent troops into the Rhondda Valley to break a miners' strike. Churchill may retain heroic status in some British and American circles today, but in Wales working people like Tom had a different view of the man.

In 1913, Tom's view of the powers-that-be hardened after a more personal experience. The 1911 Census had listed him as a Colliery Official Below Ground.[1] Translating that into perhaps more familiar military language, it made him a kind of non-commissioned officer. His specific designation was fireman, for when underground his duties included the monitoring of safety conditions. As luck would have it, Tom was not underground when at 8.00 a.m. on 15 October 1913 an explosion rocked his pit, the Senghenydd Colliery. It killed 440 coalface workers and a would-be rescuer who, together with Tom and other safety men, tried to get down to save them. The worst mining accident in British history, the blast followed an earlier explosion in the same pit that should have served as a salutary warning. The mining company

Powell Duffryn was known locally at the time as Poverty and Death. There was a cover up of the causes, and the miners believed that safety had been sacrificed to profit.

It was a hard life being a coalminer, a job fit for no man, Tom said, while still proud of his years underground. Above ground, though, he lived a life of riches. Though he had to leave school to work when still a young boy, he was bilingual, speaking English fluently in addition to his native Welsh. He was a smart dresser. He was a talented musician and, although unable to read a score, could play any tune on the piano or organ after hearing it just once. In 1915 and 1919 his wife Sarah gave birth to two daughters, both of whom, he insisted, should be university educated. For the then-princely sum of £600, he was able to buy a house at the western end of his mining village, Abertridwr, a dwelling that adjoined a farm with its green hills beyond. He worked steadily through the economic vicissitudes that affected the mining industry in the 1920s. A respected person in the community, he sat in the *sedd fawr*, meaning he was an elder in his local Nonconformist chapel. A member of his firemen's union, he was entrusted with the collection of its membership dues.

One day in 1926, Tom made his last entry in the union dues book. There was a background to the reason why. The previous year Chancellor of the Exchequer Winston Churchill, now serving in a Conservative government, put the country back onto the gold standard, a decision he later claimed to have taken in a moment of political weakness. The effect was deflationary, and the labour movement saw the gold standard reversion as an attempt to reduce wages and weaken trade unionism. The General Strike began on 3 May 1926. There was widespread alarm and, with a Big Brotherly touch, Churchill proposed that the government should take charge of radio broadcasting in order to propagandize the employers' cause (the BBC refused to cooperate).

The General Strike lasted for nine days. When it was finished the miners refused to go back to work—they called their dispute a lockout, seeing the stoppage as a well-planned employers' effort to break the union. The coal owners had indeed planned effectively for the event by stockpiling coal supplies in advance. So the union's position was weak and the spectacle of coalminers' families' suffering as the dispute wore on emboldened the employers and their sympathizers. When in September Prime Minister Stanley Baldwin offered the miners what he termed a compromise, it involved a wage cut and longer working hours. Feeling betrayed, the miners' leadership now called on the safety men to go on strike.

It was a desperate move. Members of the firemen's union, Tom included, had worked throughout the dispute to keep the mines from flooding. If they now refused to go below ground to keep the pumps and gas-extraction fans in order, the mines would become inoperable, there would be no jobs to go back to, and everyone would lose. Nevertheless, so bitter was the dispute that the firemen did withdraw their labour. As a tactical move, it was too late. With their families starving, coalminers trickled then rushed back to work, and by December the employers' victory was complete.

Tom was now fired. It required no great leap of logic for him to see that as a union man he no longer had a future in Abertridwr or Senghenydd, so he walked to the next village seeking a job, but had no luck in that quarter. He tried again. It was the same story throughout the South Wales coalfield, so he looked elsewhere.

The English coalmines were just as inhospitable. Ruining his feet in the process and already struggling because of the miners' disease silicosis, Tom now walked to Ayrshire in Scotland, another coalmining area, but there was no work for him there either.

After the 1929 Crash there was the Great Depression and a shortage of other types of work. Tom was without paid employment for well over a decade. He became a migrant snooker player. Rather like his pool-playing US counterparts, he moved from city to city playing badly to lure the bet-placers, before switching on his game and leaving town fast with the proceeds. Hustling at one point made him a small fortune, which he sacrificed on a slow horse. He had now lost his respectability, and no longer sat in Abertridwr's *sedd fawr*.

The £600 house had to be sold for £300. Sarah left the Welsh valleys and kept a boarding house in Cardiff. There, she undertook the hard work and sacrifices that helped Tom's daughters to fulfil his dream of their being university educated.

Tom Watkins was a victim of the blacklist. Across the United Kingdom, from Ayrshire to Staffordshire to South Wales, a unified system of surveillance existed to keep tabs on workers in an industry that at its peak employed 1 million men. Given that miners had large families, a sizeable portion of the British population was affected by surveillance in this one industry alone. Union troublemakers were identified through their activities, by means of scrutinizing the union and local press, and with the assistance of a league of informers—not private detectives who infiltrated the unions, but men who for economic or other reasons were willing to identify their union-active comrades to company officials. Some of these men joined a company or 'scab' union, the South Wales Miners Industrial Union, and performed the additional task of identifying men who were prepared to go back to work. The blacklist meantime extended beyond individual combines (employers' trusts) and was the product of widespread inter-employer collaboration, hence Tom's difficulties in Ayrshire. The surveillance that underpinned the blacklist was sufficiently systematic to affect deeply the lives of families right across the land.

Partly because they questioned the reliability of detective agencies, a number of companies in the 1920s and 1930s took matters into their own hands, recruiting their own informers and compiling their own blacklists. Employers' associations such as the mining combines were increasing in number—1,500 in the United Kingdom in 1914, rising to 2,400 by 1925. In the United States the National Association of Manufacturers, established in 1895, originally set out to lobby on tariff issues but then took up the challenge of fighting labour unions. According to the millionaire socialist William English Walling, manufacturers' associations established local strikebreaking employment exchanges in seven Midwestern and Western cities between 1901 and 1904. There was a subsequent boom in their number.[2]

However, in the interwar years, an additional kind of private organization emerged. Specialized blacklisting facilitators came into being partly to protect the employers' right to manage, partly because of an ideological commitment against the left, and also to exploit a business opportunity. For, once a firm had identified and indexed troublemakers, its lists could be sold to subscribers, employers who wished to keep their businesses union-free.

Ralph Van Deman, who took the lead in the United States, was a Harvard graduate and army officer with a forbidding demeanour. (See Illustration 3.) In the course of America's suppression of

ILLUSTRATION 3. Ralph H. L. Van Deman (1865–1952), seated second from the left, organized a private surveillance network that targeted labour union activists, feminists, and other 'radicals' between the 1920s and 1950s. Directly behind him stands Allen W. Dulles, director of the CIA, 1953–61. The group is the Current Diplomatic and Political Correspondence staff of the US Commission to Negotiate Peace, photographed at the Hotel Crillon, Paris, in March 1919.

the Philippines independence uprising of 1899, he had reorganized General Arthur MacArthur's intelligence system by placing the indigenous population under surveillance. He had developed an indexing and classification system for identifying insurgents, thereupon using the telegraph to disseminate his findings quickly to US commanders in the field. In the First World War, he imported his colonial system into his native America. He persuaded the government to use the military for domestic surveillance, and facilitated that process by reorganizing the Military Intelligence Division (MID) over which he presided. An Anglophile, he set up subdivisions on the British model, MI1 for administration, MI4 for 'contra-espionage outside the military service in the United States', and so on. He even used British spelling.[3]

Van Deman had a broad interpretation of his intelligence duties—for example, he kept a file on 'Negro Subversion'. Seeing him as over-ambitious, Secretary of War Newton Baker stripped him of his beloved MID command in 1918, and sent him on a fact-finding tour of European intelligence agencies. In the course of that tour and sensitive to the Bolshevik triumph in Russia, he formed lurid opinions of the communist threat—he thought the Reds had 'taken over' Belgium and that Holland was 'honeycombed' with traitors.

Van Deman found himself in harmony with his British counter-parts. The US intelligence officer Edward (Ned) Bell noted in May 1919 that Mansfield Cumming, the head of what we now call MI6, 'spoke in the highest terms of Colonel Van Deman, as in fact do all British intelligence officers who came in contact with him'. Some British intelligence officers lobbied President Wilson to give Van Deman more powers. But to the dismay of these admirers, their hero's military career declined after the war. With the waning of the Red Scare, Van Deman's hostile surveillance of radicals went out of fashion. His military superiors saw him as a danger-ous careerist and exiled him to posts in Asia and California. There was a further factor that the British may well have appreciated, as they had the same problem. With the arrival of peace, the American people—like their British allies—wanted a return to normality, or 'normalcy' as President Warren Harding put it. That meant military demobilization, less government meddling in everyday life, lower taxes, and, as a corollary to all this, less official surveillance.[4]

By the end of the decade, Van Deman had settled into civilian life in his house in San Diego, California. But he had not abandoned his commitment to anti-left surveillance. Indeed, the election of Franklin D. Roosevelt to the presidency in 1932 was a signal to him that the left was on the march, and the 1930s New Deal programme with its recognition of organized labour alarmed him even more. Using a network of volunteers and spies and with help from personnel in US military and naval intelligence, Van Deman built up a register of subversives and undesirable employees. He had the financial backing of numerous anti-communist donors. Los Angeles was an 'open shop' city with a low level of union recognition, and San Francisco industrialists wanting to achieve the same status poured millions of dollars into a local Industrial Association that backed Van Deman's union-busting campaign. The American Legion supplied him with informers and the California National Guard backed his efforts.

Van Deman's papers reveal how he deployed 'stool pigeons' or 'stoolies' to penetrate union meetings, perhaps provoke workers into unwise actions, and report back to him. For example, in 1934 a stoolie referred to only by his codename R-384 attended meetings in Sacramento of the Cannery and Agricultural Industrial Union and sent back copious notes to his boss, who indexed the names of the union's activists. Van Deman supplied the resultant names to government organizations, especially the FBI and the House Un-American Activities Committee, but his organization was essentially a private one. It grew to embrace most of the state of California, and then Van Deman extended his surveillance nationwide. His targets went beyond the Communist Party, and included such middle-class, respectable groups as the Women's International League for Peace and Freedom. The Tom Watkinses of America consequently continued to find, throughout the Second World War as well as after it, that they were blacklisted.

By Van Deman's death in 1952, there were 125,000 alleged subversives on his list. Following his demise Margaret Ann Kerr, who had helped him with filing, helped to effect a transition, and his records moved to G2, or Army Intelligence. A G2 memorandum of 1958 noted than most of the information in them 'came from private confidential sources and informants developed by General Van Deman', and that in 1955 the data had been integrated into an Army Master Personality Index. Van Deman's list of names thus circulated beyond private industry—to inform the Senate Internal Security Committee, the FBI, CIA, and State Department intelligence. A subsequent Army memorandum noted that peak usage of the files was in the late 1950s, and that there was 'a sharp decline in use through [the] early 1960s' because the names they contained were no longer properly cross-referenced with the Army's own data.[5]

In America in the interwar years, there were other organizations that paralleled Van Deman's. For example, the American Vigilant Intelligence Association, founded in Chicago in 1927, organized informers to penetrate labour unions and identify troublemakers. By 1933, there were 600 of these informers supplying information to around 5,000 businessmen who subscribed to a monthly publication, *The Vigilante*. In terms of operational scope, however, Van Deman was unmatched in his own country.[6]

In the United Kingdom, Van Deman did have a comparable counterpart in another intelligence officer, William Reginald Hall, the son of William Henry Hall who had been the first head of the British Naval Intelligence Department back in the 1880s. During the First World War Reginald Hall was in charge of a code-breaking unit named after its initial venue, Room 40 in the Admiralty. So secret was Room 40 that its first charter, drafted by Winston Churchill, existed in only two copies. Assisted by some purloined German naval codes, Hall presided over a team of mathematicians who unscrambled intercepted enemy naval communications, giving an operational advantage to the Royal Navy. His team also decoded diplomatic intercepts, most famously the Zimmermann Telegram that conveyed Germany's secret offer to bribe Mexico to come into the war on its side, should there be hostilities between Germany and America. When in February 1917 Hall asked Ned Bell to alert President Wilson and the American press to the secret offer, the resultant publication of the telegram caused an uproar that helped to precipitate US entry into the First World War.

Like Van Deman, Hall inspired his followers. His facial tic mesmerized his staff and appears to have been celebrated in John Buchan's *Thirty-Nine Steps*: 'This old man was more than just a paid spy. Those hooded eyes shone with a deep, burning love for his country.' America's ambassador in London, Walter Hines Page, reported to his president that in those eyes you could see 'the muscular movements of your immortal soul' and that 'Blinker' Hall was the world's outstanding genius in intelligence work.[7]

But Hall's manipulative conduct could give offence. Looking back at the year 1917, some Americans asked whether their country should have entered the war, and whether it had been duped into doing so by Hall's machinations in the Zimmermann affair. There were British reservations, too. Using some private help to begin with but overseeing almost 5,000 government employees by the end of the war, Hall introduced a letter-opening and mail-censorship programme directed at foreign correspondence, a move that alarmed some of his contemporaries and foreshadowed some contentious present-day practices.

Historians who have looked askance at Hall's career have also pointed to his role in connection with the Easter Rising, the Irish patriots' rebellion repressed with such needless brutality by the British in 1916. Room 40 had been one step ahead of the Dublin revolutionaries and via intercepts had enabled the pre-emptive arrest of the nationalist Sir Roger Casement. Hall saw to it that Casement did not call off the Rising to avert bloodshed, and then smeared him with leaks about his homosexuality in a manner that turned opinion against him and contributed to the decision that he should be hanged. Shown the evidence of gay activity from Casement's diaries, Ambassador Page declared that after half a page he could read no further.

Hall could turn people's minds, but some minds turned against him. At the war's end he, like Van Deman, found himself sidelined. To his dismay, the British government did not send him to the Paris Peace Conference to help shape the post-war world; his sympathetic biographer Admiral James conveyed his sense of betrayal: 'One of the least agreeable traits of the British people is their readiness to drop the pilot as soon as the danger is passed.'[8]

Some of his peers saw in Hall a person who could be a dangerous foe in political infighting and who needed to be kept in check, and for a while it seemed that Room 40 would pass into extinction. In the event, Hall's colleague Alistair Denniston achieved a reprieve for the code-breakers, but the unit was moved out of Hall's Admiralty and into the Foreign Office. It now operated under the name Government Code and Cypher School (GC & CS), and would from 1946 be known as Government Communications Headquarters (GCHQ). In future years, the expanded activities of GCHQ would generate heated debate over surveillance, but in 1919 the founders' ambitions were more limited.

This outcome was unsatisfactory to Hall. Having lost one domain, he, like Van Deman, identified a new foe in communism. Russia now had a communist government and 1919 was a year of industrial unrest in both Britain and America. With women winning the vote and a major expansion in the franchise in prospect, Hall feared—rightly—that a Labour government might be elected. He assumed—wrongly—that this would be a step away from democracy and in the direction of communism. Hall proposed that there should be a secret, £1 million subvention to pay for a new intelligence agency with the object of countering labour and political radicalism, and of frustrating the ambitions of Labour politicians. Prime Minister David Lloyd George was a Liberal who shared Hall's antipathy to communism and was similarly unhappy about the rise of the Labour Party, but he was a realist who needed the support of Labour Members of Parliament. He was against the super-surveillance plan, and there would be no official state support for it.

Hall therefore turned to the private sector. Soon after being elected in Liverpool to a seat in the House of Commons in 1919, he convened a meeting at 4 Dean's Yard. Two minutes' walk from Parliament, this was the location of the brewery owners' lobby. In attendance were another Conservative MP, John Gretton, chairman of Bass Brewery, and a selection of anti-labour industrialists representing ship owners, engineers, steel-makers, and, in the person of Evan Williams, mine owners. Hall organized these and other sympathetic businessmen to back National Propaganda, an organization with the declared aim of combating labour and the left. Wealthy supporters donated £250,000 in seed money to fund Hall's scheme.

Hall lost his parliamentary seat in the December 1923 election that resulted in the formation of the first Labour government under Prime Minister Ramsay MacDonald. Though his health was beginning to fail he continued in his active opposition to the Labour Party. For example, he was associated with a cabal within MI6 and the Conservative Party that falsely authenticated the Zinoviev letter. In the letter, a purported Comintern official urged Labour supporters to agitate for revolution and prepare the way for Bolshevism in the United Kingdom. Hall's co-conspirators caused it to be circulated just before the general election of 1924, an election that led to the fall of MacDonald's short-lived Labour government. Only later did it emerge that the letter was a forgery. The Zinoviev affair was one more reason why working people felt bitter towards the Tories in the 1920s.[9]

Hall stepped down from the leadership of National Propaganda in 1924 and went to America to advise on legal claims arising from German sabotage in the recent war—he soon developed a decided antipathy towards American liberals. National Propaganda in the meantime wanted to distance itself from the partisan politics that Hall represented. Within two years, Hall's creation changed its name to the Economic League. In spite of having formally distanced itself from the admiral, the League continued with his mission of propaganda and 'dirty tricks' against organized labour. Admiral Hall maintained his links with the organization and was a bridge between it and government intelligence agencies. There was resistance in some quarters. The head of the Metropolitan Police's Special Branch, Sir Wyndham Childs, saw private intelligence agencies like the Economic League as 'an intolerable nuisance'.[10] In other government circles there was a warmer welcome for Hall and his ilk. This was partly because of political sympathy with his anti-left, anti-labour views, and partly because the reduced capacity of MI5 and other agencies in straightened times seemed to his sympathizers to indicate a need for voluntary agents who would fill the breach. Hall thus retained his influence, and in the 1920s and 1930s he was also in demand across the Atlantic. There, he joined Van Deman in his denunciation of Franklin D. Roosevelt, and lectured and consulted on methods of countering labour insurgency.

Hall's Economic League, a nationwide organization, suggests the possibility that for a while, at least, the United Kingdom had taken the lead in the realm of private surveillance. The League had an ideological profile, being opposed to leftism and unionism in principle, making it perhaps more trustworthy in the eyes of employers than palpably for-profit detective agencies. In its propaganda activities, it operated openly, distributing millions of pamphlets and running classes on the dangers of communism and associated tendencies.

About the League's specific blacklisting activities, less is known. The picture is one of a struggle between agents and informers on the one side, and union loyalists who, on the other side, tried to deter and identify informers. Keeping tabs on informers was not always an easy task in a workforce that might be divided on ethnic and religious lines—Abertridwr, for example, was one-third Welsh, one-third English, and one-third Irish. Sometimes activists resorted to subterfuges like applying for jobs under assumed names in order to escape the surveillance of the blacklist makers. The absence of detail concerning these matters arises from the destruction of the relevant records. This destruction is unsurprising given the murky nature of the League's activities. Exposure of its collaboration with public officials would have been embarrassing and in some cases might lead to prosecution. The League refrained from going into detail about its strikebreaking activities for the further reason that some of its 1920s activists were linked to the British fascists.[11]

The deployment of spying and surveillance in the 1926 General Strike and the following miners' stoppage may not lend itself to detailed exposition, but it was certainly extensive. It is known that in Scotland coalmine owners were able to exchange lists containing the names of all those men dismissed for being activists. The Economic League demonstrably poured resources into Nottinghamshire, where the miners were less 'solid' than in other parts of the United Kingdom, and where it proved possible to start a back-to-work movement. Tom Watkins's Wales had in Evan Williams produced perhaps the most formidable of coalmine-owning leaders. For a quarter of a century from 1919 he was president of the Mining Association of Great Britain. He had been educated at Cambridge University and had a link to Scotland through his wife Charlotte. Williams had been associated with the move to return the coalmines to private ownership after the First World War. He was responsible for defeating the efforts of the 'Fed', the Miners' Federation of Great Britain, to achieve universal wage rates. It is to be assumed that he sanctioned and encouraged Economic League-style surveillance and blacklisting in Wales, where he had been chairman of the Monmouthshire and South Wales Coal Owners Association as early as 1913. The surviving records of the Economic League indicate that in the years leading up to the General Strike it had an exceptionally strong following in South Wales.[12]

Meanwhile on the national level, official MI5 records show that the Security Service's Chief Vernon Kell kept an eye on the General Strike through a dining club he had formed. By employing these gastro-bibulous means, he kept in touch with former intelligence personnel who now had their fingers in private pies. With a view to becoming privy to the strikers' tactics, one of these agents penetrated the offices of the *Daily Herald*, the newspaper jointly run by the Trade Union Council and the Labour Party. Once the strike had been defeated, Kell wrote to his staff to congratulate them on their achievement.[13]

When it came to the surveillance of British workers, then, there was private, official, and also official-cum-private activity. In this respect, the work of the Economic League should be kept in perspective. The authors of one study of the League note that it was 'just one element' of a broader attack on labour in the 1920s and 1930s.[14] For example, there was Conservative government legislation. The Trade Disputes and Trade Unions Act of 1927 (repealed in 1946) made crimes of strikes with political objectives, sympathy action, and mass picketing, and placed restrictions on unions' financial contributions to the Labour Party.

There were also other private anti-labour organizations. Nevertheless, the League continued to play a significant role, and continued its unofficial collaboration with the government. To give a micro-illustration, it received data from the Admiralty following the 1931 'Invergordon Mutiny' when Royal Navy sailors went on strike over a pay dispute at a base in north-east Scotland, and blacklisted at least one of the leaders when he sought work as a rigger outside the Navy.

Later in the 1930s, there were, on both sides of the Atlantic, public exposés of anti-labour surveillance. The La Follette Civil

Liberties Committee, a subcommittee of the Senate Committee on Education and Labor, held hearings between 1936 and 1941. It published two reports on the misdeeds of Californian employers; additional nationally orientated reports titled *Industrial Espionage*, *Private Police Systems*, and *Strikebreaking Services*; and seven further reports on associated matters. Its chairman Senator Robert M. La Follette, Jr (Progressive, WI) subpoenaed the Pinkerton National Detective Agency, the William J. Burns International Detective Agency, and other firms engaged in penetrating labour unions. The agencies destroyed their archives to conceal their practices, and so did the Van Deman-linked Industrial Association on the night before it was subpoenaed to reveal its records. Officials testifying for the Pinkerton and Burns agencies insisted that they were not union-busting but chasing down communists.

Interrogated on the point, the Pinkerton man had to confess that he had so far uncovered not a single Red. In spite of the spate of record-destruction, the anti-labour surveillance industry failed to cover its tracks. It became clear that labour unions were still saturated with private-agency spies. In addition, there were those employers who directly employed agents and informers. General Motors could not conceal the fact that in the space of two years it had spent around $1 million on informers within the United Automobile Workers union. In 1937, the socialist Leo Huberman presented a digested version of the La Follette hearings' 2,500,000 words of testimony in his book *The Labor Spy Racket*. He focused on private detective agencies, and estimated that they made $80,000,000 a year out of 'Union-Prevention and Union-Smashing'.

The La Follette civil liberties investigation of the 1930s brought home to Americans and to their representatives on Capitol Hill the need for action at the federal level. Section 8 of the National Labor Relations or Wagner Act of 1935 had already outlawed 'unfair labor practices' including discrimination in employment on the ground of union membership. In 1940 Senator La Follette promoted an even tougher bill, the Oppressive Labor Practices Act. Though the Senate approved the bill, the House withheld its support as the nation began to go onto a war footing and the mood swung against labour militancy.

In May 1937 with the La Follette inquiry in full swing, the United Kingdom's communist newspaper the *Daily Worker* ran an exposé of the Economic League. According to *The Times*, which commented on the story a month later, the story drew on correspondence that was stolen from the League, copied, and then given to the *Daily Worker*, whose staff then refused to divulge the identity of their informants. The League confirmed the authenticity of the documents when they cited them in suing the *Daily Worker* for damages.

For once, there was an authenticated glimpse into the inner workings of the League. It revealed that its regional branches kept records on troublemakers who might ask questions about safety conditions or otherwise challenge managers, and that the Central Council of the League had a nationwide card index of 'subversives' with records of their movements and activities, information that could be and was passed to League subscribers. For example, lists of men not to be employed arrived at the offices of the Devonport and Sheerness dockyards, Fairey Aviation, Metropolitan Vickers, Ferranti, and the English Steel Corporation.[15]

Labour MPs asked questions in Parliament, especially about the revelation that the Manchester police had passed information to the League, allegedly in breach of the Official Secrets Act. They demanded a prosecution of the police and the League. The Attorney General suppressed the case, but the Economic League had suffered a blow to its credibility and prestige.

The pendulum of fair play appeared to have swung at least half an inch in favour of the wage earner. By restoring higher levels of employment, British entry into another war further helped to redress the balance. Things did improve for Tom Watkins. Suddenly, his country needed him. As ever, he undertook dangerous work, this time as a dispatch rider patrolling the streets of Cardiff and then Manchester during German bombing raids. Already schooled in the use of explosives, he took an interest in the effects of blast, such as 'bouncing'—one night, a bomb fell behind him and its blast killed the man in front of him, leaving him unscathed. After the war, Tom was a white-collar worker in Manchester, played the organ for BBC Sunday worship programmes, and then retired with Sarah to live in North Wales, next door to one of his daughters. Once more, at the Methodists' Capel Moriah in Harlech he sat in the *sedd mawr*, the epitome of respectability until his death in 1968. One of his few social solecisms was his habit of spitting whenever anyone said the word 'Tory'.

Tom Watkins was not wasting his spittle, for blacklisting returned with a vengeance to post-war Britain. But although labour espionage remained a potent issue, it was the advent of middle-class concern that made surveillance a universal debating point. The arrival of the national security state hastened that concern. To illuminate the theme, the searchlight of inquiry must once again focus on the United States, and on the presidency of Franklin D. Roosevelt.

4

Franklin D. Roosevelt's Incipient Surveillance State

What kind of a man was Franklin D. Roosevelt (FDR), now regarded as the president who ushered in America's national security state with its surveillance tendencies?

Like so many of his predecessors and successors, he had a mistress. Lucy Mercer (later Mrs Rutherfurd) first engaged his attention in 1914. They managed to hide their affair from FDR's wife Eleanor until 1918, when Eleanor stumbled across a cache of their love letters. After that, the triumvirate kept the relationship hidden in spite of its long-surviving character—Lucy was still with FDR when he died in Warm Springs, Georgia in 1945. As in all such cases until the Bill Clinton–Monika Lewinsky episode, the secret endured with the assistance of nods, winks, and silence from the press corps and from fellow politicians. Not until 1966, over twenty years after FDR's death, did the story come out.

Well practiced in the defence of his own privacy, FDR was by contrast inquisitive about his fellow citizens. He was particularly curious about their voting intentions, and about their views on issues that, collectively, would determine which way they would vote. In 1933 at the beginning of his presidency, he was dependent on the White House's press office, which undertook the task of approximating public opinion from what the papers said. From the start of his second term in 1937, however, independent opinion assessment started under the auspices of the privately funded and run Gallup poll. George Gallup, its pioneer, had improved the methodology of that now-familiar form of public interrogation, the questionnaire. Gallup polls collected what in our own day would be called 'metadata'—a benign activity, yet potentially a step in the direction of the management of political beliefs.

None of the characteristics so far identified made FDR all that different from his presidential peers. Presidents kept their sexual encounters private, and all took an interest in public opinion—the White House press office had been operating since the late nineteenth century. Although CIA and other spooks are meant to be professional deceivers, top politicians like the denizens of the White House could give them lessons in the dark arts of dissimulation and public-opinion manipulation.

Yet if FDR was just like other presidents, he was like them but more so. People commented on his exceptional characteristics. Those who visited him noticed that he kept a clear desk. He wanted no paper trail to give a clue to his own thoughts. His visitors generally left his presence feeling happy. Roosevelt had the gift of making you think that he had agreed with you, even if he had just received another supplicant with views opposed to your own who had also left feeling satisfied.

FDR did lack one quality when it came to keeping tabs on the American people. Because he had been struck down with polio in the 1920s, he was unable to walk properly and to intermingle freely with his fellow Americans. Famously, Eleanor Roosevelt stepped into the breach. She remained her husband's political if not sexual partner. It was she who went to meet and listen to the Bonus Expeditionary Force marchers, the impoverished First World War veterans who early in her husband's presidency camped on the outskirts of Washington DC and demanded the back pay due to them. It was she who continued to circulate amongst the American people with her eyes and ears open, and reported back to the president. Well before the international crises of the later 1930s that prompted President Roosevelt to set up the formal apparatus of a more intrusive state, he had made use of his wife and other opinion gaugers to find out what made Americans tick.

The Roosevelt administration's main moves towards a surveillance state nevertheless occurred only when war clouds had once again thrown their shadow across Europe. There were warning signs in the Nazis' domestic intolerance and Germany's intervention in the Spanish Civil War in 1936. Now that FDR's New Deal policies had averted the immediate political crisis caused by the Great Depression, perhaps America might be ready to resume its place on the world stage.

But in America there was a deep reluctance to become involved in another European war. Between 1934 and 1936, the Senate Investigation of the Munitions Industry led by Gerald P. Nye (Republican, ND) stoked the feeling that American manufacturers and British diplomacy had manoeuvred the United States into entering the First World War. People asked, why risk American boys' lives by confronting Adolf Hitler, when the Soviet leader Joseph Stalin posed just as serious a threat to the nation's democratic values? With such feelings in evidence, distant belligerencies were not enough to undermine the isolationist spirit. It would take a more immediate trigger, an event that affected America directly.

Such an event occurred in 1938. Its beginnings occurred a long way from American shores in the shape of a German foreign intelligence (*Abwehr*) operation in Scotland. The *Abwehr* sent Jessie Jordan to spy on her homeland. A Scottish-born daughter of Irish parents, Jessie was the widow of a German who died on the Western Front in 1918. Following his death she had a rough time in Germany and would tell her lawyer that she felt rejected by all countries, and had no sense of nationality. On her return to Scotland in 1937, she responded to *Abwehr* requests for sketches of the significant naval installations around Edinburgh and Rosyth.

Jessie also had another function. In the jargon of her trade, she was a post-box. She received letters from German agents and forwarded them to her controller in Hamburg. Some of the letters came from Czechoslovakia, a country that Hitler was about to invade. Most of them came from the United States.

Jessie's activities were no secret to British counter-intelligence. At first, MI5 let her run, with the purpose of learning more about how the *Abwehr* arranged its affairs. But then '5' learned of a German spy plot to trick an American naval officer into visiting a room in the McAlpin Hotel, New York City, where he would be relieved of secret defence documents at the possible cost of his life.

The time had come to tip off the Americans. After an approach through diplomatic channels, the FBI put one of its crack special agents onto the case—Leon Turrou was a formidable linguist with a forensic mind. It soon transpired that the person behind the McAlpin plot was Guenther Rumrich (alias 'Crown'), a German-speaking Czech who had joined and then deserted from the US Army. In a similarity with Jessie Jordan, he would say at his trial that he did not know the meaning of patriotism. Though Rumrich was lower down the spy pecking order than his leader Willy Lonkowski (alias 'Sex'), the press insisted on referring to the 'Rumrich Spy Ring'. The case inspired two rounds of sensational publicity, the first in February 1938 occasioned by the arrest of Rumrich and others, the second in October when Rumrich was a witness for the prosecution in the trial.

The Rumrich spy case helped to alter the course of history by encouraging America to think again about its 1930s policy of neutrality. In particular, it nudged the nation in the direction of stronger counter-intelligence and more domestic surveillance, for Turrou had compiled a portfolio of evidence indicating that there was a serious need to tighten up US Navy security. His portfolio did also suggest the evidence could be read in another way—US naval ship design (for example, regarding aluminium hulls) was so complex that nobody could understand it, least of all a humble spy. However, it is clear in retrospect that the German spies did deliver secrets to Berlin, including the specifications of the latest US precision-bombing sight.

The *New York Times* tried to play down the significance of both the case and the need for tighter security. Towards the end of the year, it published an editorial depicting the Rumrich trial as a 'faintly humorous drama' and arguing that, in an age of open access to information, the very idea of military secrets was anachronistic. The paper had its own agenda: 'The creation of any super-espionage military agency is both unnecessary and undesirable. It is alien to American traditions, and no glorified [Soviet] "OGPU" or secret police is needed or wanted here.'[1]

Because spy stories make such good copy, it was hard to stick to the line that the Rumrich case should be played down. London's

Times had carried no fewer than fifty-four stories on the case in the first eleven months of 1938. Turrou fanned the media frenzy when he quit the FBI and sold details of the case to the *New York Post*. He kept interest alive through his book *The Nazi Spy Conspiracy in America*, published in the following year, in which he warned that Jessie Jordan had been at the heart of 'a vast, international Nazi spy ring'. In May 1939, Hollywood released the movie *Confessions of a Nazi Spy*. Its star Edward G. Robinson had won fame for acting the part of gangsters in *Little Caesar* and other films, but, of Romanian-Jewish extraction, he was aware of the nature of the Hitlerite menace, and successfully petitioned to cross the lines and play the part of Leon Turrou.

Turrou's leaks annoyed President Roosevelt who at first wanted to minimize friction with Germany. As a *New York Sun* correspondent put it, the biggest spy case since 1918 meant that 'relations between the United States and Nazi Germany may become more strained', and FDR was not yet ready for that.

But it was too late to assuage fears about national security. When most members of the spy ring escaped custody (only four out of eighteen went on trial and were convicted), indignation over American incompetence overtook anger at German perfidiousness. Analysis of congressional debate shows that there was more concern about foreign espionage in 1938 than at any point since the dying down of the First World War and Red Scares of 1917–22.[2]

Roosevelt overcame his caution and decided to put the FBI at the centre of an effort to boost American security. The decision reflected his political judgement that Americans valued security. Having delivered social security at home, he saw it as his duty to enhance national security against foreign threats. This put him on a collision course with the liberal thinking that had prevailed over the previous twenty years. Fears of FBI political meddling had been evident in the year of its foundation in 1908. The bureau's activities in the 1919–20 Red Scare rang further alarm bells in the civil liberties fraternity, and Attorney General Harlan Fiske Stone in appointing Hoover to be director in 1924 explicitly prohibited political surveillance. Then in 1934, President Roosevelt signed the Federal Communications Act banning wiretapping; in *Nardone v US* (1937, 1939) the Supreme Court ruled that this applied to federal agencies, and that wiretapped information was inadmissible as court evidence.

However, less liberal trends were in also evidence prior to the Rumrich jolt to American public opinion and leadership. In the case of *Olmstead v US* (1928), the Supreme Court had ruled that the government could conduct warrantless wiretapping without violating Fourth Amendment rights. Then in August 1936 FDR asked the FBI director to investigate communist and fascist activities within the United States. Not wishing to clutter his desk with telltale evidence, the president made it an oral not a written instruction. Hoover remembered the request as a directive to look into 'subversive activities'.[3]

Any ambiguity on that point disappeared in the wake of the Rumrich affair. At a press conference on 24 June 1938, President Roosevelt deplored Turrou's indiscretions but also said he would request bigger appropriations for the FBI's counter-espionage budget. In October, the president asked his Attorney General, Homer Cummings, to investigate intelligence security and determine whether more money was needed. Cummings asked Hoover to report on the matter. The FBI director said he already had the authority to act against foreign spies and against 'subversive' activity.

Less than a year later, the Second World War broke out in Europe. Although American entry into the war was still more than two years away, Roosevelt now issued on 6 September 1939 what is sometimes referred to as the 'Magna Carta' of FBI intelligence work. He put the FBI in charge of all counter-espionage matters and, apparently for the first time in writing, charged the bureau with investigating 'subversive activities'. The FBI began to compile a Custodial Detention Index. Later known as the Security Index, this was ostensibly a list of people who might endanger security if a war broke out, but potentially a tool of oppression in a surveillance state. The following May, Roosevelt backed the director when he issued a secret directive authorizing the FBI to tap telephone conversations in the course of national security investigations. Additional FBI offices sprang up all over America to handle the additional work. Cummings' successor as Attorney General, Frank Murphy, promised there would be no 'witch hunt' on the 1919 model, and that there would be no unruly voluntary or 'vigilante' element in the new initiative.[4]

In spite of that promise, the FBI did operate against radicals. Even before the new Rooseveltian dispensation, the FBI had kept literary radicals under surveillance; indeed the Red Scare of 1919 continued in more muted form throughout the interwar years. The bureau's file on Sinclair Lewis (author of *Babbit*, first American winner of the Nobel prize for literature) dated from 1923. Through an administrative oversight, the transcript of an FBI 1934 wiretap on Upton Sinclair (author of *The Jungle*) survives. By the end of the 1930s, there were FBI files on Clifford Odets, Ernest Hemingway, John Steinbeck, Pearl Buck, and William Faulkner.

In February 1940, the FBI refreshed its anti-left credentials by swooping on a Detroit meeting of union officials and others associated with the Lincoln Brigade, the American volunteers who had fought against the fascists in the Spanish Civil War. Commenting on this, a local Methodist pastor warned that 'the American people will not countenance even the first steps toward the establishment of a secret police that will in any way resemble the despised German Gestapo or the hated Russian Ogpu'.[5]

Hoover's equation of the left with subversion was nothing new, but he went further. His FBI increasingly placed non-left persons under surveillance. His targets included his one-time boss, Attorney General Frank Murphy, the New Dealer and future Supreme Court Justice Felix Frankfurter, and the president's wife Eleanor. A white southerner with little appreciation of the civil rights of black citizens, Hoover set the FBI to discover what Mrs Roosevelt was up to in her meetings with southern black women. Even with the war under way and many calls on the federal budget, in 1942 he found the resources to set Special Agent Howard Odum the task of discovering whether 'ER' was engaged in a conspiracy to liberate black female cooks, thus condemning southern white women to undertake culinary chores in their own kitchens.

Hoover placed prominent anti-interventionists under surveillance. The president was implicated here, obliquely. It seems to have worked like this. Hoover showed FDR political intelligence reports and Roosevelt made no complaints about receiving them. Making the deduction that Roosevelt wanted the information, the FBI director furnished the president with still more reports.

In assessing the significance of the anti-interventionist surveillance activity, the historian must make an effort at objectivity. The verdict of most people, looking back at the years 1939–41, is that the case for intervention was good, and that Pearl Harbor catapulted American into a just war. On the basis of that assumption, it would be easy to forgive the sins of the FBI and the compliant president. But, of course, those who adopt a mistaken political stance have just as many rights as those who pursue the wiser course. Furthermore, it must be remembered that in spite of the Rumrich affair and Hitler's depredations in Europe, public opinion favoured American neutrality. In May 1941, Hoover sent Roosevelt the result of an opinion poll that *Look* magazine was about to publish, indicating that there was still strong public disapproval of most forms of interventionism, including 80 per cent opposition to the use of American ships in Atlantic convoys bearing vital goods to the United Kingdom.

The FBI kept under surveillance those individuals who opposed intervention and had political influence. Charles Lindbergh, for example, was a household name. In 1927, he had achieved a solo, non-stop flight across the Atlantic in his monoplane the *Spirit of St. Louis*. In March 1932, the aviator's toddler son, Charles Augustus Lindbergh, Jr, was kidnapped from the family home in East Amwell, New Jersey. The family paid the ransom, but the 20-month-old was brutally murdered anyway. The FBI eventually got their man, the unemployed carpenter Bruno Richard Hauptmann went to the chair, and the whole nation sympathized with Charles Lindbergh. By 1940, however, Lindbergh had infuriated President Roosevelt by becoming a leader of the 850,000-strong anti-interventionist organization known as America First. FDR called Lindbergh a Nazi, and that made him an FBI target.

In July 1941, Lindbergh said that the FBI was bugging his telephone. The contention was not provable as the bureau was too canny to keep records of such surveillance, especially in the case of a high-profile target. But the FBI did seek information to discredit the flier. It circulated rumours that he had leaked national defence secrets to the anti-interventionist *Chicago Tribune*, and tried to show that the iconic family man had associated with prostitutes in Butte, Montana. In this case, the FBI missed a trick because it remained ignorant of the fact that Lindbergh secretly kept a second family in Germany. Lindbergh avoided disgrace for the further reason that he now distinguished himself as a US combat pilot. But it is plain that surveillance-cum-dirty tricks had become entrenched on the national scene.

In the summer of 1941, FBI surveillance coughed up false evidence of criminality affecting three prominent anti-intervention politicians. One of these was Senator Burton K. Wheeler (Democrat, MT), who was not only an upholder of neutrality, but also a leading critic of overweening FBI surveillance.

Known as 'Bolshevik Burt' in his youth though a fervent anti-communist in later years, Wheeler had defended civil liberties during the hysteria of the First World War. Elected to the Senate in 1922, he helped to expose the corruption of Attorney General Harry Daugherty, leading to the resignation in 1924 of Daugherty and of Hoover's predecessor as director of the FBI, William J. Burns. A New Deal supporter at first, Wheeler became chairman of the Committee on Interstate Commerce in 1935, before criticizing President Roosevelt's attempt to pack the Supreme Court in 1937. He then led the opposition to US involvement in the European war.

Wheeler had fallen within the orbit of FBI anti-radical surveillance at an early stage. In 1932, the bureau had to respond to the charge that the disgraced Attorney General Daugherty had put a tail on Senator Wheeler and two other critics. Special Agent in Charge D. Milton ('Mickey') Ladd sent Hoover a report on the case in which he exonerated Daugherty. Ladd furthermore dug up two strictly confidential reports from informers in the Soviet Union, one working for the State Department and the other for the FBI. These spies had relayed information about Wheeler's Bolshevik contacts on a visit to the Latvian capital Riga in 1923, and recorded the Senator's view that the United States should recognize the Soviet Union (an event that would occur in 1933). To put it mildly, the conservative leadership of the FBI did not regard Senator Wheeler as a friend.

The year 1940 found Wheeler and the FBI re-sharpening their swords. An initiative to clarify the law on wiretapping in the wake of the *Nardone* case arrived at its climax. The administration had wanted clearer authority in the matter. But the government's resultant bill (S. 3756) came before Wheeler's Interstate Commerce Committee, which in its report upheld the principles of the Fourth Amendment. The committee stated that, regarding the 'interception of radio and wire communications', authority should be granted 'only after' the head of the relevant government department 'certifies that through a "gang, confederacy, or group of two or more persons" a crime has been or is about to be committed'. Thus, general warrants were unacceptable to Wheeler's committee. Two senior Hoover aides gave the director a briefing report on 'Wire Tapping by the Federal Bureau of Investigation' in case he should be called to testify before the committee, but the legislative effort did not even get that far. The administration's bill died.[6]

This was not the only bone of contention between Wheeler and the administration. Another disagreement arose from FDR's immigration policy. A contrived xenophobia lay at the back of that policy. Just as in the previous war public opinion had been mobilized against German-Americans and socialists who were accused of being anti-war, so in the Second World War the administration whipped up public anxiety by warning of 'fifth column' activities. These were acts of sabotage and espionage by Nazi sympathizers working undercover in the USA. British spies operating from their base in New York helped to manipulate public-opinion polls in a way that suggested that the American people were afraid of the German Trojan horse in their midst. It was an example of opinion sampling operating as a form of pseudo-surveillance, producing an artificial result. British front organizations such as Friends of Democracy additionally organized anti-fifth column demonstrations. By no means every American was taken in by these British initiatives or open to deception by them, but a siege mentality began to develop.

In reality the fifth column menace was virtually non-existent. But the provision of an obnoxious 'other' was a good way of rallying public support in favour of a stance against Germany, and, after Pearl Harbor, against Japan—the US government interning almost the entire Japanese-American population in February 1942.

To back up its fifth column propaganda, the Roosevelt administration proposed a bureaucratic reform. The Immigration and Naturalization Service, hitherto run by the Department of Labor, would now fall within the Department of Justice. Senator George W. Norris (Republican, NE), not an admirer of J. Edgar Hoover and soon to be a champion of the incarcerated Japanese-Americans, saw this as a sinister move that would allow the FBI 'to operate upon thousands and thousands of poor, ignorant, helpless people'. Senator Wheeler admitted he could not stop the anti-fifth column juggernaut, but recorded his feeling 'that a very serious mistake is being made in turning this bureau over to the Justice Department'.

This most senior critic of Roosevelt's foreign policy continued by making a series of charges against the FBI. He reminded his fellow-Americans about the FBI's actions in the Red Scare and more recently against the Lincoln Brigade, and added:

> I am prejudiced against the FBI for some of the things it has done to me. They have raided my office time and time again…They had a file on me in the Department of Justice, which I found when I came down there. They have files on this Senator and that Senator…on Senator Robert M. La Follette (Prog., Wis)…They have gone through the offices of every liberal senator…[7]

Wheeler had identified a behavioural trait that would become familiar to politicians over the years. To instil fear into the powerful Mr Smith, Hoover would show him the compromising information he had on Mr Jones, with the unstated but clear implication that he had similar information on Smith himself. Proving that the FBI had conducted politically motivated raids would not be easy—the bureau disguised telephone taps by referring to them in its records as 'confidential sources'—and might well prove impolitic as the FBI director could deploy embarrassing information to exact his revenge.[8]

Hoover used dirty tricks to advance the political interests of his master in the White House in the course of the debate over interventionism. Senator Nye was a high-profile target as his congressional inquiry had discredited the arms industry and the rationale for US entry into the First World War, and because he continued to advocate the cause of neutrality, becoming a leading speaker and radio broadcaster on behalf of the anti-interventionist America First Committee. The FBI scoured every available source to obtain embarrassing information on Nye—and on Congressman Hamilton Fish (Republican, NY).

A decorated veteran of the last war and critic of the New Deal, Fish had in 1939 formed the National Committee to Keep America

Out of War. British Security Coordination, London's intelligence outfit in New York, paralleled the FBI's efforts and through the secret dissemination of disinformation tried to secure Fish's defeat in the election of 1940—he survived, but with a reduced majority. In the following year, the FBI launched an investigation into all three politicians—Wheeler, Nye, and Fish—with a view to charging them with abusing their mail-franking privileges to send out anti-war propaganda. In the event, it turned out that the plot had been hatched in the German embassy, and had nothing to do with the anti-interventionist members of Congress.

After Pearl Harbor, the former anti-interventionists supported the war effort. However, they remained under surveillance. When in January 1942 Wheeler made some off-the-record remarks criticizing the Roosevelt administration for being Anglophile and for covering up the truth about Pearl Harbor, President Roosevelt's secretary Stephen Early asked Hoover to investigate. The FBI director obliged, and the White House received a report partially based on Senator Wheeler's 'facial expressions'.[9]

Politically motivated FBI investigations targeted people in several walks of life. Harry Elmer Barnes was an influential historian whose book *The Genesis of the World War* (1926) had challenged the view that Germany alone should bear the responsibility for the start of the 1914–18 conflict. With another war on the horizon, he was an anti-interventionist who attracted Hoover's attention. Once the war broke out, the time had arrived for what George Orwell would later describe as 'newspeak'; history had to be rewritten and contemporary events had to be recorded in a 'groupthink' script. In 1942–3, Hoover sent the Justice Department four reports claiming that Barnes was a pro-communist Anglophobe. However, he failed to convince the department's lawyers that there was enough evidence to charge the hitherto respected historian with sedition.

Another FBI target was the anti-interventionist campaigner Robert E. Wood. The bureau denied Wood's charge that it was tapping his telephone conversations, but it did have him under surveillance. In February 1942 the FBI processed a report that recorded Wood's career: he had retired from the Army in 1918 while serving as acting Quartermaster General and with the rank of Brigadier General. In peacetime he enjoyed a career in merchandizing, becoming chairman of Sears Roebuck and Company, then was chairman of American First. The report probed into ways in which Wood might have broken the law, but on balance gave him a clean bill of health, and noted that he quit his isolationist stance as soon as the war started.

This particular report was chiefly based on newspaper stories. So it is notable not as a secret method of surveillance but because it was so political. Another point of interest is that although the FBI processed the report, it originated with the War Department's Military Intelligence Division. The president had charged the FBI with coordinating counter-intelligence, and the report is an example of how the FBI did not rely solely on its own resources, and utilized the manpower to be found elsewhere in the intelligence community.[10]

Such developments later caused a bipartisan storm of criticism of Franklin D. Roosevelt for presiding over the start of an American security or surveillance state. Early on, the more serious attacks came from American conservatives who took exception to the president's use of executive power, and to the New Deal's creation of a tangle of federal agencies that, they complained, rode roughshod over the rights of private businessmen and prepared the way for a police state. Later on, American liberals seized the baton. Frank Church (Democrat, ID) chaired the 1975–6 Senate investigation into federal intelligence. It published five volumes of hearings on domestic surveillance and reviewed its pre-1945 history. Civil libertarian historians like Athan Theoharis, a staff member for the Church inquiry, rewrote national security history in a way that threatened to knock FDR off the pedestal on which liberal historians had previously place him. The indictment has continued in more recent times. The historian Ellen Schrecker points to the multiplication of informants in the Second World War—the Army's G2 had 250,000, and the FBI 80,000—informants whose contribution to national security was, according to the FBI's Mickey Ladd, 'practically negligible'.[11]

Nevertheless, in assessing the FBI's political surveillance in the early 1940s there is a need for a sense of proportion. The fifth column scare was allowed to subside once it had achieved its objective, the preparation of public opinion for another war. And the resources of the FBI were relatively limited. Partly because of resentment of Hoover's ambitions, cooperation with military and naval intelligence was less satisfactory than FDR had hoped, and the bureau had to rely largely on its own resources.

These did include an army of private informants. But the limited reach of full-time FBI professionals can be demonstrated by making some comparisons. By the end of the Second World War, the FBI had 4,370 special agents, one for every 32,037 citizens. This was a higher ratio than in the United Kingdom, where in 1943 MI5 reached a wartime peak of 332 officers, one for every 138,554 subjects. But in Hitler's Germany, there was a Gestapo agent for every 2,000 citizens; after the war, Stalin's KGB had one officer per 5,830, and East Germany's Stasi one for every 175.[12]

Even under the duress of all-out war, America was far from being a police state. Care must be taken not to assume that the concealment of evidence by the president and the FBI director meant they were engaged in a deep-seated conspiracy to spy on all Americans.

Yet, in spite of these qualifications, it is difficult to resist the conclusion that the Rumrich spy case and its after-effects helped to set the nation on a new course. Roosevelt's appetite for information and J. Edgar Hoover's intrusive instincts and desire to please the president contributed to some significant developments. Citizens' Fourth Amendment rights and freedom from surveillance were certainly less secure in 1945 than they had been before the Rumrich case.

5

McCarthyism in America

Lewis Compton was of New Jersey 'old stock', an aspiring politician, and a Franklin D. Roosevelt protégé. President Roosevelt from time to time delivered intimate and persuasive 'fireside chats' on early evening radio, and Lewis would sit his son Jim down to listen to them. James V. Compton duly grew up an FDR fan. He took pride in his father's service as FDR's Assistant Secretary of the Navy, a post in those days regarded as a stepping stone to the presidency; he shared Compton, Sr's sense of tragedy and shock over Pearl Harbor, and, following his father's death in 1942, found solace in the launch of a warship bearing the family name.

Jim Compton later attended Princeton University, and upon graduation in the early 1950s found himself on the labour market. His mother had remarried, and his stepfather was a rancher out West, so the job Jim applied for was in the Arizona public school system.

It was there that his troubles began. Students of 'McCarthyism' will have recognized already that Jim was a potential victim of that era's hate discrimination—born with the proverbial silver spoon in his mouth, Ivy League educated, an adherent of FDR and his allegedly socialistic practices. To this, could be added the fact that Jim was gay—as is becoming increasingly evident in the light of continuing research, McCarthyism was aimed at homosexuals as well as those perceived to be on the left. The particular stumbling block in Jim's case was the teachers' loyalty oath. The Committee on Un-American Activities in the lower house of Arizona's legislature had drafted loyalty oaths in 1948 with the result that, in common with forty other states by 1953, Arizona required its teachers to abjure communism as a condition of employment.

So here was the problem. If everyone who was not a communist took the oath, it would by process of elimination leave the actual communists exposed. The communists thus isolated would consequently find it impossible to find employment even if they were qualified to teach and had committed no crime. To uphold the principle of fair play, Jim and others across the nation refused to take the oath.

Arizona therefore would not hire him. On the reasonable assumption that the same fate would await him elsewhere in the teaching profession, Jim now sought and found manual work in the Hughes Aircraft Company in California. However, the long arm of popular surveillance snaked out to the West Coast and found him out. When managers at the defence contractor discovered that Jim had refused to take the Arizona loyalty oath, they fired him.

Traumatized, Jim left America for Europe where he purchased a leather jacket, revved up his motorbike, and hit the roads throughout the continent. Having tasted the lifestyle portrayed in *The Wild One* (Marlon Brando's movie), his next step was to acquire a PhD from the London School of Economics. With this in hand, he obtained a teaching post and promoted the study of America at the University of Edinburgh where his charismatic lectures on FDR's New Deal would be long remembered—an accidental benefit of American McCarthyism.

Jim's lectureship initially depended on funds from the American Council of Learned Societies. Though Edinburgh University made the appointment, the provenance of the funds seemed like at least a partial US exoneration of Jim. In the late 1960s James V. Compton in a reciprocal vein 'forgave America' on the basis that McCarthyism was dead. In 1968 he returned to the USA and secured a teaching post at San Francisco State University. Thereafter, he lived happily in the Castro district of his adoptive city.[1]

The Jim Compton story—it is by no means extreme or exceptional—feeds into a number of questions about the surveillance ingredient in McCarthyism. The surveillance of Jim Compton appears not to have been organized by the federal government or by the State of Arizona. Rather, the surveillance was of a private and informal nature. People kept their eyes open, the word went around, and the secret blacklist tracked him to California. At the back of this lay developments in national and local politics. But as far as the Jim Comptons of this world were concerned, McCarthyism was also something the American people did to themselves.

This touches on a contentious historical theme: who or what accounted for McCarthyism with its invidious surveillance practices? The word is taken from the surname of Senator Joseph McCarthy (Republican, WI). While McCarthy's investigating committee sowed seeds of terror in the early 1950s, it based its identification of radicals more on hearsay than on systematic government surveillance. However, the Wisconsin senator was just one of the people involved in McCarthyism or, as some prefer to say, the Great Fear. A historian of religion might be tempted to see the phenomenon as a secular manifestation of American revivalism, with millions of Americans prying into the affairs of their neighbours in search of the sin of 'un-Americanism'. A little more prosaically, historians have pointed to the preceding role of the Truman administration, which, in the 1940s, placed dissenters under FBI surveillance.

Whatever one's emphasis, there has been a tendency to view McCarthyism as an episode in the history of American exceptionalism. Seen from this perspective, America gave birth to McCarthyism and then destroyed its own baby-monster. A corollary holds that the United Kingdom, by comparison, looked askance at the antics of its transatlantic cousin, claiming to be immune from such nonsense. However, as we shall see in the next chapter, America was not so very different. In the United Kingdom, the dual phenomena of denial and then the absence of a purging process contributed to the perpetuation of a lower-level, longer-lasting, and 'silent' British McCarthyism.

The phenomenon often referred to as McCarthyism started before McCarthy discovered it. In its modern form it can be traced to President Harry Truman's sales pitch when he found himself with his back to the political wall. With both houses of Congress under Republican control following the 1946 mid-term elections, the president faced two problems. The first was Republican Red-baiters who charged that his administration was soft on international communism and in favour of creeping socialism at home. The second was wavering public support for his foreign policy. Truman apparently calculated that it would be possible both to outflank the Red-baiters and to scare his fellow Americans into supporting his policies.

The historian Ellen Schrecker has consequently observed that what 'transformed the Communist threat into a national obsession was not its plausibility, but the involvement of the federal government' (the American Communist Party had by now shrunk to miniscule proportions). She further argues that 'McCarthyism was not a private venture', and that Washington 'led the way'. In another work, Schrecker does point to a private factor—the way in which universities fell into line with the Great Fear. But on balance there is a good case for saying that the government in the shape of the Truman administration, like the Roosevelt administration that preceded it, strengthened the sinews of the surveillance state.[2]

The timing of Truman's loyalty programme confirms its link with foreign policy. In March 1947 the president announced what came to be known as the Truman Doctrine, the policy of propping up anti-communist regimes in Greece and Turkey. In June of the same year, he launched a scheme to bolster the economies of the democratic countries of Western Europe—the European Recovery Plan was usually referred to as the Marshall Plan after its eponymous promoter, Secretary of State George Marshall. Both of these policies, and the Marshall Plan especially, required large-scale US expenditure and thus the support of Congress. By talking up the Soviet threat overseas, Truman hoped to achieve bipartisan support for his foreign policy, and this was indeed the outcome— but at the same time the president gave an unintended opportunity to the Red-baiters he had hoped to silence.

Truman legitimized the Red-baiters not just rhetorically, but also through his actions. On 21 March 1947, a presidential executive order established the loyalty programme for federal employees. The government presented it as an effort to root out Soviet spies—there had been a rash of spy cases in the war and its aftermath and Moscow had acquired some of the USA's atomic secrets—and to expunge communist influences. The task of checking on the loyalty of employees and potential employees fell to the FBI.

The programme worried even those who were responsible for it. FBI director Hoover was not overjoyed at the prospect, and dragged his heels when it came to investigating one of the most sensitive categories, those being hired to work for the recently formed Central Intelligence Agency (CIA). Truman himself was wise to potential repercussions. The FBI had recently come under attack for being an incipient 'American Gestapo', so the president authorized the creation of a Loyalty Review Board to guard against FBI excesses.

Regardless of Hoover's initial reservations, the FBI put a programme into effect. By 1952 it had doubled its number of special agents and had conducted 2 million loyalty investigations, 20,000 of them intensive. Gestapo worries about the FBI had by now been forgotten. In his book of 1951 exposing the excesses of the loyalty programme, the *Washington Post* journalist Alan Barth ruefully noted that the FBI 'is undoubtedly the most popular of all federal agencies'. If the Truman-FBI loyalty programme supplied the framework for a surveillance regime, it was with the approval of the American people.[3]

The Attorney General's List of Subversive Organizations (AGLOSO) was a further dimension to the Truman administration's surveillance policy. AGLOSO had existed since 1903, but from the end of 1947 the Justice Department applied it with greater vigour. Dozens of organizations were now listed as being subversive. Membership in an AGLOSO club or organization could be a reason for exclusion from federal or other public employment. The FBI engaged in surveillance, ranging from wiretapping to burglaries, to see who might be involved in proscribed organizations, and what organizations might be added to the list. 'Mini-HUACs', state level legislative committees taking their cue from the US House Un-American Activities Committee, reinforced the loyalty programme and AGLOSO list, promoting legislation to control 'subversives', and hounding individuals. The framework for surveillance was in place. Private employers and agencies had for decades compiled blacklists and now had official encouragement, while individuals acted on their own initiative. American campuses were riddled with such informers, and people became afraid to join societies, sign petitions, or express their views—a silent generation was in the making.

Another federal development occurred during the Truman administration that would have repercussions for domestic surveillance. This was the creation, through the National Security Act of September 1947, of the CIA. Debate on the formation of such an agency had been continuous since the end of the war. The president and Congress agreed that, to avoid an over-powerful agency, powers would be divided between the FBI, which would be limited to a domestic remit, and the CIA, which would take care of foreign intelligence and would be banned from domestic operations.

But the exclusion of the CIA from domestic operations would never be absolute. In August 1947, with debate on the shape of the prospective CIA reaching its climax, two men met on the steps of Columbia University's library and exchanged views on the matter.

One of them was Navy Secretary James V. Forrestal, who would soon be the first incumbent of the new post of Defense Secretary under the terms of the National Security Act. The other was William J. Donovan, formerly director of the wartime Office of Strategic Services (OSS) and now a keen promoter of the CIA proposal. Donovan was worried about the private money being poured into the anti-communist campaign. 'I am sure', he wrote to Forrestal just after their meeting, 'you would think it unwise to let this pass beyond your control.'[4]

To avoid chaos in foreign relations, Donovan wanted private initiatives to be brought under federal control, and this is precisely what the CIA set out to achieve. The agency secretly coordinated the activities of 'voluntarist' (non-governmental) organizations operating overseas, ranging from women's groups to business associations. But the problem was that, while these organizations may have operated abroad, they were headquartered in the USA and staffed by Americans. In future years, it would be a short step from the clandestine management of foreign-orientated private organizations to instituting the surveillance of domestic groups.

Still another development affecting the future of surveillance was the emergence of the National Security Agency (NSA). Established in 1952, this entity had a history of predecessor code-breaking agencies stretching back to the First World War. In fact, the NSA had a potential problem that was rooted in history. Communications executives had been reluctant to cooperate with the NSA's 1920s precursor, the American Black Chamber, partly because of respect for the law and partly because they valued customer confidentiality. Western Union president Newcomb Carlton protested to Congress in 1921 that his company had never in peacetime betrayed the interests of its clients engaged in

US–European messaging.[5] Here, there was a further consideration. Major companies were becoming multinationals, and felt a tug of loyalty that went beyond the narrower confines of US national security.

History repeated itself in the Second World War, with private communications once again coming under government control. After the war and in light of tensions with the Soviet Union, US code-breakers wished to continue the arrangement, but as in the 1920s the company executives voiced objections and pointed to the illegality of what was proposed. However, this time, with considerable variations in enthusiasm yet with a fairly uniform result, the major cable companies Western Union, RCA, and ITT agreed to continue their wartime practice of supplying American code-breakers with copies of the messages they handled. This peacetime arrangement was known as Project SHAMROCK.

Cooperation with the British was a significant feature of the new dispensation. The United Kingdom's code-breaking agency was known after 1942 as GCHQ. Under the terms of the 'UKUSA' intelligence-sharing agreements of 1946 and after, wartime cooperation between the UK and US code-breakers continued into peacetime. The prime objective of GCHQ, NSA, and UKUSA was to keep a vigilant eye on Soviet capabilities and intentions. However, as in the case of the CIA, it was impossible not to involve Americans—or, in the United Kingdom, Britons. Once an instrument existed that could track Moscow's communications with persons within the United States, the capability existed to put those US citizens under surveillance for reasons having no bearing on national security. Should that prove to be politically risky, NSA could turn to GCHQ and ask the British to keep tabs on targeted Americans—this was second nature to the Brits, who had long maintained an espionage capability in the USA. And, of course, the Americans could return the favour. The tactic could be a means of avoiding the scrutiny of Congress and Parliament respectively. That is not to say that the Truman administration resorted to such stratagems—but it did put the machinery in place and it would be a bone of contention in future years.

The impact of Joe McCarthy needs to be assessed and kept in perspective within these broader contexts. But the Wisconsin senator's career does need to be considered. It is the story of a Democratic FDR supporter who saw political advantage in becoming a populist Republican. It is further the tale of a son of one of America's then most progressive states, Wisconsin, who twisted Midwestern egalitarianism into a bitter anti-communist creed that won the loyalty of private groups ranging from We the Mothers Mobilize to the Sons of I Shall Return.

McCarthy took advantage of a national mood inflamed by continuing spy scandals (the Alger Hiss trial of 1949 and the Rosenbergs case of 1950–3), by the 'fall' of China to communism in 1949, and by the Soviet detonation of an atomic bomb in the same year. The Wisconsin senator also profited from the tacit support of a Republican Party desperate to regain control of the White House for the first time since 1933. Elected to the Senate in 1946, he discovered the communism issue late but in a spectacular fashion—in a widely publicized speech in February 1950 he claimed that the State Department was infested with Reds. McCarthy served prominently on Senator Millard Tydings' committee investigating that problem, and then in 1953 took the chairmanship of the Committee on Governmental Operations and of its inquisitorial Permanent Subcommittee on Investigations.

Programmes of surveillance have often attracted criticism for their inaccuracy, and McCarthy's data-gathering system was vulnerable to that charge. Variously reported as saying there were 205, 81, 51, or 'a lot' of communists in the State Department, the senator actually found none. He likewise drew a blank in his attempts to uncover disloyalty in the US Army and the CIA. He relied on the unbalanced testimony of ex-communists who betrayed their former comrades to save their skins or because they had abandoned one messianic mission for another. He relied also on a shambolic system of surveillance based on informers known collectively as the 'Loyal American Underground'—civil servants who informed (or misinformed) on their colleagues and people or organizations who defined patriotism not as the defence of Fourth Amendment and other civil rights but as anti-communism—and communism as pretty much anything that disturbed the tranquility of the complacent mind.[6]

But not all of McCarthy's informants were amateurs. The more professional FBI secretly played a role. It was a dangerous game, for the FBI's confidential files were supposed to be just that, confidential. Furthermore, open support for McCarthy could have been suicidal for the bureau, as it was a blatant act of disloyalty to the Democratic president of the United States, Harry Truman, who remained in office until January 1953. But as he had shown in the earlier Red Scare of 1919–20, Hoover was adept at playing the anti-communist card at the opportune moment.

McCarthy's original list of suspected State Department 'communists' came from a list compiled by FBI veteran Robert E. Lee when he was working for the House Appropriations Committee. Current FBI officials also leaked files to McCarthy or to his assistant Roy Cohn, and fed information to other Red-baiters in the

Senate. One of these Red-baiters was Pat McCarran (Democrat, NV), author of the Subversive Activities Control Act of 1950, which gave official blessing to some of the surveillance activities of the FBI. McCarran claimed on the floor of the Senate on 25 March 1953, 'I have had dozens of [FBI files] in my possession and have taken them home and used them for Sunday reading.'[7]

The House of Representatives ran a parallel programme of anti-communist persecution, and informers obliged both the upper and lower chambers of Congress. The House's Committee on Un-American Activities (HUAC) twice investigated radicals in the Hollywood movie industry. Ten studio writers and directors who refused to testify before HUAC in 1947 were fired and blacklisted. A further investigation took place in 1951, and many screenwriters suffered the same fate. In the course of what amounted to a reign of terror, Hollywood workers were under duress to deny their radical affiliations or to express contrition and inform.

The movie actor Sterling Hayden (*The Asphalt Jungle*, *Dr Strangelove*) wrote an autobiographical novel relating his experiences as an informer. *Wanderer* told how the 6' 5" veteran of wartime special operations joined the Communist Party in 1946 at a time when it was the chic thing to do in Hollywood. In 1951 to his subsequent regret, he betrayed his former comrades to McCarthy's team of investigators. Scared that they would be denounced as communist sympathizers, others in the movie industry similarly testified to the lower chamber. To prove their anti-communist sincerity they named names, betraying to HUAC with varying degrees of accuracy the identities of colleagues who had shown signs of deviation from Cold War conformity.

Some of the victims were famous. Charlie Chaplin, for example, was the world's best-known actor. The involvement of 'stars' distracted attention from the fact that this was another chapter in labour history. The FBI had an estimated 12,000 informers in the unions nationwide. In Hollywood, Screen Actors' Guild president Ronald Reagan was an informer who had testified against the left in the opening HUAC hearings of 1946. The atmosphere was intimidating and conducive to the silence of compliance. Those who did not lose their jobs tended to mellow their messages. John Ford, director of *The Informer*, the gritty 1935 movie about the Irish civil war, lapsed into productions like *The Quiet Man* (1952), a movie dripping in Irish sentimentality for which he won the best director Oscar. Its title was an unwitting commentary on the quietened men of Hollywood.

A few, for example Arthur Miller, resisted. The American Legion organized a boycott of Miller's Pulitzer Prize-winning play *Death of a Salesman*, but the playwright took his revenge by writing *The Crucible* (1952). Ostensibly about the infamous Salem witchcraft trial of 1692–3 and the hysterical young girls who fingered the innocent, the drama fooled no one—it was a condemnation of McCarthyism and its informer-based system of surveillance.

Other opposition to McCarthy came from what might seem to be a surprising source, the CIA. McCarthy had the agency in his sights in spite of the fact that it was fighting communism overseas. It was stuffed with too many blue-bloods for the senator's liking, and the agency's officers were courting the European democratic left as part of their war on Moscow. Given McCarthy's loose definition of communism, that made the CIA itself communist. In July 1953, Hoover informed the senator that CIA official William Bundy had contributed to the Alger Hiss legal defence fund. Thinking that this gave him the perfect opportunity, McCarthy tried to subpoena Bundy to appear before his subcommittee on investigations. However, the CIA's recently installed new director, Allen Dulles, refused the request. Vice-President Richard Nixon had to step in to work out a compromise. According to this compromise, the CIA conceded in principle the committee's right to subpoena CIA officials, on the understanding that they would never do so. That concession by McCarthy was a sign that, with their own President Dwight D. Eisenhower now safely installed in the White House, the Republicans' need for McCarthyism was over.

The Senate was slower to react to changing times. As early as June 1950, it is true, there had been a warning shot. This was fired by the first woman to be elected to the Senate in her own right. In the Republican primary in Maine in 1948, Margaret Chase Smith had projected a fairly conservative image yet was comprehensively smeared by opponents on the right. Anonymous leafleteers claimed to have watched her closely and to have proof that she had dispensed sexual favours for political gain; she was variously accused of hiring a gay political adviser, William C. Smith, Jr, and of sleeping with him; the *Bangor Daily News* excoriated her for having 'opposed machinery for congressional investigation of un-Americanism'.

The trauma of 1948 affected Smith's outlook, and she opposed McCarthy's inquisitorial campaign at an early stage. In June 1950, she spoke in the Senate against Red-baiting, and six of her fellow Republican senators signed her 'Declaration of Conscience': 'It is high time that we stopped thinking politically as Republicans and Democrats about elections and started thinking patriotically as Americans about national security based on individual freedom.'[8]

With new signals coming from the Republican White House two years later, Congress finally came around to Smith's way of thinking. According to a Gallup poll McCarthy still enjoyed an impressively high 50 per cent of public support in January 1954 and in February only Senator William D. Fulbright (Democrat, AR) voted against a further appropriation of $214,000 to his permanent subcommittee (politically damaged by her earlier stand against McCarthy, Smith dared not support Fulbright on this occasion). But by the year's end, the Senate had passed a vote of censure. McCarthy lost his confidence, succumbed to his old seducer alcohol, and finally died of a liver complaint in 1957.

It would be perfectly possible to imagine that McCarthyism ended right there. Within a decade, Jim Compton and doubtless many others had 'forgiven America'. The very word 'McCarthyism' became a term of abuse. To a discernible degree America—unlike its British cousin—had purged itself of a great sin and was the better for it.

Yet some cautions are in order. Only 10 per cent of Hollywood's blacklistees got their jobs back. There were by the late 1950s no more than a few thousand members of the Communist Party, and many of them were FBI informers. This virtual extermination of the Old Left meant there was no credible target to aim at, and it weakened the case for surveillance. However, by the 1960s there was another target for McCarthyist persecution, the New Left, and its adherents found themselves placed under renewed surveillance.

Meanwhile, private labour surveillance and blacklisting continued. In the present century, the American Federation of Labor-Congress of Industrial Organisations (AFL-CIO) still persistently complains about blacklisting. Moreover, the private sector kept workers under surveillance and disciplined them for any signs of divergent thought, a form of silent McCarthyism that affected millions but attracted relatively little attention.

If governmental institutions had stepped back from blacklisting by the late 1950s, the unions allege this restraint did not last. On behalf of twenty-five Milwaukee County Courthouse janitors, a local AFL-CIO affiliate in 2014 filed a suit against Milwaukee County. In a case that was watched across the nation, it charged that Governor Scott Walker of Wisconsin, when first elected to office in 2010, had with 'his cronies at Milwaukee County' recommended that the county privatize its custodial services as a step to identifying and not rehiring employees who were members of labour unions. In a compromise three years later, Milwaukee officials agreed to consider some of the dismissed janitors for re-employment, but in the meantime Governor Walker had won acceptance for Wisconsin Act 10, which provided for the annual recertification of union representation of public employees. In his 2015 bid for the Republican presidential nomination, Walker committed to making this a national policy.[9]

6

McCarthyism in Britain

Senator McCarthy's communists-in-government speech to the Republican Women's Club of Wheeling, West Virginia, took place on 9 February 1950. Not long afterwards, on 29 March, Robert Vansittart rose to speak in the House of Lords: 'I have full particulars of sixteen Communists and 100 per cent fellow travellers who have got themselves into good jobs in the Department of Inland Revenue.' Distancing himself from McCarthy's guesswork, he added 'I am not talking from gossip or hearsay. In some cases, I have actually seen the Communist Party cards.'

The two men were markedly different. McCarthy dropped out of high school aged 14 to help on the family farm; Vansittart went to Eton. As the journalist Karen Potter put it, 'The ageing Vansittart (69 in 1950) was aggrieved by his lack of a future; the upstart McCarthy (41) was aggrieved by his lack of a past.' There were differences, but the question still arises—was there a British form of McCarthyism?

From the beginning, there were those who feared this might be the case. In the 1930s when there was a vogue for communism, MI5 had kept a number of left-wing writers, musicians, and directors under surveillance, including W. H. Auden, Stephen Spender, Christopher Isherwood, Ewen McColl, Joan Littlewood, John Cornford, and George Orwell (in another similarity with the FBI, it also watched right-wingers like Ezra Pound). In 1940, Orwell confided to his diary his fear that if Hitler invaded England and started liquidating the left as he had done in Germany, he would find local allies: 'The police are the very people who would go over to Hitler once they were certain he had won.'

In a report on the future of MI5 drafted in 1945, the former civil servant Sir Samuel Findlater Stewart reflected a parallel fear. He issued the Cassandra-like warning that the agency should be 'concerned with the Defence of the Realm from external and internal danger, and with nothing else'. It should really be no surprise that five years later, the *Manchester Guardian* articulated the fear, 'we should hate to see Lord Vansittart becoming another Senator McCarthy'. McCarthy may have been 4,000 miles away, but there were jitters about his possible impact in Britain. When the FBI sent a two-man mission to Europe in 1953, there was parliamentary concern that they were going to inspect the British Broadcasting Corporation (BBC), McCarthy-style.[1]

In Britain as in America there were spy scares that encouraged the Red-baiters. On the eve of Vansittart's 1950 speech, Klaus Fuchs admitted to having been a Soviet atomic spy—he had probably delivered to Moscow more important information than any other British or American secret agent. But this did not guarantee support for Lord Vansittart. The British left had a tendency to dismiss the significance of Soviet espionage. Like the *New York Times* in 1938, some UK leftists saw spy scares as an anachronism. The *Daily Herald* had in 1946 published a spoof nursery rhyme when

Igor Gouzenko defected to the Canadians and told of the Soviets' efforts to obtain Western atomic secrets:

> Sing a song of spy rings. Spies are in the news
> All the States have secrets other states can use
> Espionage disclosures come as no surprise
> Why become excited when it's headlines for the spies...
> Why not open dealing?
> Bid the spies good-bye
> While nations make a secret, the Secret makes a spy.

Consistently with this, the pro-Labour Party newspaper, *Reynolds News*, portrayed Vansittart's House of Lords speech as a baseless series of allegations by 'Lord VanWitchhunt'.

Condemnation of Vansittart went beyond the left. The Lords as a whole did not support him. The Labour Lord Chancellor, William Jowitt, spoke crushingly of his allegations. Viscount Jowitt was a defender of Alger Hiss and believed that America overreacted to spy scares. Britain was a more reasonable country. It was stalwart in its opposition to communism abroad, but would not overreact to a conjectural threat at home. Replying to Vansittart's speech, he declared, 'There is no complacency, no panic, no hysteria.' Vansittart had himself anticipated that he would be seen as hysterical, declaring that his appeal for measures to be taken against domestic communism had 'nothing to do with the shy-making ballyhoo of Senator McCarthy'.[2]

Disclaimers from these diverse sources contributed to the impression that if the United Kingdom was suffering from a dose of McCarthyism, it was relatively mild. Yet if there was no full-blown Great Fear in the United Kingdom, there is nevertheless a case for saying that the nation operated a kind of 'silent'

McCarthyism. Why the silence? It sprang at least in part from the muted nature of the opposition to McCarthyist tactics, meaning that the British McCarthyists had no need to shout from the rooftops. There was no expectation of resistance except from a few on the left—and no great reaction against the British version of McCarthyism to parallel what happened in America. Thus British McCarthyism not only existed, but also endured.

The reasons for the Great British Silence were various. In the case of MI5, for example, it is instructive to contrast it with the FBI and its arrest culture. The FBI special agent was essentially a policeman who was keen to get his man and, in an open process, put him behind bars. The MI5 man was trained to follow and observe, and not to shout about the story of his successes in publicized court cases. His was still an oppressive presence—MI5 observers taking notes at the back of left-wing Theatre Workshop meetings were an encouragement to self-censorship, and some (like the Workshop director Joan Littlewood) abandoned the left out of fear of being blacklisted.

The Great British Silence sprang also from differences between American and British society. First, America had a Constitution with its 'Bill of Rights' that included the Fourth Amendment, and a tradition of vociferous reaction against any infringement of those rights. Although the United Nations in 1948 and the Council of Europe in 1950 had adopted conventions on privacy, the inhabitants of the United Kingdom, called subjects not citizens, had no such national constitutional guarantee. Secondly, in spite of its reputation for class differences, Britain had a sense of social cohesiveness reinforced by collective wartime suffering and sacrifice that had been much greater than in the United States. Thirdly, Britain was still fighting a rearguard battle to preserve remnants of its empire, and its government suppressed news of the ruthless undercover tactics it was using in its rebellious colonies. Its domestic security service was (and is) called *Military Intelligence 5* (MI5), in contrast with the civilian FBI which could more easily be called to account in the less deferential United States. Britain did have a history of social and political protest, but it also had a population whose majority was prone to silent obedience.

The silence in the United Kingdom on the issue did not, then, signify the absence of something resembling McCarthyism in that country. There were, in fact, parallels between the United Kingdom and the USA. As in the case of America, for example, there is a case for saying that the main government surveillance initiative in the United Kingdom emanated not from the national legislature in the 1950s, but from the national executive in the 1940s.

The Labour government of Clement Attlee (1945–51) resisted the persistent demands of Conservative MP Sir Waldron Smithers for a UK version of HUAC, a parliamentary select committee on Un-British Activities. But in the wake of the Gouzenko defection in 1945 the government was conscious of the dangers posed by Soviet espionage. The top-secret US interception-cum-code-breaking programme called Venona indicated there was continuing treason afoot in the United Kingdom, and, as the decade advanced, the Americans increased their demands for tightened security on the part of their ally. In May 1947, a new UK Cabinet Committee on Subversive Activities resolved to weed out communists from sensitive government jobs. In March the following year, Prime Minister Attlee announced in the House of Commons what came to be known as the 'Purge Procedure'—in due course (after the defection of the 'Cambridge spies' Donald Maclean and

Guy Burgess in 1951), this would harden into the stringent security checking process known as 'positive vetting'.

Just as responsibility for vetting fell to the FBI in the USA, so it became the responsibility of MI5 in the United Kingdom. Like the FBI, MI5 had concerns about the new policy. These concerns arose partly out of its leaders' misguided faith in the Old Boy system, the belief that persons from one's own social class were trustworthy and that new procedures that challenged their integrity were not needed. There was also some worry that MI5 informers might be outed in the effort to purge the civil service.

Additionally, MI5's leadership and their superiors in government were concerned there might be charges, damaging to their agency, that Britain was on the road to a police state. To meet that worry, the Attlee government established an Advisory Tribunal, the government-appointed 'Three Wise Men', to handle appeals and to act as a political buffer. The loyalty programme was under control in the days of Attlee, but, as in the case of the Truman administration, a procedure had been established. Politically motivated vetting, that dark cat of the surveillance state, was almost out of the bag.

Any discussion of surveillance in the years of the Attlee government needs to touch on the Information Research Department (IRD) and George Orwell. The IRD was a secret branch of the Foreign Office established in 1948 to wage propaganda warfare against the Soviet Union. In 1949 the IRD approached Orwell, who had just completed *Nineteen Eighty-Four*, to see if he could help. The novelist was ill, as it turned out within six months of death, and could not help by writing. But he supplied the names of possible communist collaborators in Britain and America—and added a list of thirty-five people who could not be trusted. When the IRD records were partially declassified in 1996, journalists pounced on the seeming inconsistency and shocking headlines appeared: 'Orwell is revealed in role of state informer', 'Orwell offered blacklist', 'Socialist icon who became Big Brother'.[3] Perhaps it was an exaggeration to imply that Orwell had sold out to the very Thought Police that his forthcoming book was about to denounce, but the terms of his cooperation with the IRD do suggest the way in which the unlikeliest of individuals might participate in surveillance as Cold War psychology exerted its grip.

The Attlee government's policies were strands in the development of a surveillance that was both public and private, and in the latter respect there is a case for looking at Vansittart more closely. The attempts to belittle Vansittart do not detract from the role he played or the trend that he exemplified. If he was a less sensational character than Joe McCarthy and if there was no such thing as Vansittartism, it should be remembered that McCarthy's career, too, was one link in a chain of events, and that historians have reservations about the applicability of the term 'McCarthyism'. Vansittart begs attention as a person who was indicative of a vindictively prurient tendency in British society.

Sir Robert Vansittart, as he then was, had been Permanent Under-Secretary of State for Foreign Affairs from 1930 to 1938. Then he became chief diplomatic adviser to the government—it was a demotion, for in the vehemence of his opposition to appeasement he had departed from the neutrality expected of civil servants. There was general agreement that Vansittart was obsessive. The former Foreign Secretary Sir Anthony Eden recalled that 'Vansittart was seldom an official giving cool and disinterested advice based on study and experience.' Cabinet Secretary Maurice Hankey thought Vansittart was 'jumpy' and paid 'too much attention to...S[ecret] S[ervice] information'. The socialist (and Jewish) political scientist Harold Laski rebuked Vansittart for his racial stereotyping of the Germans in wartime propaganda radio broadcasts, and as a cautionary reminder of the imperfections of the civil servant's own nation, quoted Thomas Jefferson: 'England's selfish principles render her incapable of honourable patronage or disinterested co-operation.'[4]

Vansittart was closely interested in intelligence matters. He had overseen UK–US liaison over the Jordan–Rumrich spy case of 1938, was a strong partisan of MI5 and MI6 and a personal friend of both their directors, and built up a private intelligence capability to gather data on the Nazi threat. He maintained his intelligence links during and after the war, when they helped him to campaign, in a private capacity, against the communist enemy. Unlike Hall and Van Deman he did not run a formal organization, but he was influential nevertheless in stigmatizing and in naming names.

The Vansittart records in Churchill College, Cambridge, show that as a post-war member of the House of Lords the former civil servant searched for communist/socialist influence not only in government, but in other British institutions, too. One of them was the Church of England. Scoffed at by the left as the Tory Party on its bended knees, the Church of England nevertheless contained some socialists. If America had its 'Red Dean' (McCarthy's mocking label for Secretary of State Dean Acheson), so did the United Kingdom—the Dean of Canterbury Cathedral, Hewlett Johnson, leader from 1948 of the Great Britain–USSR Friendship Association.

Though Vansittart later on denied being a McCarthyist, in his attack on the Church of England he took heed of American trends.

For example, he had in his possession a pamphlet attacking the US Federal Council of Churches, a Protestant ecumenical organization established in 1908. The author of the pamphlet encouraged the idea that HUAC and the FBI should investigate the council because of its leftist tendencies. Vansittart also had an article by the best-selling conservative polemicist John T. Flynn, who attacked the Federal Council for its importation to America of Attlee-style British Fabianism or 'creeping socialism'. No doubt influenced in part by these materials, Vansittart collected the publications of left-wing British clergy together with related data such as a list of the seventeen executive committee members of the Society of Socialist Clergy and Ministers.[5]

In his March 1950 House of Lords speech, Vansittart laid into the Red Dean of Canterbury as well as other Church targets he thought were virtually communist, for example the Bishop of Bradford, 'a particularly murderous priest called Canon Gilbert Cope', and an organization called the Council of Clergy and Ministers for Common Ownership. The Bishop of Ely in a defensive reply felt obliged to draw a distinction between the Church of England and some of its leftist clergy—he pointed out that the Archbishop of Canterbury was embarrassed by his Dean, especially as in America and Canada people mistook Dr Johnson for the Archbishop himself. In May 1950, in spite of the support of American liberals who wanted him for a lecture tour, the Red Dean finally lost his struggle to obtain an American visa—MI5 and the FBI had collaborated in opposing the application. Hewlett Johnson stuck it out as Dean until 1963. However, feeling the hot breath of British McCarthyism breathing down his dog collar, more than one British clergyman must have wondered who was watching him.

In his Lords remarks, Vansittart denied that the firing of forty-five civil servants had amounted to a 'purge', ridiculed the idea that MI5 was a British Gestapo, and insisted that '5' was under-funded and needed more support. Engaging in a standard form of self-exoneration, he pointed to communist bloc practices, in this case the blacklisting activities of the Bureau of Supervision at the Bucharest headquarters of Cominform, international communism's propaganda unit. It was not too soon to fear that anti-communists on the blacklist would be 'bumped off': '[Communist intimidation] in this country is in its infancy, but it would be unwise to overlook entirely the fact that the beginnings are there.'

Vansittart broadened his range of fire to take in targets other than the civil service and the Church, complaining, for example, about the presence of communists in the military and in the universities. But he aimed a special salvo at another venerable UK institution, the BBC. (See Illustration 4.)

Nicknamed 'Auntie' for its prudish, Auntie-knows best tenor, the BBC nevertheless commanded respect because of its commitment to journalistic objectivity—it bent the knee to the opinions of no private owners or advertisers. But some of its critics believed that the Cold War called for something more than objectivity. For example, under the secretaryship of retired naval officer C. H. Rolleston, the Listeners' Association objected to the BBC's deadpan reportage of opinions expressed in the Soviet press. In 1949, the same officer together with Listeners' Association president Lord Craigavon closely questioned Major General Sir Ian Jacob, director of the BBC's overseas service, when Jacob asserted, in a lecture, that there was no ground for the dismissal of any communist from the BBC, so long as he did his job properly.

ILLUSTRATION 4. Big Brother is listening to you. In December 1954, BBC television broadcast Nigel Kneale's adaptation of George Orwell's novel, *Nineteen Eighty-Four* (1949). There was already a campaign of intimidation against the BBC, and now the broadcaster's telephones never stopped ringing. One media critic said the objectors who cried 'horror' were 'in pretty much the same state as though the screen were indeed two-way, and they were forced by fear to sit and watch it' (*Manchester Guardian*, 16 December 1954). As the cartoonist David Low suggests, though, some people like to be watched.

Vansittart took note of these exchanges, and in his 1950 Lords speech gave full vent to his views.[6]

Vansittart complained that the BBC 'ought to be, but is not, the most potent weapon in the Cold War'. It had refused to purge itself of communists, and its reporting on the Soviet Union was particularly contaminated. Here, his complaint was reminiscent of the attacks in America on Owen Lattimore, who had committed the sin of being an expert for the State Department on China, a country that had turned communist. Falsely accused of espionage, Lattimore finally had to leave for England where he became a professor at the University of Leeds. In parallel purging mode, Vansittart wanted the BBC to replace the alleged communists with refugees from communism who would be qualified to say the right things to and about Europe east of the Iron Curtain.

In June 1952, Waldron Smithers complained about the BBC to his fellow-Conservative Winston Churchill, who was back in office as prime minister (1951–5). Smithers was a die-hard Tory backbencher who opposed those in his party who sought the middle ground in politics. He averred that communists in the Corporation could sabotage broadcasting in a national crisis. He complained about a 'Jew...who controls the selection of programmes and is a communist'. This turned out to be Anatol Goldberg, head of the Russian service, whose approach to anti-communist propaganda was too subtle for his critics to comprehend. On the advice of MI5, Churchill rejected the demand for a more spectacular purge of the BBC, though '5' continued to vet the Corporation's staff.

In terms of immediate impact, 'Vansittartism' (broadly defined) did not compare with 'McCarthyism' (ditto). By 1954, 4 million civil servants had been screened in the United States. Some 4,353 lost their jobs through being fired, or because they resigned after being investigated by the FBI or named to loyalty boards. In Britain in the same period, 10,000 had been screened and 124 removed from their posts. The smaller population of the United Kingdom by no means accounts for the scale of difference.[7]

Nevertheless, there was a slow-burning and long-lasting tendency in the United Kingdom to put people under government surveillance. Vansittart died in February 1957 and McCarthy three months later, but the McCarthyism that Britain experienced was no flash in the pan. And that surveillance showed a tendency to be political in character, sometimes having little to do with national security.

As in the USA, the story of surveillance is one with many scapegoats. To focus too heavily on any of them would be a distraction from the unsettling truth that Britons as a whole, no less than Americans, were willing to accept transgressions against privacy and civil liberties. For example, while it would be possible to point the finger at Vansittart or MI5 for what happened at the BBC, it must be acknowledged that Auntie was a compliant victim. In 1957, its mandarins eased Anatol Goldberg out of his job. Sir Hugh Greene became Director General of the BBC in 1960 and was keen to be seen as a reformer. But, anxious not to be sidetracked by security scandals, Greene pressed MI5 to redouble its vetting efforts.

Although it might be tempting to see threats to civil liberties as emanating from the political right, the 1960s Labour Party was also prepared to undertake surveillance beyond the needs of national security. Its leader, Hugh Gaitskell, had no qualms about informing on colleagues. In 1961 his party supplied MI5 with a list of Labour MPs and asked the agency to find out whether they were communists. After thirteen years of Conservative government, Labour resumed office in 1964, with Harold Wilson as prime minister. Two years later, Wilson had the seamen's strike on his hands. He asked MI5 to put its surveillance machinery into action and find out about the strike leaders' tactics.

In 1964 the Cold War still had a quarter of a century to run. It was not all doom and gloom. From time to time, there were indications that political surveillance might fade. In March 1965, Prime Minister Wilson called MI5 director Roger Hollis to 10 Downing Street and announced a new doctrine, that MI5 should not tap the telephones of Members of Parliament. In the 1970s, MI5 began to refocus on anti-terrorism, a mission that would become the priority once the Cold War ended. In 1985, following an exposé, MI5 vetting of BBC employees came to an end.

But there were also renewals in MI5's political surveillance activities. It transpired that the Wilson Doctrine was not legally binding, and left-wing Labour MPs remained under surveillance. Edward Heath, Conservative prime minister from 1970 to 1974, said he suspected communist influence was behind the strikes taking place on the docks and in the coalmines. In September 1972, his government established a Committee on Subversion in Public Life. The committee investigated the major trade unions in the United Kingdom, with MI5 supplying data from its past and current surveillance files. A BBC documentary later revealed that Special Branch had in the 1970s recruited twenty-two senior union officials as informers, including the president of the National Union of Mineworkers, Joe Gormley. While there were ostensibly legitimate fears that Moscow's agents would insinuate themselves into the United Kingdom's industrial troubles in an attempt to sabotage capitalist enterprises, and with a view to obtaining strategic information, the intention of the Heath government was also to weaken the union movement by questioning the patriotism of its leaders, to minimize the occurrence of politically damaging work stoppages, and, as ever in the case of powerful men, the exertion of political control.

The list of politically inspired MI5 surveillance targets extended beyond the labour movement. The MI5 renegade Peter Wright recalled how his agency had two undercover officers in the

Newcastle offices of the National Insurance service, men who could be relied upon to identify all kinds of protestors—the agency was beginning to computerize its National Insurance links when Wright published his whistle-blowing memoir *Spycatcher* in 1987. As we now know for sure from Christopher Andrew's authorized history of MI5, its 1980s targets included the leadership of the Campaign for Nuclear Disarmament (CND), which had as its primary aim the unilateral relinquishment of nuclear weapons by the United Kingdom. MI5 amassed files on Joan Ruddock, chair of CND 1981–5 (and later a Labour MP and cabinet minister), and on Bruce Kent, CND chair from 1987 to 1990. Another target was the National Council for Civil Liberties, or Liberty. Liberty officers who came under surveillance included Harriet Harman and Patricia Hewitt, who would both become prominent leaders of the Parliamentary Labour Party.

Margaret Thatcher (Conservative prime minister, 1979–90) portrayed the miners' strike of 1984 as a subversive act, and under her aegis MI5 intensified its efforts to collect information on the National Union of Mineworker (NUM) leaders. MI5's hackers did not always have an easy time. NUM President Arthur Scargill used to shout at them down the phone, while the communist Scottish NUM official Mick McGahey spoke in such a strong dialect that the line tappers found it hard to comprehend him. But the listeners' discomfort was trivial compared with the penalty paid by those under surveillance. MI5 surveillance foiled the attempt by the NUM to save its funds from restraining legal action, and contributed to the defeat of the strike and the devastation of the coalmining communities.

According to Athan Theoharis, who served as the FBI expert on the 1970s Church inquiry into intelligence matters, the bureau was ineffectual in stopping Soviet espionage and then failed in its later mission of preventing terrorist attacks on the USA. Instead, it had been complicit in McCarthyism and was a consistent threat to American civil liberties. Could a parallel indictment be made of MI5? Its record of counter-espionage against Germany in two World Wars was reasonably good; it failed to foil significant Soviet spying, but did record some successes; it claims to have foiled terrorist plots, but some bombers have got through. On the civil liberties front, its record is patchy in spite of the presence in its crest of the portcullis, depicting parliamentary democracy.

Writing in 1988, the *Guardian* journalists Mark Hollingsworth and Richard Norton-Taylor estimated that by then there were the names of a million 'subversives' in MI5's files. They made an international comparison: 'Britain, according to the conventional wisdom, has escaped relatively unscathed from the scourge of the political witch-hunt', but a difference was that blacklisting in the United States had 'been a much more open affair. It is also easier to detect in America because of Freedom of Information and Privacy laws.' Recently the British authorities had admitted that vetting was taking place, but 'much is secret, especially in the private sector'.

Hollingsworth subtitled another of his publications *The Silent McCarthyism*.[8] He was here referring to the Economic League. The exposures of its activities in 1937 had been a setback for the League, but it began to recover with the approach of the war, when it cooperated with Mass Observation in its efforts to assess civilian morale. After the war, it also cooperated with Attlee's loyalty programme and the IRD and, with a Red Scare in progress, picked up business clients worried about militancy in the workforce.

So, political surveillance was not limited to MI5. It occurred also in private business, and not only through the auspices of the Economic League. For example, the John Lewis Partnership, though a progressive, cooperative venture, proposed a political test for its employees. The unions blocked that move, but, in spite of the secrecy that surrounded such matters, other instances came to light of companies that used surveillance as a tool for encouraging compliance.

An initiative by Gilbert Hunt, a director of Rootes Motors and a member of the council of Warwick University, was one infamous case. Hunt organized the infiltration of a Labour Party meeting addressed by David Montgomery, an American lecturer at the university suspected of working up discontent amongst the workers in the Coventry car manufacturing industry. Following discovery of evidence of this during a student protest occupation of the university's administration buildings, the student body as a whole started a strike that closed the university for a lengthy period.

As for the Economic League, it went from strength to strength. In the north-west of England there were 6,000 names on its blacklist by 1986. In 1988, 200 companies subscribed to its surveillance service. The list read like a who's who of British industry: Balfour Beatty, Barclays Bank, Christian Salvesen, Ford Motor Company, Glaxo, Royal Bank of Scotland, and so on. As ever, the police and particularly Special Branch were accused of cooperating with the League, and in a pioneering book of 1986 on surveillance and computers, the *New Statesman* journalist Duncan Campbell wrote that some Economic League personnel worked from within MI5 headquarters.[9]

The main thrust of the Economic League's activities was, however, private. This may help to explain its resilience in a nation devoted to private enterprise engaged in a Cold War against communism. For whatever reason, it survived a whole series of exposés: in the *Daily Express* in 1961, and in *The Guardian* (1964 and 1974), *The Observer* (1969), and *Sunday Times* (1974).

In 1987–9, Granada TV broadcast an unusually thorough exposé of the Economic League. Parliament now renewed its interest, and an official inquiry took place. Under pressure and with the Cold War over, the Economic League dissolved itself in 1993. It was, however, a ruse. A new organization, The Consulting Association (TCA), came into being very quickly under the direction of Ian Kerr. A parliamentary Scottish Affairs Committee report of 2012–13 found that the construction firm Sir Robert McAlpine Ltd had been the prime mover behind the TCA. The association like its predecessor claimed to have an educational role, and it also served as one of the Conservative Party's funding channels. Its main function, though, was surveillance that resulted in blacklisting. Its clients bore a striking resemblance to those of the Economic League.[10]

Taking a broad definition of McCarthyism, as is now standard practice, and keeping in mind the fact that the practice extended beyond the activities of Joe McCarthy and Robert Vansittart, it is evident that the phenomenon existed in Britain as well as in America, and that it survived the deaths of the two individuals who might erroneously be thought to be the main culprits. Surveillance that resulted in the blacklisting of members of the workforce, whether in the studios of Hollywood or on the construction sites of the United Kingdom, caused distress to its victims that was at least as acute and extensive as that caused by the more high-tech recent practices of the surveillance state.

7

COINTELPRO and 1960s Surveillance

The intelligence agencies that subject us to surveillance can normally rely on blanket secrecy. From time to time, however, their secrets leak out. Occasionally this is because rivals who have penetrated them choose to spill the beans. At other times, it's because of the actions of apostates who have turned against them, or of whistle-blowers who want to expose malfeasance. But on 8 March 1971, the FBI suffered a breach of its security for another reason—burglary.

Bill Davidson was the person responsible for the break-in. A physics professor at Haverford College on the outskirts of Philadelphia, Davidson was an opponent of the Vietnam War. He had become an admirer of the peace activist Father Daniel Berrigan and adhered to the views of the Catholic left. In his circle, there was a growing conviction that the FBI had conducted a programme of surveillance and disruption against the anti-war movement and political dissenters generally. However, because a cordon of secrecy surrounded the bureau, it was difficult to prove such charges.

Davidson and his covert Citizens' Commission to Investigate the FBI decided on a new strategy. They took their cue from the anti-draft movement. Those wishing to resist the drive to recruit young men into America's army in Vietnam had broken into a number of local draft offices and destroyed their records. Davidson's group decided to pursue that tactic, but with exposure not destruction in mind.

They were aware that the FBI had tight security, so they decided to raid one of its smaller, ancillary offices. The one they chose was located on the second floor of a suburban apartment block opposite the Delaware County Courthouse in Media, Philadelphia. Just two days before the date of the projected burglary, Davidson met with President Nixon's national security adviser, Henry Kissinger. Dr Kissinger had heard rumours that Davidson planned to kidnap him. He had rejected those suspicions but, perhaps guided by a sixth sense, had still been curious to meet the activist. Little did he know that another Davidson plan was about to come to fruition.

Keith Forsyth, who had dropped out of college to oppose the war and drove a cab part-time, had by this time received a request from Davidson to pick the locks at the Media office. He remembers thinking, 'Yeah, OK, let's go break in. Then, after we finish that, let's go down to Fort Knox and steal a few million.' Forsyth applied himself to the task of learning the locksmith's trade.

On the evening of 8 March, the nation was glued to the Muhammad Ali–Joe Frazier heavyweight 'fight of the century' in Madison Square Garden. As war protesters mourned the defeat of draft-resister Ali over a gruelling fifteen rounds and others celebrated with Smokin' Joe, the amateur lock-picker at first fumbled with no result, and then succeeded. The Media burglars removed a large number of documents from the FBI's filing cabinets. They sent them in batches to politicians and newspapers they thought might be sympathetic. Attorney General John Mitchell discouraged this in words that, to those who followed the history of such revelations, had a familiar ring: publication 'could endanger the lives or cause other serious harm to persons engaged in investigative activities on behalf of the United States'.

But the criminality of the act itself would fairly soon become a side issue. Only the greatest hypocrisy could drive forward the rhetoric of condemnation, for the White House was about to damage its own reputation in the matter of burglary. It formed a break-in team, the Special Investigations Unit, or 'plumbers', whose task was to plug leaks and whose first job was to burglarize the office of the psychiatrist of the military analyst Daniel Ellsberg—the man who, with sensational effect, had leaked the 'Pentagon Papers' showing White House decision-making on the Vietnam War in a bad light.

Whether or not because he was averse to hypocrisy, Attorney General Mitchell refused to accede to J. Edgar Hoover's request for an injunction against publication of the Media documents. Denied this avenue of defence, the FBI tried to hunt down the Media burglars. It concentrated on the right area, the Catholic left, but failed to make any arrests.[1] The *Washington Post* journalist Betty Medsger noticed that one of the Media documents sent to her was headed 'COINTELPRO' (a contraction of COunter INTELligence PROgram). Hoover was aghast when he learned of this leak. He shut down COINTELPRO as soon as he realized the cat was emerging from the bag. He was too late. The NBC reporter Carl Stern launched Freedom of Information requests and over the next three years details of the programme emerged. The FBI had put hundreds of thousands of non-criminal citizens under surveillance. The bubble of bureau sanctity had finally been pricked. From a popularity rating of 71 per cent in 1970, the FBI slumped to 37 per cent in 1975.

COINTELPRO was in part a development from the secrecy-shrouded Security Index, first established in 1939. By 1970, the index contained 26,000 names and an undetermined number of them, Bill Davidson included, were in it for political not military reasons. In 1956, Hoover had taken the decision to develop the principles behind the list. Over time, he devised a number of separate but linked programmes mostly with the justification of being anti-communist 'counter-intelligence'. The original target was the Communist Party. Then in 1961 a new programme aimed at the Socialist Workers Party. In 1964 the Ku Klux Klan was added to the list, in 1967 black nationalist groups, and in 1968 the New Left, especially its anti-war component. The COINTELPRO programmes like the Security Index aimed at surveillance—but they were aggressive and meant to disrupt as well.

Quite why Hoover decided to launch a new offensive against the communists just as they were on the verge of extinction invites explanation. Though he was no admirer of communism, he had in the past blown hot and cold on the issue depending on political circumstances. On this occasion, he may have felt under pressure to pick on a soft target because the FBI's war on organized crime was going badly. Though Hoover tried to disguise his ineptitude by claiming there was no such thing as a nationally organized Mafia, it was becoming increasingly clear that the opposite was the case and that the Mafiosi were outwitting the FBI. Yet Hoover did not really need an artificial boost to his prestige, for in spite of his lack of progress against organized crime, he remained popular. And, in any case, COINTELPRO could not really enhance his reputation. It was a closely guarded secret, and it is difficult to claim credit for something few people know about. So in launching COINTELPRO, Hoover may have been attempting to prove himself not to a wider audience, but to himself and to his immediate colleagues and confidants.

To understand it more fully, however, it is helpful to put COINTELPRO into a broader context. For a start, there was presidential involvement. In the estimate of the lawyer Frederick A. O. Schwartz who advised Congress on the issue, 'all administrations from Franklin D. Roosevelt to Richard Nixon asked for and got political information from the FBI. But there was a marked increase during the Johnson and Nixon administrations.' Examples of this behaviour were President Johnson's requests for a list of people helping Senator Barry Goldwater (Republican, AZ) in his presidential campaign of 1964, and for a report on long-distance telephone calls made by Republican vice-presidential candidate Spiro Agnew in 1968. President Nixon's White House demanded wiretaps on a spectrum of the administration's critics, including prominent Democratic politicians such as Senators Edward Kennedy (Democrat, MA) and J. William Fulbright.[2]

A further indication of presidential interest is the fact that federal surveillance activities expanded beyond the confines of the FBI programme. When President Lyndon B. Johnson encountered a mounting tide of protest against his policy in Vietnam, he claimed—and at the time probably believed—that international communism was to blame. He asked the CIA to investigate the protest movement with a view to uncovering how it was being run from Hanoi, Beijing, and Moscow. Though under law the CIA was prohibited from operating domestically, in 1967 the agency launched the programme codenamed CHAOS. This operated within the unit headed by the CIA's counter-intelligence chief, James Jesus Angleton. Angleton's counter-intelligence staff collated files on thousands of war protesters, black nationalists, and campus activists within a special, central registry. Armed with information derived from CHAOS, the CIA's analysts concluded that the protest movement was spontaneous and not externally directed.

But when President Richard Nixon inherited the war and the protest movement against it, he promoted a similar programme known after its author, White House aide Tom Huston. The language of a 1970 Huston document, even in its redacted version, conveys the programme's chill: 'President [Nixon] has...made the following decisions:...The intelligence community is directed to intensify coverage of individuals and groups in the United States who pose a major threat to the internal security...Restrictions on...covert [mail] coverage are to be relaxed...Restraints on the use of surreptitious entry are to be removed.' Hoover at the FBI balked at the Huston Plan's illegality, but nevertheless proceeded with his intensive monitoring of activists.[3]

The US Army, whose domestic surveillance activities were meant to be restricted to the protection of military installations, similarly extended its remit and, in an era of anti-war protest, began to collect data on civil disturbances. In 1971, Senator Sam J. Ervin (Democrat, NC) initiated hearings into army surveillance, computers, and data bases, and how they complied with the Bill of Rights: 'It has become increasingly clear that unless we take command of the new technology...we may well discover some day that the machines stand above the laws.'

Senator Ervin faced opposition from a senior colleague who demanded more, not less scrutiny of radicals. James O. Eastland (Democrat, MI), the segregationist and FBI stalwart who chaired the Senate Committee on the Judiciary, furthermore revived an old if by now decaying source of surveillance. He noted that 'for a considerable time the Army has been holding the private files of Colonel Ralph Van Deman'. As this was a private collection there could be no restriction on the use made of the information, and Eastland demanded that the files be made available to the Internal Security Subcommittee. This subcommittee, which he chaired, was the Senate's equivalent of HUAC. The Army handed over the documents.[4]

So COINTELPRO was not the only extension of government surveillance in the 1960s. McCarthyism and its snoopers were still around, and government surveillance was becoming an ingrained tendency in American life. Such surveillance in being secretive attracted little opposition. Though Bill Davidson and a minority like him knew in their hearts that the FBI was conducting political surveillance, there was no general uprising against it for most of the decade. Indeed, appearances can be deceptive in retrospect. While the 1960s were a time of rebellion, protest as a whole was a minority activity. Government officials might be forgiven for thinking there was tacit support for federal surveillance. The rebellion against mass snooping, when it came, would be all the more dramatic for that.

J. Edgar Hoover launched the FBI's first COINTELPRO against the Communist Party on 28 August 1956. According to Athan Theoharis, a leading authority on the bureau's civil liberties infractions, he did so 'unilaterally'. He does at first appear to have bypassed executive oversight by the White House and the Department of Justice, as well as congressional procedures, though he did in 1958 inform all three parties about his initiative. At any rate COINTELPRO was an FBI initiative, and it was not until the mid-1960s that first Johnson and then Nixon placed their presidential foot on the surveillance accelerator.

Bureau officials justified COINTELPRO by referring to the effect of recent Supreme Court decisions culminating in *Yates v United States* (1957) that established the need for greater clarity of evidence in prosecutions under the provisions of the Smith Act (1940), which had outlawed advocacy of the violent overthrow of the US government. In future, proof of violent intent would be required. There was now a fear that FBI informers would have to clarify the evidence by testifying in court, thus blowing their cover—at the time, an estimated 1,500 of the Communist Party's decimated membership of 5,000 were FBI agents. Although a Hoover-approved treatise had in 1955 conceded that the party by then posed only a 'potential' espionage or sabotage threat, the same treatise maintained that the communists could still exert 'influence over the masses'. With this in mind, bureau officials feared that the Supreme Court's delicate regard for civil liberties could result in a revival of the party's fortunes.

The COINTELPRO against the Communist Party thus conducted surveillance not with its customary view to arrests and prosecution, with but the aim of disruption. The FBI used the information at its disposal to sow dissent within the party, for example by planting rumours concerning comrades' marital infidelity and homosexual activity. It also encouraged machinations against the party by those on the left of it. Alan H. Belmont, the FBI's third in command, noted in his memorandum launching COINTELPRO in 1956 that the 'Socialist Workers Party (SWP) is making an all-out effort to win over CP members who have become disillusioned with Stalinist communism…This SWP program could very definitely benefit the Bureau provided we can achieve through our informant coverage in the SWP some degree of control and direction over it'. Thus, surveillance was to be reinvigorated beyond the boundaries of the Communist Party—in fact, a variety of people having contact with the communists even if they were not communists themselves came under surveillance.[5]

The Socialist Workers Party could trace its rationale to the 1920s, when followers of Leon Trotsky had fallen out with the mainstream communist movement, and particularly to the 1930s, when Trotskyists opposed Joseph Stalin's genocidal purges. Although in February 1956 the Moscow regime finally admitted to the evils of Stalinism, by the end of the very same year it had sent tanks to crush the stirrings of freedom in Hungary and blown its chances of reforming the image of Soviet communism. As FBI strategists rightly deduced, there was now a renewed opportunity for the SWP to attack the Communist Party. Even with this advantage, though, the SWP's membership never rose beyond 2,000.

By 1961, nevertheless, the FBI had redesignated the SWP as a national security menace in its own right. One reason for this was the SWP's Trotskyite commitment to 'permanent revolution', which meant that the party supported Fidel Castro's seizure of control in Cuba—an event that President John F. Kennedy and other mainstream politicians saw as a communist incursion into the Western hemisphere and a threat to the principles of the Monroe Doctrine. Hoover's memorandum launching the SWP COINTELPRO called for 'a disruption program along similar lines' to that against the Communist Party and condemned the SWP for 'openly...running candidates for public office...supporting such causes as Castro's Cuba and integration problems arising in the South'.[6]

That last phrase referred to the civil rights upheaval then taking place in the former Confederate states. Hoover is sometimes portrayed as irrational in his assumption that civil rights equated with

communism, but that portrayal is itself partly based on irrational-
ity arising from the wishful thinking of non-communist liberals.

Two points invite attention here. First, Hoover was correct in his
perception that the Communist Party, as well as other socialist
movements, promoted the cause of black freedom. Socialism had
been a significant ingredient in the 'Harlem' Renaissance that, in the
1920s, stamped American identity with the imprint of black culture. In the 1930s, the communists fought against the South's neo-
slavocracy. In spite of the persecution and decline of the Communist
Party, the legacy endured. In the words of the historian Mary Helen
Washington, 'nearly every major black writer of the 1940s and
1950s was in some way influenced by the Communist Party or other
leftist organizations'. This historian regarded the FBI files as so
thoroughly researched that they were 'invaluable biographical aids'.

Secondly, it is incorrect to say that the FBI did nothing to protect the rights of black Americans. When subcontracted to the
Justice Department in the 1870s, its antecedent the Secret Service
had smashed the Ku Klux Klan and ensured the freedman's ability
to vote. Ninety years later, Hoover launched his White Hate
COINTELPRO to suppress white racist terrorism, the resurgent
Klan included. Starting in 1964, the programme violated the privacy rights of southern extremists just as other COINTRELPROs
offended against more liberal prerogatives. An authority on White
Hate has concluded that the FBI suppressed both leftist challenges
and white supremacist vigilantism in order to 'ensure domestic
tranquility'.[7]

All that having been said, the FBI's surveillance and disruption
of the black rights and black power movements is a case study in
the dangers of an over-intrusive state. The bureau routinely tapped
the telephone calls of two charismatic black leaders of the 1960s,

Malcolm X and Martin Luther King. Attorney General Robert F. Kennedy authorized the latter tap in October 1963, and extended the authority to King's Southern Christian Leadership Conference, the preeminent civil rights organization of its day. The FBI placed fifteen listening devices in King's hotel bedrooms and anonymously sent his wife Coretta an aural anthology that purported to show him engaging in marital infidelity and sexual orgies—this on the eve of his receipt of the Nobel Prize for Peace, and in the hope that he would kill himself when placed under such extreme personal pressure.

Hoover and King were clashing personalities, and the FBI director believed there was a pressing need to rein in the civil rights leader. His presumption was that King was bending his ear to the traitorous pleas of his adviser Stanley D. Levison, who had formerly been a communist. When in April 1967 King condemned US participation in the Vietnam War, it seemed to confirm that he sympathized with communists, in this case the North Vietnamese and their Chinese and Soviet backers. As is so often the case where surveillance is concerned, there are issues with accuracy and propriety. An ordained Baptist minister, King was no communist. And even if he had been a communist, was the nature of the surveillance to which he was subjected appropriate or justifiable? There is a further twist to this conundrum. In the final year of his life, King began to focus on the problem of social inequality in American society. Just before his assassination in April 1968, King confided to a colleague that he was a democratic socialist. But at the time there was no information in the public domain on that subject.

A further COINTELPRO launched in 1967 called BLACK HATE targeted black nationalist groups, believers in racial separation and armed resistance. Like other COINTELPROs, it went beyond surveillance. For example, the Chicago police in December 1969 raided a house used by the Black Panther Party, killing the Illinois chairman of the party, Fred Hampton. They planned the raid with the assistance of Hampton's bodyguard, who was an FBI informer.

The overall effectiveness of COINTELPRO-BLACK HATE surveillance is open to question. In spite of the recent passage by Congress of the Civil Rights and Voting Rights Acts (1964, 1965), prejudice remained deeply entrenched and only 40 of the FBI's 6,000 special agents were black. There was no way in which a white FBI special agent could penetrate a black radical movement, so the bureau depended on secondary, less reliable informers. Furthermore, the new black radicalism had departed from the familiar lexicon of communism and, being in this way a new puzzle, was more difficult for the formulaic FBI to police. One of the few privileges enjoyed by the black community was its relative impenetrability and imperviousness to blanket surveillance.

The FBI director nevertheless attempted to recruit African American informants, apparently without telling his boss. When Attorney General Ramsey Clark in September 1967 asked Hoover to recruit 'urban ghetto' informants within Black Nationalist organizations and the Student Nonviolent Coordinating Committee, Clark appeared to be in ignorance that such a programme was already under way but involved difficulties. Perhaps for this reason, the Attorney General set up his own organization within the Justice Department, the Interdivisional Information Unit. It generated computerized dossiers on black persons of interest. These consisted of biographical profiles, and recorded the political opinions of those 'ghetto' dwellers whom the administration feared.[8]

The creation of Clark's unit further illustrates the fact that J. Edgar Hoover did not single-handedly spread the tentacles of federal surveillance in the 1960s. It was in fact a general tendency. The CIA had its CHAOS programme and in 1968 would start a counter-terrorist effort. The Army kept an eye on domestic dissidents. The NSA had a watch list that by now included American protesters. Known as Operation Minaret from July 1969, it had as its objectives 'communications concerning...antiwar movements/demonstrations' and, because of the programme's marginal legality, the restriction of 'knowledge that information is being collected and processed by the National Security Agency'.[9]

If further proof of the width of the tendency were needed, one could turn to Congress. As a rule, southern Democrats had historically opposed the expansion of federal powers including those of the Secret Service (in the nineteenth century) and the FBI. But in the wake of the riots and protests of the 1960s and a soaring crime rate they teamed up with Republican colleagues to pass, in 1968, the Omnibus Crime Control and Safe Streets Act. Senator John McClellan (Democrat, AR) led a successful initiative to insert a special provision that came to be known as Title III. Subject to the granting of court-approved warrants, the bureau would henceforth be able to use wiretaps and bugs in its war against crime. At the same time, the president would have the power to authorize wiretaps in the interest of national security, a power that President Nixon would utilize extensively. The legislation regularized surveillance procedures, and potentially opened the way to more political surveillance.

Like its counterparts directed at black Americans, COINTELPRO-NEW LEFT bore the imprint of failure. The label

'New Left' adhered to post-Marxian campus-based protesters who rejected the 'old' left's links to what young radicals regarded as over-conformist organized labour. New Left activists demanded racial justice and an end to US involvement in the Vietnam War. In December 1967, national security adviser Walt Rostow told President Johnson there was a 'link' between the communist Viet Cong and 'US politics'. White House advisers asked the FBI to find out why the anti-war demonstrators were 'so well organized'. After a spectacular student protest at Columbia University, COINTELPRO-NEW LEFT launched in May 1968.

The FBI conducted psychological warfare against the New Left as it had against other groups. For example, it planted stories in the *Cincinnati Inquirer* indicating that protesters at Antioch College were causing campus disruption that would ruin the career prospects of all students affected. The bureau then arranged for clippings to be sent to parents in the hope that they could induce the college authorities to clamp down on dissident students. But its COINTELPRO was ineffective. Unlike the static Communist Party, about which FBI personnel had become quite authoritative, the students were a moving target. They changed each year with the influx of freshmen, and adhered to no defining ideology. Reflecting that state of flux, Students for a Democratic Society (SDS) had a standard quip about why the Communist Party had failed to penetrate their movement—'They can't take us over because they can't find us.' The FBI would have seconded this analysis.

To appreciate the full scope of the FBI's surveillance activities in the 1960s, one has to look beyond the COINTELPROs, and to programmes that had earlier origins. In the 1930s, the populist press had laid some high-profile child kidnappings at the door of 'degenerates', as homosexuals were then called. The FBI opened a file on 'sex offenders' in 1937 and then, feeding off additional fears that gays were a security risk because they might be blackmailed (though there is no recorded case of this happening in America), a 'sex perverts in government' file. At the height of the 'Lavender Scare', the bureau in 1951 established what became a 330,000-page 'Sex Deviates' file. Leaks from this file resulted in gay men and women losing their jobs in government and in the private sector. Daughters of Bilitis, a lesbian advocacy group active in the 1960s, harboured suspicions that it was under COINTELPRO surveillance, but in truth such organizations had been targeted long before COINTELPRO.[10]

The same can be said about the FBI's surveillance of feminist organizations. There had for decades been a patriarchal suspicion that the women's movement was a threat to national security in being pacifist and left wing, and since the 1920s first military intelligence and then the FBI had amassed files on feminists. Thus, to consider a single example, the surveillance of Roberta Alper after 1968 fell within the ambit of COINTELPRO-NEW LEFT, but was equally the continuation of previous business. The reasons for her surveillance? She had visited communist Cuba, had taught pioneering courses on women's studies, and advocated the closure of *Playboy* magazine. Local FBI agents in Pittsburgh and San Diego labelled Alper a 'subversive' and proposed that she should be included in the Security Index.

The levels of federal surveillance in the later 1960s would be surpassed in future decades because of the arrival of new technologies, but they were nevertheless at an all-time high compared with earlier periods of American history. Responsibility for the situation rested not with a few individuals, but with many, and to a degree with society as a whole. Public toleration of surveillance was in part based on ignorance of the facts. To be sure, there had been a steady trickle of exposés. The civil liberties lawyer Max Lowenthal in 1950 published a book, *The Federal Bureau of Investigation*, that was a searing indictment of its subject. Responding to his temerity, Hoover organized an effective counterblast of pro-FBI publicity. When in 1952 Alan Barth of the *Washington Post* depicted the Attorney General's List of Subversive Organizations as a form of tyranny, the nation was in thrall to McCarthyism and in no mood to welcome his book, *The Loyalty of Free Men*. The *Nation* magazine regularly published accounts of the bureau's phone-tapping activities, but Americans with middling political views dismissed such articles as a liberal grumble. In 1964, the journalist Fred Cook followed in Lowenthal's footsteps with a critique of the FBI's malpractices, but the title of his book was all too accurate: *The FBI Nobody Knows*.

In 1970–2, however, the veil of secrecy lifted. The nation was on the eve of a muck-raking era that would be fuelled by revelations about excessive surveillance and other intelligence malpractices. Millions of Americans were now ready to listen. There were some underlying reasons for this. Political upheavals over the civil rights issue at home and the Vietnam War in Asia had troubled the Cold War consensus. Rapprochement with Moscow and Beijing was in the air—Nixon would soon agree to limits in the nuclear arms race, and he made a pioneering visit to Red China. The need for national unity in the face of a dangerous foe was no longer so apparent, and Americans could afford the luxury of a critical look at their security agencies.

An early sign of fracturing consensus over intelligence activities was the furore over the CIA's subsidization of the National Students Association (NStA for short, to distinguish it from the

NSA, the National Security Agency). In 1967 *Ramparts,* a Catholic investigative journal published on the West Coast, showed that the CIA had recruited US students, and paid for the activities of the NStA in a manner that was illegal, given that the agency was banned from operating domestically. The story splashed all over the national press, and continuing investigations revealed that the CIA had its financial fingers in several other domestic pies, ranging from journalists' associations to women's groups. It was not a story about surveillance per se, but it prepared opinion for future revelations about intrusive practices in the American homeland.

The Army, as well as the FBI and CIA, experienced pre-1970s criticism. By the end of the 1960s, Christopher Pyle decided he had had enough. Pyle had been a US Army intelligence instructor at Fort Holabird on the outskirts of Baltimore. He was no radical, but was shocked when he visited the army's CONUS (Continental United States) Intelligence Section. He learned that the Army kept millions of computerized dossiers on dissident citizens and organizations, and maintained a nationwide force of 1,000 plain-clothes officers whose job was to keep tabs on critics of US foreign and domestic policy. He quit his post and in January 1970 published an article on the Army's domestic surveillance programme in the *Washington Monthly*. It was an instant media sensation.

The revelation kindled familiar worries in the mind of the Senator Sam Ervin (Democrat, NC). Ervin launched on a trajectory that would in due course have him in charge of the Watergate Committee that helped force the resignation of President Nixon in 1974. On the road to that destiny, he demanded an inquiry into the Pyle revelations. There was firm resistance from the administration, but the senator's grandfatherly demeanour, conservative credentials, and southern drawl proved to be an irresistible force. The hearings began in February 1972. It was in the next month that Bill Davidson and his fellow burglars showed that the FBI, too, was engaging in domestic political surveillance. A very American rebellion had begun.

8

An Age of Transparency

At the end of 1974, Pulitzer Prize-winning journalist Seymour Hersh published a story that helped to usher in a new age of transparency. On the front page of the *New York Times*, he announced that the 'CIA, directly violating its charter, conducted a massive illegal domestic intelligence operation during the Nixon Administration against the anti-war movement and other dissident groups in the United States'.

Following the resignation in August of President Richard Nixon (1969–74), it had become open season on the intelligence community, and Hersh's story marked the peak of a spate of embarrassing revelations. The new president, Gerald Ford (1974–7), knew there was a problem. He requested an explanation from the director of the CIA, William Colby. The director at first replied that it is 'not accurate to characterize [the Agency] as having engaged in "massive domestic intelligence activity"'. But in a meeting with the president and his advisors on 3 January 1975, Colby acknowledged that the CIA had compiled files on almost 10,000 dissidents. Starting in 1967, it had watched protestors to see if they were externally directed. It had concluded that they were not, but there had been 'unease within the Agency—was it done for the foreign connections or was it anti-dissident?'[1]

Ford now faced a dilemma. Should he launch a cover-up? That would have been a standard political reaction. However, the very reason for his elevation from the vice-presidency to the White House had been the exposure of President Nixon's attempt to suppress the truth about the burglary by his 'plumbers' of the Democrats' offices in the Watergate complex, Washington, DC. The scandal was so recent that it would have been foolish to attempt another cover up. Should he instead try to find out what had been going on and confess to it all? Or should he follow the advice of his advisors Philip Buchen and William Casey, and go for selective revelation plus partisan flashback, pointing out that earlier Democratic administrations had been just as guilty of surveillance excesses as that of the Republican Nixon?

Ford listened to his advisers. On 4 January, he established a Commission on CIA Activities within the United States, known as the Rockefeller inquiry after its chairman, Vice-President Nelson Rockefeller. His goal may well have been to delay and deflect more intrusive probing. Pillars of the Republican establishment including the Wall Street banker C. Douglas Dillon joined former California governor Ronald Reagan on the commission. According to Colby, the commissioners did not exhibit excessive curiosity. He recalled that he had offered some files to the inquiry only to be rebutted by its chair: 'Bill, do you really have to present all this material to us?' Then on 15 January, President Ford rolled out his flashback, revealing what was perfectly true—the Democratic president, Lyndon Johnson, had initiated the CIA's surveillance of domestic protesters.

Ford's response made political sense, but in the excited atmosphere of the day it was not enough. With domestic issues at stake, Congress felt it had to investigate. On 27 January, the Senate set up what would be its biggest-ever inquiry, the Select Committee to Study Governmental Operations with Respect to Intelligence Activities. Frank Church (Democrat, ID), an aspiring presidential candidate with a gift for oratory who had served as an intelligence officer in the Second World War, chaired what came to be known as the Church Committee. A corresponding probe in the House sat under the chairmanship of Otis G. Pike (Democrat, NY).

Surprisingly President Ford now poured oil on the flames. CIA director Colby had previously briefed him on the 'Family Jewels', a list of the agency's misdeeds. It was unusual for a security-minded intelligence officer like Colby to be so open. He may have been influenced by the recent tragic death of his daughter Catherine, who had suffered from a nervous disorder and had been critical of US foreign policy and of her father's doings—Colby had been responsible for some ruthless policies, including the mass execution of suspected communists in South Vietnam. He was certainly swayed by political calculation—better to confess to the CIA's misdeeds and to tough it out than to risk a botched cover-up with the nation in a revelatory mood. So he was candid with his president—and, genuinely shocked, Ford let slip a public confession. At a White House function for senior *New York Times* editors, he explained that the Rockefeller inquiry had to be a blue-ribbon affair—because, otherwise, there might be irresponsible leaks about dreadful events. Asked to explain what he meant, he said assassinations.

This was an ultra-sensitive admission that inspired sensational headlines. Fears would in due course be ventilated about the CIA's involvement in assassination plots against foreign leaders such as Cuba's Fidel Castro. Such plots were shocking to public opinion, as Americans were not yet inured to the later policy of routine assassination of foreigners by drone. However, the real sensitivity of the admission arose from domestic assassinations. Americans were deeply troubled by the 1960s killings of President John F. Kennedy, Senator Robert F. Kennedy, Martin Luther King, Jr, and Malcolm X. The suggestion that there might be hidden stories behind these tragedies was media dynamite. America's leading 137 newspapers had carried no editorials about the CIA in 1970; in the calendar year 1975, there were 227—and the itchy fingers of suspicion pointed far beyond the agency itself.[2]

The mid-1970s inquiries into intelligence malpractices were a powerful plea for greater transparency. The intensity of the reform impulse sprang from a number of causes. US relations with the Soviet Union were improving in the wake of strategic arms limitation treaties, and it did not seem quite so unpatriotic to criticize the intelligence establishment. There was a general disillusionment with government in the wake of Nixon's Watergate transgression— that break-in had been privately organized, but it was still an example of political surveillance. The stalemate in Vietnam was a new experience for a nation that expected universal military supremacy, and further undermined faith in government. Revelations by Hersh and others about domestic surveillance affected citizens' lives directly, giving millions of Americans an interest in reform.

Finally, there was an unusual harmony between liberals and conservatives over the need for a shake-up. Americans for Democratic Action (ADA) were a left-leaning advocacy group that measured congressional voting behaviour on a scale from zero (perfect conservative record) to 100 (perfect liberal record). Church with a score of 75 was an intelligence reformer—but so was the ranking Republican on his committee, Senator John Tower (TX), who had an ADA score of just 20. Conservatives would in future years be supportive of the CIA and its sister agencies, but in the 1970s they still suspected that the CIA might harbour liberal tendencies. They were not being irrational—the CIA had courted European democratic socialists, cleared anti-war demonstrators of charges of communism, and prepared the way for detente with Moscow.[3]

Although the US Constitution vests the House of Representatives with relatively more domestic responsibilities and the Senate with foreign policy powers, the two branches of Congress on this occasion reversed their roles. The House committee concentrated on foreign intelligence. In spite of some good work, it had a poor reception because of its inattention to the domestic matters that really worried Americans. The better-received Senate committee issued two interim reports on foreign intelligence and assassination plots, but its hearings and final report more closely reflected the concerns of the nation. One volume of the hearings was on foreign covert action and another on the domestic-cum-foreign issue of the storage of poisons, but the other five volumes were all about domestic surveillance. Two books of the six-book final report were on foreign matters or mixed, and the other four on domestic matters, three of them on surveillance. One reason why the Church Committee devoted only 35 per cent of its report to foreign matters was its determination not to leak information about overseas intelligence in an irresponsible manner. But another reason was political—its members, the ambitious Senator Church included, attempted to deliver the domestic transparency that the public craved.

Via leaks to the press and then through the Church Committee's hearings between 16 September and 5 December 1975, Americans learned a great deal about what had been going on in their intelligence community. They heard a cluster of hitherto unfamiliar terms associated with surveillance. These included COINTELPRO (the FBI's mass spying on dissent), CHAOS (the CIA's equivalent), SHAMROCK, the telegram interception programme run on behalf of other agencies by the National Security Agency (NSA), and MINARET, a sister project whereby the NSA compiled a watch list of US citizens on the basis of SHAMROCK data, all without judicial oversight or authorization. Until recently, not many Americans would have known what NSA meant, let alone SHAMROCK. Now, they learned from NSA director General Lew Allen that 'some [intercepted] circuits which are known to carry foreign communications necessary for foreign intelligence will also carry personal communications between US citizens, one of whom is at a foreign location'.

Officials from a wide spectrum of federal agencies had to submit themselves to cross-examination. The Church Committee's chief counsel was F. A. O. 'Fritz' Schwartz. This grandson of a toy manufacturer had crewed at Harvard and rewritten the Nigerian constitution—he was a formidable presence. On 21 October 1975, he interrogated Thomas Abernathy, who had served on the staff of the CIA's Inspector General (IG). The IG staff have the duty of probing into and assessing the workings of the agency and they have a reputation for doing effective work, but Schwartz was not intimidated by reputation.

Schwartz wanted Abernathy to explain to the committee how the CIA had arranged for the Post Office to intercept mail between private US citizens and correspondents in the Soviet

Union. Initially, the objective of this 'HTLINGUAL' programme was to accumulate what in more recent years we have called 'metadata'—the names and addresses of senders and recipients on unopened envelopes—but then the CIA began unsealing selected letters and reading them. In a secret inquiry of 1961, its IG office had investigated the practice, and concluded that no information had been gleaned that was helpful to national security. Schwartz elicited this information from Abernathy and then continued his interrogation:

MR SCHWARTZ. Did you make another recommendation in connection with this project?

MR ABERNATHY. The second recommendation was that the Agency should be prepared to explain the project, if it should ever become public knowledge.

MR SCHWARTZ. Now, would you characterize that as a cover story?

MR ABERNATHY. That is correct.

MR SCHWARTZ. What did you mean by a cover story?

MR ABERNATHY. Plausible explanation for what was happening.

MR SCHWARTZ. You mean, a misexplanation?

MR ABERNATHY. In this particular case...

MR SCHWARTZ. All right. You did not recommend that the project be turned off.

MR ABERNATHY. No.

Observers of the intelligence community were receiving a painful education. Metadata collection could descend into letter opening, and the CIA ran disinformation tactics against not just the communist foe, but also the American people. Still another lesson could be gleaned from the mail-opening hearings. Here, as in other hearings, there was an issue of disclosure—had the CIA explained to its political masters what it was up to? Schwartz asked former CIA director Richard Helms whether the CIA had informed Postmasters General, Attorneys General, and presidents about the real extent of the mail opening programme. Helms confessed that there might have been some confusion in the minds of his superiors about the distinction between mail cover operations and mail-opening operations.[4]

This related to a further controversy that generated heat in the 1970s but has also been important at other times. It centred on the idea that the CIA was out of control, and it bore a similarity to the much-ventilated view that, over at the FBI, J. Edgar Hoover (who died in 1972) had been a law unto himself. On 19 July 1975, Senator Church had told the press that the 'CIA may have been behaving like a rogue elephant on the rampage', especially as it seemed to have been plotting assassinations without the knowledge of presidents. Committee member Senator Barry Goldwater (Republican, AZ, ADA rating zero), contradicted Church and insisted that intelligence misdeeds, whether to do with surveillance or foreign policy, resulted from presidential authorization. The evidence over many years does point to the correctness of Goldwater's view. Presidents hid behind circuit-breaking committees that concealed their role, and used intelligence officials as scapegoats for their own failures and misdeeds. Congressman Pike declared in a House hearing in November that the CIA 'was no rogue elephant', and Church's own inquiry finally admitted, if with some reservations, that 'The Central Intelligence Agency, in broad terms, is not "out of control".'[5]

At the end of the hearings and deliberations came the reports and the recommendations. The Rockefeller inquiry was the first in the field. Published in June 1975, it failed in its purpose to preempt other more hostile inquiries. But it did show that the post-Nixon Republican administration was capable of at least some candour. It confirmed that the CIA's Operations Directorate had indexed 7.5 million individuals, of whom 115,000 were Americans. Its Office of Security had 900,000 files, 90 per cent of them on individuals, most of whom were American. In 1971, it had computerized its records—surveillance had entered the age of modern technology.

The Rockefeller commission recommended that the CIA should stick to its original brief of foreign operations, with only a limited counter-intelligence remit involving domestic surveillance. It favoured mail coverage, but not mail openings. It recommended the destruction of the CHAOS files, and the purging of 'improper materials' from agency files with 'constant vigilance' by the CIA in future years against the gratuitous collection of personal information. It wanted a 'Joint Committee on Intelligence' drawn from both houses of Congress to replace the separate and reputedly supine House and Senate subcommittees hitherto charged with the legislative oversight of the CIA.

The report of the House inquiry into intelligence chaired by Otis Pike was leaked to the press in January 1976 after Congress had voted to suppress it, a circumstance that undermined the impact of an investigation that had otherwise been thorough and insightful. Pike and his colleagues had concentrated on foreign intelligence, making their deliberations less important for the history of domestic surveillance. The hard-hitting Pike report subscribed to the 'plausible denial' doctrine—the White House would cover its tracks and let the blame fall on others for mistakes and misdeeds. The authors of the report also worried about the politicization of intelligence. They were thinking, for example, of Secretary of State Henry Kissinger's alleged manipulation of CIA data on Soviet compliance with nuclear accords, resulting in congressional approval of arms limitation treaties. Though the committee was looking at foreign policy, the politicization charge touched a nerve as it applied also in the case of domestic surveillance. To be watched in the interest of law enforcement is one thing, but to be watched politically quite another. Pike and company added to such concerns when, acting on the House's constitutional duty to protect the taxpayer, they revealed that the amount of money spent on domestic intelligence was five times higher than the admitted figure.

The Church Committee published its report in a more sedate manner in April 1976 and expanded the data offered by the Rockefeller inquiry. It stated that there had been 1.5 million names in a CIA database derived from the opening and photographing of almost 250,000 first-class letters between 1953 and 1973. It stated that the FBI opened and photographed a further 130,000 letters in eight US cities and indexed 300,000 individuals in a computer system. Prominent figures like Congresswoman Bella Abzug, a forceful opponent of the Vietnam War, had had their correspondence opened. The NSA had obtained sight of 'millions of private telegrams'. The Army had files on 100,000 Americans.

The committee took a more sympathetic view than its House counterpart of the contributions made by the CIA to national defence, but insisted that the CIA, the military, and the NSA should refrain from domestic operations. The committee wanted 'all three techniques' of domestic surveillance, 'mail opening, electronic surveillance and unauthorized entry', to be under 'judicial warrant procedures'. They should be centralized in the FBI under the supervision of the Attorney General. Congressional oversight should be 'intensified', and the Senate should establish its own permanent oversight committee.[6]

Loch Johnson and Kathy Olmsted, leading authorities on the mid-1970s congressional investigations, both refer to the Senate's 'Orwellian' vision of the problem their nation faced. Although the Church report does not cite Orwell, its worries did parallel those of the English novelist. Notably, Church and his colleagues feared the encroachment of Big Government on individual freedom.

Also in common with Orwell, they undervalued the role of the private sector. The Church Committee was at least aware of the private dimension of surveillance. Though about foreign intelligence, Book I of its report deploys the word 'private' on 124 occasions. That section of the report recalled that the Anti-Pinkerton Act of 1893 had banned the federal use of private eyes, but noted that this had not restrained the CIA from engaging three private firms in the 1960s to help with domestic security duties—including a project called MERRIMAC that monitored dissident groups in Washington, DC.

However, the Church Committee was less worried about what private companies did to civil liberties than about what the federal government might do to private companies. The concern ran back to the history of CIA proprietaries, with the committee's perception being that the CIA connection had contaminated private companies, student organizations, and newspapers:

> The important line between public and private action has become blurred as the result of the secret use of private institutions and individuals by intelligence agencies. This clandestine relationship has called into question their integrity and undermined the

crucial independent role of the private sector in the American system of democracy.

The Church Committee did not consider the impact that the private sector had had on federal surveillance. Such influence had occurred through personnel exchanges—the 'revolving door' process—and through the influence of the private sector on government attitudes. For example, the tendency to 'hype up' threats to security in ways that sometimes led to excesses of surveillance sprang, in part, from the 'boosterism' of private business. Church and his colleagues did not investigate worker surveillance or companies' use of computers for the purpose of consumer surveillance. It was inclined to the sanctification of the private, and to the Orwellian view that it was government alone that needed to be reformed.[7]

The Rockefeller, Pike, and Church investigations contributed to what the historian Jason Arnold has called a 'Sunshine Era' in American politics extending from 1972 to 1978. This was a period of legislation that aimed to open up government and to guard the privacy of the individual from the activities of federal snoopers at a time of galloping digitalization. The reform impulse was evident in government policy and in judicial decisions as well as in legislation, and, as the Church reports suggest, the emphasis was on the protection of citizens from government, not corporations.

Agency officials could see the train coming down the line. Having regard to his posthumous reputation, J. Edgar Hoover worried about the 'Personal and Confidential' file behind his desk that contained information gleaned from the surveillance of political and other personalities. He instructed his secretary to shred the file in the event of his death, and this happened in 1972. He had already announced the shutdown of COINTELPRO in 1971.

The programme title disappeared from official usage. Hoover's successors destroyed the 'Sex Deviates' file in 1977–8. Officials in other agencies closed programmes to avoid being told to do so, in some cases leaving the way open to resume operations in the future. CHAOS closed in 1973, HTLINGUAL the following year, and SHAMROCK/MINARET in 1975.

The federal courts helped to curb some of the excesses of unwarranted surveillance. Heard in the Supreme Court, the case *United States v U.S. District Court*, 407 US 297 (1972) addressed an attempt by the radical White Panther Party to dynamite a CIA office in Ann Arbor, Michigan. The case is also known as 'Keith' after the district court presiding judge Damon Keith. The Supreme Court upheld the Keith ruling that a warrant was needed for electronic surveillance except where a foreign power was involved, and that wiretap evidence used in the preparation of a prosecution had to be made available to the defence. In the following year, another federal district court upheld a Freedom of Information Act request for all COINTELPRO documentation to be released. The Justice Department challenged the ruling, but had to give way.

Meanwhile, the legislators on Capitol Hill had been sharpening their pens. The Privacy Act of 1974 amended the Freedom of Information Act (FOIA) of 1966, which with various exemptions had opened up to public scrutiny the files of government agencies. The FOIA was important to those who opposed excessive surveillance because the more questionable types of surveillance were so often undertaken in secret. The Privacy Act now made it illegal for federally gathered information on individuals to be made available to third parties except with the consent of the individual concerned. The law also gave citizens the right to see the files kept on them, and to offer corrections to the information contained in those files. Inaccurate surveillance had long been a complaint in a variety of contexts, and the aim was to curtail this abuse.

In March 1976, the White House launched an executive reform initiative. It owed a great deal to an appointment President Ford had made back in January 1975. In that month, Chicago University president Edward H. Levi had accepted the post of Attorney General. Though he had conservative credentials, Levi could also claim centre-ground status, as he had at one point been counsel for the Federation of American Scientists, a private body that was then, and still is, a voice promoting open government. In office, Levi countered the attacks on the FBI and stated that it was not a 'runaway agency', but he also resolved to reform the bureau.

Levi proposed that the Attorney General should be put in charge of surveillance reform and thus by implication surveillance itself. At a meeting of top security officials in the Oval Office on 13 October 1975, Secretary of Defense James R. Schlesinger, who had formerly enjoyed a brief period in charge of the CIA, questioned the plan. Here are excerpts from a release of the debate:

SCHLESINGER: The Attorney General should not be the one to approve NSA surveillance.

PRESIDENT: In the case of telephone taps [REDACTED] you sign each one. For [REDACTED] you would sign a general one that is within the law.

LEVI: Yes, but I think it should be periodically reviewed...

PRESIDENT: I think trying to get a statute would be a disaster in today's environment. Maybe we can try to get passage of a statute in a year or so, but now we'll just have to use guidelines...

LEVI: I think we have to have some guidelines.

Levi was not given the power to write guidelines for the intelligence community as a whole, but on 10 March 1976, he did issue the FBI's first-ever executive charter. At the time there were demands for a legislative charter for the FBI, and the Church inquiry favoured that outcome. But, as President Ford had foreseen, political disagreements would mean that neither the FBI nor the CIA received such a charter. This by default gave Levi's guidelines a unique role. The very issuance of his charter asserted the Attorney General's authority over the FBI, diminishing the autonomy of the bureau's director in reality and, as importantly, in public perception. The words in the charter clarified the matter of control—instructions from the White House were in future to be in writing, making it more difficult for presidents to use the FBI for purposes of political surveillance and then deny responsibility. The charter's language also made it clear that surveillance was for the purpose of combating crime. The charter applied to the FBI, but it would now be difficult to resist the idea that the NSA and other surveillance agencies, too, should be subject to at least some form of tighter control.

Congress addressed this issue. In 1976, the Senate established its permanent successor to the Church inquiry, the Select Committee on Intelligence (commonly known as the Senate Intelligence Committee). The House followed suit in 1977 with its Permanent Select Committee on Intelligence. Oversight of the intelligence community through Senate and House subcommittees had existed previously, but Congress had now signalled a step-change in intensity. The national legislature had taken a step in the direction of openness and accountability.

Congress attacked the obfuscation behind surveillance when it passed yet another amendment to the FOIA. The Government in the Sunshine Act of 13 September 1976 supplied a historical label for the 'sunshine era'. This Act broadened citizens' rights to information by specifying the exemptions to those rights (these had to do with national security, but there was also an exemption that further protected the privacy of individuals from the over-inquisitiveness of other individuals exploiting the FOIA procedures). The law also made it clear that the FOIA covered the whole of federal government, including Congress.

The 'apex' of the anti-surveillance movement of the 1970s according to historian Katherine Scott was the Foreign Intelligence Surveillance Act (FISA) of 1978, which applied to all government agencies. On the one hand, FISA legitimized the use of wiretaps and bugs in fighting foreign espionage. It allowed them for another purpose, too. 1978 was a year in which the Senate Committee on Governmental Affairs showed awareness of a new threat, and produced a report on international terrorism. FISA paralleled that concern and legalized electronic surveillance in the fight against terror. On the other hand, FISA stipulated that, whatever its purpose, electronic surveillance would be lawful only when authorized by newly created special judges. There would be no blanket surveillance, for these judges would issue warrants only on a case-by-case basis.[8]

From the beginning, there were cynical and sceptical attitudes towards the 1970s reforms. Henry Kissinger at least gave FOIA a backhanded compliment: 'Before the Freedom of Information Act, I used to say at meetings, "The illegal we do immediately; the unconstitutional takes a little longer". But since the Freedom of Information Act, I'm afraid to say things like that.' Seymour Hersh had little faith in the efficacy of the Rockefeller inquiry: 'They'll clean up their shop a little, but in 10 or 20 years it'll start again.'

The *Washington Post* had this editorial comment on the Attorney General's guidelines: they 'may be effective as long as Mr Levi is in office, but could be scrapped by any future Attorney General'.

The impermanence of politics was certainly a problem. In the 1970s, there had been a consensus for change. To use broad-brush labels, liberals who might previously have favoured expansive government had come to believe in reining in federal agencies' powers. Conservatives had always tended to be suspicious of Big Government, and in a period of detente extended that attitude to the intelligence services.

But the election of 1980 was a watershed. Once in office, President Ronald Reagan revived a different element in the conservative agenda and initiated America's final confrontation with Soviet-orchestrated international communism. All of a sudden, the FBI, CIA, and NSA found themselves restored as precious assets whose freedom to act—and to monitor radical groups— returned. In December 1981, Reagan signed Executive Order 12333, weakening the FISA-imposed controls on federal surveillance and directing government departments to furnish requested data to the CIA. With his approval, the FBI watched the activities of domestic opponents of US policies in Central America. When details emerged and the House Committee on Civil and Constitutional Rights investigated in 1987, the bureau admitted to ninety-three break-ins at premises such as the Cambridge, MA, office of a Christian organization, the Sanctuary for Central American Refugees. The *San Francisco Chronicle* later calculated that the FBI had placed under surveillance over a hundred organizations whose members had criticized US foreign policy.

The Levi charter was in danger of becoming a meaningless scrap of paper, and the Sunshine reforms a mere memory. In

Congress, it is true, each house retained its supervisory intelligence committee, and that carried the promise of enforcement of measures guarding against over-surveillance. But the separate oversight committees were not manifestly robust. More committee members meant a greater likelihood of leaks. A joint oversight committee, the Rockefeller recommendation, might have commanded more trust and authority. Another problem was that the 1976–7 transition from investigation of specific cases to permanent oversight carried the danger of institutionalization. Congressmen and Senators sitting on the intelligence committees got to know the CIA and other officials they were supposed to supervise, had lunch together, swapped stories about their kids, and failed to ask tough questions. That was when they actually attended committee meetings, and often they did not. A problem here was that much intelligence committee work was secret, so legislators could not win plaudits for it from the press and voters.

On top of this, there was the impact of the Republican electoral sweep on the leadership of the Senate Intelligence Committee. Between 1981 and 1984, Senator Barry Goldwater served as its chairman. He helped to water down the FOIA provisions, and repeatedly called for his own committee to be abolished. A committee staffer offered this comparison: 'It would be like the chief of staff of the air force saying: "I don't believe in flying".'

However, the chairmanship of a committee can nourish proprietorial instincts. The Republican Goldwater ultimately defended his turf and launched an offensive that would bring bipartisan credibility to a committee that had been the brainchild of 1970s Democrats. The showdown came over foreign policy. When the CIA neglected to tell him in advance that it was going to mine the harbours of left-leaning Nicaragua, he publicly declared to the CIA director William Casey that he was 'pissed off' and extracted an apology. Commenting at the end of the decade on his change of heart, the senator expressed his opinion that the 'honest exchange of views [with the oversight committee] has probably done more for the agencies than anything in the last five years'. Intelligence oversight reform had come to stay.[9]

The campaign for surveillance reform did not stand still in the years of the Reagan presidency (1981–9). In 1988, Congress passed the Computer Matching and Privacy Protection Act. An amendment to existing privacy legislation, the law addressed the problem of record linkages, where officials could find out more about you than you might care to reveal by using computers to match data from different sources. Through automated matching of federal and state data sets, officials had since the 1970s been identifying fraudulent claimants of public benefits and debt absconders. The new law aimed to limit gratuitous invasions of privacy through the powerful matching tool. The limitation applied only in a limited sphere, did not apply to the private sector, and suffered from weak enforcement because it was administered from within a unit dedicated to chasing down miscreants as well as protecting their rights, the Office of Management and Budget.

The Matching Act nevertheless reflected developing concerns for privacy, as did the outcome of the debate over the NSA's 'clipper chip' proposal. The development of public key encryption meant that private citizens could communicate via encrypted messages that were harder for the NSA's computers to read. This presented criminals, terrorists, and cyber-saboteurs with an opportunity. The NSA's idea was that digital devices like mobile phones should by law carry a 'clipper' chip enabling federal officials to keep track on what was going on. By the 1990s, however, the proposal had been defeated.

The efforts of 1970s lawmakers with their respect for privacy did not, then, fade from sight. The 1970s restrictions on federal surveillance would be a benchmark for future political discourse regardless of the ebb and flow of politics. The 1970s US reforms stand out in still higher relief when they are considered in an international context. Furthermore, they impress because of their international impact. (See Illustration 5.) These last two points are demonstrable in the case of the United Kingdom.

Until the 1970s, Britain was a super-secretive country. People did not know about GCHQ. The intelligence and security services were famous through fiction, but the government still did not admit that MI6 existed and even 007 did not refer to it by name. The name of 'C', MI6's director, was kept from the public. In 1968 Special Branch, the police unit that looked after domestic security and cooperated with MI5, established a Special Demonstration Squad. As its name suggested, it took its cue from American operations like COINTELPRO and CHAOS—it targeted protesters. But whereas CHAOS and its like became public knowledge in America, the Special Demonstration Squad continued its work incognito until exposed in the early years of the present century.

The United Kingdom did, however, have its very own Seymour Hersh. The young journalist Duncan Campbell admired the work of his fellow professionals in the USA. He had technical competence in such arts as 'phone freaking' (today known as 'hacking'). In May 1976, he and the American journalist Mark Hosenball combined to write an article called 'The Eavesdroppers' for the alternative culture magazine *Time Out*: 'Britain's largest spy

ILLUSTRATION 5. Italian surveillance. This sign, photographed in Ferrara, Italy, in 2016, reads 'Building site under video surveillance'. The US and the UK may have established a lead in surveillance practices by the mid-twentieth century, but such practices are now becoming universal. Unusual in international terms, the small print at the foot of this notice is a reminder to Italians that they have privacy rights under their nation's legal code.

organisation is not MI5 or MI6 but an electronic network controlled from a country town in the Cotswolds'. Thus was exposed for the first time the existence of GCHQ. Writing mainly for the *New Statesman*, Campbell went on to reveal the working relationship between GCHQ and the NSA. He documented the existence of US listening stations all over the United Kingdom. To begin with, he was less concerned with domestic surveillance than with his country's dangerous status as an 'unsinkable aircraft carrier' at the disposal of the NATO command—Churchill had warned back

"Arthur! You're not under surveillance again!"

ILLUSTRATION 6. Arthur! By the time *Punch* carried this cartoon by J. W. Taylor in June 1981, people in the UK were beginning to worry about surveillance, though some remained nonchalant.

in 1951 that the American presence made Britain 'the bull's eye of a Soviet attack'. As a consequence of his journalism the GCHQ genie was, however, well and truly out of the bottle.[10]

By the 1980s, there was heightened awareness in the United Kingdom of the powers of government and businesses to intrude on privacy. (See Illustration 6.) In opposition to the Conservative government of Margaret Thatcher (1979–90), the Labour Party in its 1983 election manifesto committed itself to the creation of a select parliamentary committee to oversee intelligence matters.

The following year, Parliament defied Orwell's *Nineteen Eighty-Four* prediction and enacted a Data Protection Act in an attempt to limit the harmful collection of data on individuals. It aimed specifically at computerized data, and raised the possibility of further safeguards to protect data about the racial, political, religious, psychological, and sexual characteristics of individuals, as well as about persons' criminal records. It provided for a Data Protection Registrar, later known as the Information Commissioner, created a right to compensation for the effects of the collection of inaccurate data, and gave people the right to challenge and correct information held about them by the police.

This did not satisfy civil libertarians. In 1986, Campbell asked a series of questions, one of which reflected parallel worries across the Atlantic: 'What suspicions about your sexual life, family relations or friends may have been put in a databank by government investigators who are checking your entitlement to government benefits?' He believed that while there were many potentially harmful data banks held in the private sector, the chief threat came from officialdom. He estimated that one citizen in five was the 'subject of police local intelligence files'. He drew attention to the 'most secret computer in Britain', run by MI5's Joint Computer Bureau in Mayfair, which had 20 million people in its system.[11]

Then Campbell outed the NSA's Echelon programme. Derived from the French word for ladder, 'echelon' refers to the hierarchical sifting and analysis of intelligence. Its methodology took forward the signals traffic analysis techniques developed in the United Kingdom's Bletchley Park in the Second World War, and in America's MINARET, the project for processing secretly obtained data that became public knowledge at the time of the Church investigation. It 'matched' and 'linked' evidence from disparate sources and made sense of it. The codeword MINARET had fallen out of the watchers' lexicon when it became politically toxic, and the programme was ostensibly terminated in 1973. In his *New Statesman* article of 1988, Campbell revealed that the NSA and GCHQ collected 'billions' of messages, achieving 'near total interception of international commercial and satellite communications in order to locate the telephone or other messages of target individuals'. He referred to the Echelon project by name, and identified the Menwith Hill listening complex in Yorkshire as one of its major facilities.

Gradually such stories took effect, and the pace of reform picked up with the election of Tony Blair's Labour government in 1997. The Data Protection Act was strengthened in 1998, and in the same year Parliament adopted the Human Rights Act, giving force to the European Convention on Human Rights (1953), Article 8 of which protects the privacy of family life and personal correspondence. In 2000, the United Kingdom enacted its own Freedom of Information law—sharing Kissinger's attitude, Blair ruefully remarked that 'the power it handed to the tender mercy of the press would be gigantic'.[12]

In the same year, however, the Regulation of Investigatory Powers Act (RIPA) entered the statute book. It was a response to the growth of the internet and of encryption, and authorized a variety of public bodies (not just the security services) to demand data and encryption keys from internet service providers. A warrant from the Home Secretary would be required for wiretaps, letter reading, and the bugging of vehicles and houses. But MI5 and GCHQ would not need a warrant to monitor the 'clickstream', the pattern of an individual's clicks on chat and websites, and the addresses of emails sent and received. The Act prompted criticism on the grounds that it was unenforceable, presumptive of guilt in the case of those who fell under surveillance, unparalleled in the USA or other countries, and injurious to e-commerce. There was less discussion of the fact that it legalized employers' surveillance of their employees. Overall, RIPA recognized government activities that, being now on an open legal footing, could henceforth be regulated, but it was also a commentary on the degree to which the United Kingdom had assumed a stronger resemblance to a surveillance state than some of its allies.

In the regulation of government surveillance abuses, at least, the United States had pulled ahead of the United Kingdom while at the same time helping to inspire reform in the United Kingdom and elsewhere. Canada, Australia, and the Scandinavian countries debated the issue, but were slow to introduce concrete measures. These comparisons confirm that, whatever their weaknesses, America's 1970s investigators and reformers had pioneered a rebalancing of national security and civil liberty.

9

The Intensification of Surveillance Post-9/11

Of North African heritage, Zacarias Moussaoui was notionally a citizen of metropolitan France with all the rights and privileges that that conferred. In practice he came from the wrong side of the tracks, and grew up in the kind of *banlieu* that people drive through quickly, with the doors locked. His mother had married a stranger named Omar when she was 14, left him with her four children after suffering his violence, and worked as a cleaner in Narbonne. The career adviser at Zacarias's school told him to have no aspirations, and the father of his girlfriend let him know that he would never get his Arab feet under the family table. Even before he began to hear stories about Palestine and American policy in the Middle East, Zacarias was a boy with neither father nor fatherland, and a potential recruit for a terrorist group such as al-Qaeda that disavowed any national allegiance.

Moussaoui arrived in the United States in February 2001, and by August the FBI had him under surveillance. It seemed odd that he drew on unaccountable funds and that he took a course on how to pilot take-off and landing with a Boeing 747 passenger jet. A Minneapolis special agent concluded that he was 'an Islamic extremist preparing for some future act in furtherance of radical fundamentalist goals'. An FBI supervisor in the same city justified an application to the FISA court for a warrant to search Moussaoui's laptop computer and other communications, explaining that he was 'trying to keep someone from taking a plane and crashing into the World Trade Center'. But his warrant application was refused because he could not credibly argue, as required in the 1978 legislation, that Moussaoui was agenting for a foreign power.[1]

The Moussaoui affair was a double failure for America. There was a failure to appreciate what made Moussaoui and many other Moslems unhappy with the West and to adjust foreign policy accordingly, and more immediately a failure to see what was coming. Following through on Moussaoui could well have led the FBI to some of his confederates, and to those who planned and executed the attack on the World Trade Center on September 11, 2001. The Moussaoui oversight would feed into the logic that led to an intensification of surveillance post-9/11.

The 9/11 attack sent shock waves across America and beyond. When the al-Qaeda-hijacked aircraft crashed into the Manhattan twin towers, almost 3,000 people died. It was the start of a trend. The Madrid train bombing of 11 March 2004 (known locally as '11-M') killed 191. Then in the '7/7' attack in London, on 7 July 2005, there were fifty-six fatalities.

The force of the response to these events was in one way out of proportion to the number of deaths that occurred. Deaths from traffic accidents far exceeded the toll from the terrorist events in all the countries involved. More than 42,000 people lost their lives on America's roads in the year of 9/11—and 8,000 via handgun homicides.

But 9/11 was different in being premeditated murder of a kind that constituted a calculated attack on America and what it stood for. It was also a single, dramatic episode. Politicians do not always respond to eye-catching events such as mass shootings by the psychologically disturbed, but they do when they can make a link to the delivery of public security in the face of external threats, one of their prime *raisons d'être*. Policy-makers in the Bush administration also exploited the publicity attendant on 9/11 to promote their own ends, such as the imposition of more authoritarian government, the suppression of dissent, and the reshaping of foreign policy. All this was easier because they could truthfully blame the attack on foreigners. It mattered little that between 2001 and 2015 right-wing domestic extremists in the United States would kill more people in terrorist attacks (forty-eight) than did Jihadists (twenty-six). Americans remembered 9/11 for what it was: an alien attack on US citizens. This and America's ability to act on the world stage would ensure that history turned on 9/11.[2]

Reacting to 9/11, Washington's governing politicians would launch a whole new foreign policy, the 'war' on terrorism. More immediately, they fell back on a stratagem they had used before. If there is an attack, don't show weakness by trying to understand why it happened or admit that US policy may have provoked it. Blame it on the enemy, on the policies of your political opponents, and on the intelligence community—and then fortify the intelligence community, rewarding failure, as it were, to prevent accidents in the future and give credibility to the pointed finger of blame.

The opponents of good Republican order (so the argument ran) had been responsible for FISA and all its weaknesses. Democrats had drafted the Foreign Intelligence Surveillance Act in 1978 with its restraints on surveillance. Then, made complacent by the ending of the Cold War, they had allowed the intelligence community to run down. At the end of the 1990s 37,000 cars still parked daily at Fort Meade, but the NSA's annual budget had stagnated. According to Seymour Hersh writing in the *New Yorker* in 1999, the NSA was in bad shape. Once upon a time, Hersh had complained about over-surveillance, but now his gripe was about ineffective spying. He averred that, having been in the vanguard of code-breaking and eavesdropping technology during the Cold War, NSA had become 'a victim of the high-tech world it helped to create'. He asserted that other nations like India were racing ahead. He quoted a CIA veteran on the difficulties NSA headquarters had with high-speed data transmission and double encryption: 'The dirty little secret is that fiber optics and encryption are kicking Fort Meade in the nuts.' Hersh claimed that the NSA had become dynastic and complacent, that Echelon was 'a fiscal black hole', and that President Bill Clinton (1993–2001) had no inclination to pour further dollars into that cavity.

According to its critics, the long-term effect of the Democrats' FISA was to weaken the counter-terrorist effort. In 2002, Congress released a statement indicating that the FBI had been at war with the FISA courts in the period leading up to the loose surveillance of Moussaoui. FBI special agents had been admonished for using information from intelligence intercept programmes to further criminal prosecutions. Those wanting to rein in their power had insisted that 'there was supposed to be a "wall" between separate intelligence and criminal squads in FBI offices to screen FISA intercepts'. In the opposing camp, those now wanting to reform FISA argued that over-strict application of court supervision had made the FBI 'risk averse'. Rebuked for applying loose intelligence surveillance standards to criminal cases, its special agents had shown a tendency to apply strict, civil-libertarian criminal case standards all round, even in gathering intelligence on suspected terrorists. Risk aversion had deterred it from tightening surveillance on Moussaoui.[3]

The post-9/11 policy was to curtail liberty in order to defend it. In the wake of the attack, Congress voted by large majorities for a measure titled Uniting and Strengthening America by Providing Appropriate Tools Required to Intercept and Obstruct Terrorism (USA PATRIOT), signed into law by President George W. Bush on 26 October 2001. The Patriot Act modified some of the safeguards spelled out in the 1978 FISA legislation. There would now be reduced court oversight of the interception of internet surfing, email, and voice mail. Secret searches would henceforth be permitted, though in a nod to the Fourth Amendment those subjected to the searches would have to be notified retrospectively. Non-US citizens could be detained for a week without warrant, and incarcerated indefinitely if deemed a threat to national security. As it was emergency legislation, the Patriot Act had a 'sunset' clause and would be up for renewal in 2005.

Bush's Attorney General, John Ashcroft, was keen to press home the FBI's new powers. A graduate of Yale and the University of Chicago, Ashcroft was an adherent of the evangelical Assembly of God Church. Liberals regarded him as a 'no' man: he had over the years said no to racial integration, no to abortion, no to gay rights, and no to gun control. Now, though, he was saying yes to the death penalty for terrorism and yes to the revival of formerly discredited practices. For example, to the dismay of some FBI personnel but with the support of others including FBI director Robert Mueller,

Ashcroft revived religious surveillance. By the end of 2001, 5,000 Arab Americans between the ages of 18 and 33 had been summoned for interrogation, and 1,200 individuals with connections to Islamic groups had been detained. Arrests continued over the next nine months. Mostly, according to one law enforcement official, those detained were 'hangers-on and wannabe terrorists'.

In those nervous times even Hussein Ibish of the American-Arab Anti-Discrimination Committee agreed that there might be as many as thirty possible terrorists amongst the Arab American population of the United States. An unnamed FBI official told the *Washington Times* that the bureau was penetrating US al-Qaeda cells and pursuing a disruption programme, a tactic that went back to 1956, when the first COINTELPRO was launched. To destroy their efficacy, individuals and groups were being pitted against each other 'like Gladiators in ancient Rome'.[4]

Section 215 of the Patriot Act spelled out new surveillance powers for the federal government. It supplied the legal framework for the FBI to exploit the device of 1970s origins known as a 'national security letter'. Through the legal vehicle of an administrative subpoena and without judicial oversight, the bureau could now on behalf of itself or other federal agencies issue such letters demanding information about who called whom and when, though not about what was said, and could insist that internet service providers and others did not disclose that the information had been sought. Within four years, it was issuing 30,000 such letters per annum. To the same end, Section 215 authorized searches and wiretaps in counter-terror cases, not a new provision but this time on the understanding that the Foreign Intelligence Surveillance Court would in the normal course of events be sympathetic.

Branches of the federal government traditionally associated with surveillance redoubled their efforts. The United States Postal Service expanded the mail covers operation that had been so controversial in the 1970s. Warrants were still required to open and read mail, but the Post Office responded to requests from local and federal authorities to monitor Americans' correspondence—at first it reported 8,000 such monitoring exercises per annum, then in 2014 had to confess that the number was closer to 50,000. A Mail Imaging programme made this possible—computers recorded and stored every item passing through the system, mainly to help with sorting, but also making the data available for surveillance purposes.[5]

The NSA redoubled its efforts to secure information from the communications companies, and as in previous emergencies the companies felt obliged to cooperate. Though the government did not repeat the First World War measure of taking over the companies, executives allowed the penetration of their own corporations, sometimes to the dismay of their employees. In the summer of 2002, AT&T technician Mark Klein arrived to take up his duties in his company's Geary Street, San Francisco office. An email arrived saying to expect someone from the NSA to arrive on business. 'That struck me as a little odd to begin with, because I remember from back in the seventies, the NSA is not supposed to be doing domestic spying, so what were they doing in an AT&T company office?' Then in 2003, Klein transferred to his company's large switch facility on Folsom Street to install and repair new fibre-optic circuits. He discovered a splitting mechanism that double-routed all internet data to a secret room that had been constructed for the NSA on the floor below. As soon as he saw the splitter, Klein felt he was looking at something very disturbing, 'because they were copying everything'. Klein's experience was not unusual, as the NSA had or was installing surveillance equipment in seventeen of AT&T's internet hubs within the USA. In the 'war' against terror, the NSA and FBI were allowed to overlook the niceties of citizens' privacy.

On 1 March 2003, the Department of Homeland Security came into being. Epitomizing the Bush administration's response to the terror emergency, it soon boasted 180,000 employees, though most of these were in existing agencies that now came together under the one administrative umbrella for the purpose of better communication and 'connectivity'. The department brought together foreign and domestic security policy in ways that had hitherto been avoided for fear of creating an over-powerful police capability. Homeland Security relied on existing agencies' capabilities, for example CIA and FBI counter-terrorist intelligence assets.

All this cost more money, and budgetary support for the surveillance effort was strong. The FBI's appropriation rose by 76 per cent between 2000 and 2006. The NSA, with its 60,000 employees across the globe, by this time had a $6 billion per annum budget, rising to $10.8 billion by 2013. Total intelligence spending reached $64 billion by 2007, rising to $80 billion in 2011, and declining thereafter.[6]

Higher-level surveillance was no flash in the pan. The Patriot Act came up for renewal in 2005, and received a further lease of life. Some of its provisions survived into the second decade of the twenty-first century. Not every measure met with approval. In the wake of 9/11, the president had authorized an emergency data-mining programme. When the House of Representatives on 28 September 2006 approved a bill consolidating his powers to authorize warrantless surveillance subject to minor restrictions, seventeen Congressmen complained that 'nine months after we first learned of the warrantless surveillance programme, there has been no attempt to conduct an independent inquiry into its legality', and the measure failed in the Senate. But then the 2007 Protect America Act gave communications companies immunity from FISA prosecution if they handed over data to federal agencies. So did the FISA Amendment Act of 2008. In a sign of bipartisan shift, the ambitious Senator Barack Obama (Democrat, IL) voted against the 2007 bill but for the 2008 Amendment. The NSA was sufficiently confident of its mandate to start construction, in 2010, of a giant new data storage facility in the state of Utah.[7]

Opponents of surveillance expansion ran into obstacles. One of these was the Bush administration's ability and vigour in defending itself. Two influential members of the administration, Vice-President Dick Cheney and Secretary of Defense Donald Rumsfeld, had advised the Ford Administration when it came under fire from the Church intelligence committee. The deployment of 1970s tactics like flashback was again in evidence in the Bush administration even if they were sometimes clumsily expressed, as in Alberto Gonzales's erratic historical reference in defending the NSA. Ashcroft's successor as Attorney General, Gonzales remarked that 'President Washington, President Lincoln, President Roosevelt have all authorized electronic surveillance on a far broader scale' than President Bush.

Another obstacle facing the critics was the patriotic mood affecting the nation after 9/11. The Iraq War that started in March 2003 and continued throughout the Bush presidency further strengthened the emphasis on loyalty and patriotism in public life, and for much of the decade Democrats on Capitol Hill voted with the Republicans on surveillance measures. US involvement in Afghanistan hostilities only strengthened the tendency. Afghanistan was linked to international terrorism, and to Bush supporters US domestic and foreign policy seemed part of a logical, holistic approach to national security. Opponents of surveillance nevertheless voiced their concerns and deterred those who would have introduced even greater infringements on Fourth Amendment liberties. They formulated a critique that would gather force in subsequent years.

As relative calm descended in between the panic of 9/11 and the American invasion of Iraq, there was an outbreak of criticism of the government's real and imagined surveillance practices. The Columbia University law professor Patricia Williams weighed in at the end of 2001 with the statement that 20 million US resident aliens now lived under virtual martial law, and that recent federal measures mirrored 'the worst excesses of some dictatorships'. A journalist for the alternative press publication *Spiked* suggested that the FBI was back to its old habit of ethnic profiling and 'already running riot over Americans' civil liberties'. The African American novelist Walter Mosley complained he was being stopped and questioned every time he passed through an airport because he looked 'vaguely Arabic'.

James Bamford, a journalist with the *New York Times* and a leading historian of the NSA, was alarmed by post-9/11 initiatives. In an op-ed for his paper on the effect of the FBI's unnotified surveillance he quoted Franz Kafka's novel *The Trial*: 'Someone must have slandered Joseph K., for one morning, without having done anything truly wrong, he was arrested.' Joseph K. never finds out why he fell under suspicion, and gradually loses the will to resist.[8]

Joseph K. languished in the realm of fiction, and concrete stories of NSA or FBI abuse were hard to come by. The lack of evidence was to some sinister in itself. But one did not have to be conspiracy-minded to fear that the Bush administration's policies posed a potential threat to Fourth Amendment rights. When the Patriot Act came up for renewal in 2005, the Senate dragged its feet over some of its clauses and was still debating the matter when *New York Times* journalists James Risen and Eric Lichtblau on 16 December published what would be a Pulitzer Prize-winning exposé. The title of their article indicated its theme: 'Bush Lets US Spy on Callers without Courts'. They proved that starting in 2002 the NSA, President Bush, and Vice-President Cheney had systematically circumvented the courts in authorizing domestic surveillance. (See Illustration 7.) Searching for 'dirty numbers', the NSA had monitored the international emails and telephone calls of people within the United States without first seeking warrants, a practice that was disturbing (they argued) in an agency that was meant to deal with foreign matters. Additionally, the FBI was using the lower standards of proof in FISA cases (compared with criminal cases) to push for domestic surveillance warrants—1,754 in the year 2004—and was finding the FISA court a pushover, with few requests turned down.

President Bush had tried to suppress the article and when it appeared he denied its authenticity before finally agreeing he had executed the policy and claiming he had done nothing wrong. The Patriot Act remained in force and survived other challenges, too. But questions continued to be asked, and not just by outsiders. In 2009 the Inspectors General of the Justice and Defense Departments, of the CIA and NSA, and of the Office of the Director of National Intelligence combined to report on the President's

ILLUSTRATION 7. UnAmerican Leaker. This Steve Breen cartoon for the *San Diego Union-Tribune* followed in the wake of 2005/6 press disclosures about the president's surveillance programme, secretly introduced after the 9/11 terrorist attack of 2001. Vice-President Dick Cheney is talking to President George W. Bush (2001–9).

Surveillance Program (PSP). When President Bush had introduced this emergency data-mining provision (codename Stellarwind) as an emergency measure after 9/11, it was on the understanding that more regular procedures would ensue. It had included measures such as warrantless wiretapping aimed at al-Qaeda, and this continued until 2007 when it was partially discontinued. The Inspectors General noted that the PSP 'involved unprecedented collection activities' and 'should be carefully monitored', especially because of the divided opinion amongst intelligence professionals as to the utility of the effort. Senior officials believed that the PSP filled an intelligence gap left by the old FISA system, but analysts in the FBI and CIA 'had difficulty in evaluating the precise contribution of the PSP', perhaps a euphemism for saying that it achieved little and was not worth the incipient threat it posed to civil liberties.[9]

If America was slipping back into more intrusive ways, the United Kingdom had not fully extricated itself from those ways in the first place. Britain had used secret intelligence to prop up colonial rule, and surveillance practices continued in Northern Ireland even though Britain claimed that region as part of its body politic. When the Irish 'Troubles' resumed in earnest in 1969, 14 Field Security and Intelligence Company, part of the British Army Intelligence Corps, took up the job of penetrating nationalist organizations. The informer resumed his customary position as an all-Irish figure of contempt. British intelligence was constantly accused of being in league with loyalists. At an early 1970s dinner party in my home, a veteran of British intelligence in Northern Ireland looked at another guest, a mild-mannered man from Dublin, and remarked that the only good view of an Irishman was down the sights of a gun. The Dubliner gently indicated his disagreement with the remark, whereupon the officer drew back his jacket to reveal his handgun. The peace process that finally began to take hold in Northern Ireland in the 1990s had a moderating effect, but old attitudes survived. America had little to teach its British partner about ethnic profiling.[10]

As the foregoing suggests, the British tended to worry less about alleged domestic trespasses by MI6 and GCHQ than about police and security malpractices. The security services had been assiduous in their compilation of files on those active in the Campaign for Nuclear Disarmament and the anti-apartheid movement, and continued to monitor Greenpeace, animal rights groups, and other protest movements. It would in due course be revealed that former activists remained on file even after they became 'respectable' members of society. In the 1990s and later there were Special Branch files on three Members of Parliament: Diane Abbott, Jeremy Corbyn, and Bernie Grant. Other major political figures who had been under surveillance included Ken Livingstone, Tony Benn, Joan Ruddock, and Dennis Skinner. A 'domestic extremist' unit within the Metropolitan police ('the Met') kept a log on the political activities of Green Party activist Jenny Jones between 2001 and 2012, recording in seventeen reports her views on such matters as public-spending cuts and police violence—this political surveillance came to light when, by now a member of the House of Lords, Lady Jones became deputy chair of the Met's supervisory committee and received a letter from a police whistle-blower. The police were in general accessing phone call and email records with little supervision— by the second decade of the twenty-first century, they were requesting such access once every two minutes. Such evidence suggests that the police were singling out the broadly defined Left as a surveillance target—old habits died hard throughout the British isles.

Influenced by the United States, the United Kingdom had begun to review its policies on surveillance and privacy in the last decades of the twentieth century (exemplified by the passage of the Freedom of Information Act in 2000). But just as it was on the cusp of catching America up, 9/11 happened. The new attitudes and policies scarcely had a chance to bed down. Like the NSA, GCHQ beefed up its capabilities in a manner meant to give it greater surveillance capacity against the new terrorist target.

In Parliament as in Congress, there was support for this idea, and in 2005, the year of the London bombing and of the renewal of the Patriot Act, MPs almost legalized the use of intercepts as court evidence. From the government's point of view, this was misguided enthusiasm. GCHQ opposed the legitimization on the ground that it would shed too much light on their murky corner, and possibly drag NSA data into British courts, contrary to the Anglo-American intelligence understanding whereby each nation guarded the other's secrets.

In 2008 the Labour government, now led by Prime Minister Gordon Brown (2007–10), proposed to boost the capability of GCHQ with an Intercept Modernisation Programme initially costed at £12 billion. Like America, Britain planned a new storage facility. Running into opposition, the government withdrew its bill from Parliament but proceeded informally on a reduced scale. Retaining the private security firm Detica, it aimed to develop 'deep packet sniffers', devices that hoovered up information on individuals from phone calls, texts, emails, internet use, and credit card activity, and combined the data to form profiles of individuals.[11]

While there was opposition to such policies, the general drift pointed to a British inclination to trust the public intelligence services with greater surveillance powers. However, as we shall see in the next chapters, British faith in the private surveillance sector would have certain limits.

10

Private-Sector Surveillance in the Twenty-First Century

At the age of 13, a girl looks forward to many excitements in life. Milly Dowler never experienced them. Levi Bellfield alias Yusuf Rahim abducted Milly when she was on her way home from school in Walton-on-Thames, England, on 21 March 2002. Bellfield was a former nightclub bouncer with convictions for assaulting a police officer and other offences. He raped and killed Milly, and in the next two years murdered two other women. In 2008 juries found him guilty of the later crimes, and in June 2011 another jury convicted the serial killer of Milly's murder.

In the interval between Milly's disappearance in March 2002 and the discovery of her body in September of that year, Milly's parents Bob and Sally came under intensive press scrutiny led by the Sunday newspaper, the *News of the World*. Sally Dowler later testified to the level of pain that this press surveillance inflicted. 'What we did not appreciate was the extent to which the newspapers would intrude on our private turmoil and how little control we would have over where the lines were drawn in this respect.'

One day in the period when Milly was missing and hope still lingered, Sally and Bob retraced their daughter's footsteps from school to home to put out leaflets and inspect missing-person posters that had been displayed around the neighbourhood. Sally touched one such poster with her fingertips. That moment yielded to a hidden telephoto lens, with the sentimentalized result displayed on the pages of the *News of the World*: 'Face etched with pain, missing Milly's mum softly touches...' The Dowlers asked, 'How on earth did they know we were doing that walk on that day?' One inference was that the paper had been tapping their phone. Even more damagingly for the *News of the World*, it emerged that the newspaper had tapped Milly's mobile (cell) phone in the months when she was missing. Such was the public outrage upon the disclosure of these charges and events, that in July 2011 the newspaper closed down.[1]

Shortly after this, another form of private surveillance hit the headlines, as allegations were made about Crossrail, the project to tunnel under London on an east–west axis in order to provide the city with improved rail transport. Europe's largest publicly funded construction project was a wonder of engineering. Starting in 2009, huge drilling machines bored new tunnels passing in some places within millimetres of Victorian subways through which commuters strolled undisturbed. Crossrail Limited, the publicly owned company overseeing the project, employed private subcontractors to undertake its work.

The project ran into one of Britain's more immovable objects, a union steward. Frank Morris thought that there were safety issues on the section of the tunnelling project where he worked, and indeed a gantry did collapse on the site after he lodged a complaint. In September 2012 he was dismissed. In subsequent Employment Tribunal proceedings, Mr Morris, supported by the union, Unite, claimed it was on the ground that he had caused trouble and was on a blacklist.

Meanwhile, in December 2012, Crossrail had to deal with the fallout from the finding of an industrial tribunal that its industrial-relations manager, Ron Barron, had previously refused employment to workers who were on a secret list while with a previous employer, the multinational Chicago Bridge and Iron Company. There, he had referred to the list on more than 900 occasions in 2007 alone. The Consulting Association, the modern reincarnation of the old Economic League, ran the list, containing the names of 3,000 troublemakers in all. Just before his death in 2012, the Consulting Association's chief officer Ian Kerr gave evidence to a parliamentary select committee saying that he advised extensively on who should be employed at Crossrail and that, prior to being disbanded in 2009, the Association had sold its surveillance service to twenty large companies and had helped to blacklist workers at other prestige building projects that included the Olympic Park, the new Wembley football stadium, and GCHQ.[2]

After some agitation and a BBC TV programme, Frank Morris settled his Employment Tribunal claim. He regained his position on the Crossrail project and Unite and Crossrail issued a joint statement in which the union accepted that there was not a blacklist.[3]

Allegations of blacklisting nevertheless did not disappear. In 2014 MindSafety, a consultancy firm specializing in occupational safety, produced a report at the behest of a group of Crossrail's private contractors. In findings that the commissioning companies disavowed, it claimed that an atmosphere of fear pervaded the Crossrail project and that workers were too scared to report injuries to management because they feared being dismissed as troublemakers, so that dangerous conditions went unrectified. The report further claimed that there was a 'negative spy culture'. It stated that 'to actively watch people who may be in danger, photograph or video it and then email it around with unmasked glee is not the way to keep the project safe'. Crossrail responded that the report was inaccurate, and that its safety record was 'better than the UK construction industry average'.

As the Dowler story and whole history of blacklisting indicate, if one's criterion is the degree of distress inflicted by surveillance, one could argue that the main threat to privacy is private, and not the public apparatus of an Orwellian state. The private threat extends beyond the press and labour espionage. The Canadian political scientist Reg Whitaker highlights the way in which the consumer is targeted—when you use a Tesco card, Tesco is watching you. Whitaker argues that there is a Faustian deal between corporations and potential purchasers that has put an end to privacy in Western civilization—'open yourselves to our gaze...so that we will be better able to...deliver to you the precise goods and services that you most desire'. He believes that the 'surrender of the self' has been to the 'Little Brothers and Little Sisters of the corporations' and not to Orwell's statist Big Brother.[4]

Because of corporate secrecy it is hard to estimate the precise extent of the activities of those ever-curious Little Brothers and Sisters, but they were not minute. Private firms spied not just on crime victims, workers, and consumers, but on others as well. Industrial espionage—spying on the commercial secrets of competitors—has long been a thriving industry, and sometimes has had a political dimension. For example, a group of US Secret Service veterans in the 1990s formed the firm Beckett Brown International, working behalf of a number of major US firms. It spied on its clients' competitors, but also on profit-disruptors such as Greenpeace and gun-control activists.

The silhouette of the state can still be discerned behind some private malpractices. The state has in fact become the progenitor of a boom in the private security industry. The spy novelist John Le Carré drew attention to the phenomenon of US security outsourcing. 'War's gone corporate', one of his characters declared in *A Delicate Truth*, and the novel's protagonist noted that the US 'carpetbagger' tendency had spread to the United Kingdom. By 2006, 70 per cent of the $28 billion US national intelligence programme consisted of private contracts—and that did not include military intelligence. According to US government figures, some 37,000 'core contractors' worked for the intelligence community as a whole in the fiscal year 2007. By 2013, 3 million US citizens had security clearance, and almost a third of them were contracting their services to intelligence and surveillance branches of the federal government.[5]

Outsourcing had been attractive to the Clinton administration as a way of achieving economies. When the 9/11 attack demanded a stronger government security response, influential politicians inside and outside Congress were still reluctant to invest in federal bureaucracy. They instead favoured the hiring of hundreds of companies such as Palantir, a small firm located near the CIA's headquarters in Virginia that supplied analytical software to help in the pursuit of terrorists. Contracting out services in this way offered more flexibility. Its supporters saw the policy as a solution to the need for an intelligence surge and as offering bigger bang for the buck. Their critics, however, saw privatization as a step that facilitated profiteering and avoided the oversight mechanisms that restrained publicly operated agencies.

The unease arose, in part, because privatization was a break with standard political reflexes. At times of crisis, nationalization has been the recourse of governments regardless of colour—the liberal Woodrow Wilson presided over the takeover of the communications companies in the First World War, and the more conservative George W. Bush would bail out and effectively nationalize a significant sector of banking in the financial crisis of 2008. So why the urge to privatize intelligence resources?

The unease arose also because of questions about the reliability of the private sector, with worries, for example, that the FBI relied on private digital search engines like ChoicePoint and LexisNexis without double-checking the data. And was the private contractor more loyal to the bottom line than to his or her country of citizenship? Big corporations were often multinationals. Their international reach was an advantage in that they could match the globalization of terrorism, but did their multinationalism undermine their patriotism?

The outsourcing issue came to the fore when Edward Snowden, an employee of the consulting firm Booz Allen Hamilton, started to blow the whistle and sprayed the media with classified information. Stewart Baker, a former official at the Department of Homeland Security, thought that the Snowden revelations would 'produce some soul-searching about how many contractors the intelligence community has'.[6]

In spite of the clear ubiquity of sweetheart contracts, the state–private relationship has been fraught on a number of occasions. Internet service providers' reluctance to help with surveillance was one source of friction. Some of their officials held libertarian views; others had a missionary vision of an internet service that would be freely accessible and free from political control. There were those also who could see that their customers wanted privacy and would refuse to buy products featuring inbuilt government 'snooping'. Founded in 1990, the Electronic Frontier Foundation, partly funded by communications companies, had played a significant role in the opposition. The 1990s proposals to make it compulsory for 'clipper chips' to be installed in cell phones and other devices had been defeated.

Intelligence agencies on both sides of the Atlantic dropped the idea of universal counter-encryption. A British report in 2015 concluded, with an aside on the pre-1990s era when public encryption was not available and the government could read everything: 'The Agencies do not look to legislation to give themselves a permanent trump card: neither they nor anyone else has made a case…for encryption to be placed under effective Government control, as in practice it was before the advent of public key encryption in the 1990s.'

In the aftermath of 9/11, digital service providers did bend their collective knee to the need for pre-emptive federal snooping, but their commitment to client privacy continued. In 2014, FBI director James B. Comey opened fire on Apple and Google for their plans to market fully encrypted cell phones and hinted that the Obama administration might seek ways of forcing companies to unlock contacts, messages, and images kept on the phones. There was an immediate hostile reaction from those who argued that the NSA and even foreign intelligence services might exploit such access to the detriment of the civil liberties of the purchasers of Apple and Google products. Taking a stance that President Obama described as 'absolutist', in 2016 Apple successfully resisted the FBI's efforts to force it to unlock existing encryption to assist in an investigation following a terrorist attack in San Bernardino, California.[7]

Yet, the fact remains that the very same private sector that defended the privacy of its clients invaded the privacy of its employees in both the USA and the United Kingdom. In the latter country, born-again surveillance-and-blacklist policies blighted the industrial scene. Ian Kerr's Consulting Association had swung into action shortly after the dissolution of its precursor the Economic League in 1993. The passage of the Data Protection Act in 1998 in response to a European Union directive had little effect on his activities, nor did the Employment Relations Act of 1999. In 2006 the parliamentary Home Affairs Select Committee commissioned a report on 'The Surveillance Society' and by 2009 there was sufficient awareness of Kerr's activities for the Information Commissioner's Office (ICO) to raid his business premises in Droitwich. The raid revealed that about forty major companies used the Consulting Association's Services and that there were files on 3,213 construction workers.

Kerr's two-room office suite contained a top-of-the-range photocopying machine. Otherwise the 66-year-old Consulting Association director's premises were showing signs of age, with shabby decor, an electric typewriter instead of a computer, and furniture that went back to the 1970s. Its technology was antiquated and in the wake of the ICO raid Kerr had to pay a modest fine for offences against the data protection law. But he remained in business and his tried and trusted methods continued to impact on workers' lives.

Kerr's office kept card indices on workers of interest, sometimes with photographs attached, together with newspapers clippings, national insurance numbers, and other identifying data. Code numbers disguised the identities of those on the blacklist, and Kerr had a list of names corresponding to the code numbers.

Similarly he was able to shield the identities of his informers within the labour movement. Upon payment of a £3,000 annual subscription, an employer wishing to take on only compliant workers would be able to phone a special telephone number to get the lowdown on potential employees at a cost of £2.20 per check. TCA received 40,000 such requests in 2008.

Examples of comments about individual workers in the TCA files were 'Glasgow, pipe fitter, bad all round', 'Do not touch!!', 'Changed name...to get work', and 'Organised petition over homelessness'. With such information in their files, workers found they were unemployable, and went for years without finding jobs. Unite activist Frank Morris summed up what he saw as the potential human consequences: 'Missus goes, house goes, then suicide.'

In parliamentary hearings, allegations of blacklisting were directed at prestige projects across the United Kingdom, from London's Crossrail to construction work in Dundee.[8] Unions also complained that blacklisting was widespread in the North Sea oil industry, where workers were afraid to raise safety issues, and where there occurred a number of fatal helicopter crashes. In the construction industry, with an average of fifty-three workers per annum dying in accidents, many people were afraid to complain about lax safety practices. Itinerant workers moving from one major project to another knew each other less well than those in stationary industries, and there was an atmosphere of distrust. 'Someone will always point their finger at you', said Scottish building worker Stephen Kennedy having been blacklisted in London. But blacklisting was not confined to one industrial sector or to one organization. Gail Cartmail of the Unite union warned a parliamentary committee in 2013: 'We know that there were lists other than the Consulting Association list.'[9]

Kerr's methods of surveillance were effective but primitive. Beyond the confines of his outmoded office, information technology was racing ahead, and it did so within a permissive framework. The Regulation of Investigatory Powers Act (2000) established a system of oversight aimed at the intelligence services, but it also allowed any private business secretly to intercept employees' digital communications if it had a 'legitimate interest' in doing so. Firms had various reasons for conducting such surveillance, such as the guarding of trade secrets, but a significant number of them were interested in the maintenance of productivity by countering union activity and tightly regulating the behaviour of the workforce. In 2015 in the wake of its front-page story of such practices at the retail firm Sports Direct, *The Guardian* ran an editorial suggesting that 'surveillance' had become 'the British way of business'.[10]

Across the water, the United States had legislated against blacklisting in 1935. However, the Taft-Hartley Act of 1947 flagged a changing mood when it restricted the rights of organized labour and reinstated the legality of employers' anti-union campaigns. New blacklisting organizations began to flourish. According to a local American Federation of Labor-Congress of Industrial Organizations (AFL-CIO) official, by the 1970s in Southern California alone ten detective agencies were supplying labour spies to anti-union employers. Former detectives testified to having used clandestine methods of information gathering, for example by wiring workers' cafeterias. They identified union activists, who would then be fired.

Specialist private 'consultancies' were beginning to hold sway. Van Deman's operation survived, but was being eclipsed. For example, in the 1950s Labor Relations Associates (LRA) supplied union-infiltration and blacklisting services on a nationwide basis. Originally established by the chain store Sears, Roebuck in 1939, LRA had 400 business clients by 1957.

In that year, Senator John L. McClellan (Democrat, AR) opened hearings into labour union corruption. He came across the activities of LRA and found that the firm was caught up in labour racketeering as well as in anti-union activity. Just as in the 1930s, legislation followed in the wake of dramatic disclosure. Section 203 of the Labor Management Reporting and Disclosure Act of 1959, known as the Landrum-Griffin Act, required employers to disclose to the Department of Labor any payments to consulting firms engaged in labour espionage with a view to blacklisting.

It was a declaration of public attitude, but enforcement was weak and old practices continued. By 1980 Modern Management, Inc. claimed to be the biggest in the anti-union business and to have defeated organization drives in 93 per cent of 647 cases since 1977. Robert Georgine of the AFL-CIO estimated that there were by now 1,000 anti-union consulting firms in business with a turnover of half a billion dollars.

In the present century, the AFL-CIO has issued repeated alerts about the problem of blacklisting, claiming in 2005 that a number of media giants 'blacklist performers who speak their minds', charging in 2008 that seasonal labourers were routinely blacklisted, and in 2012 holding that taxi drivers in Manhattan were blacklisted if militant. In 2014, twenty-five former Milwaukee County Courthouse janitors went to court charging that they had been fired and blacklisted when Scott Walker was governor of Wisconsin (2002–10). Blacklisting and the surveillance that lay behind it has attracted widespread censure over the decades, but has by no means been eradicated.[11]

New forms of workplace surveillance had also become prevalent. In the 1980s, the US National Association of Working Women concluded that call-centre workers were stressed out because they were so continually and easily surveilled by management trying to make them work harder. The workers sometimes resisted by resorting to sabotage, for example by misleading customers, by leaving lines open after customers had hung up, and by pretending to talk on the phone.

According to an estimate published in *Business Week*, almost 75 per cent of American companies monitored worker communications. A survey of 294 American companies in 2006 suggested that over a third of the larger companies employed staff to read through employees' emails. Worldwide, an estimated 27 million workers were subject to electronic monitoring. The most intensively surveilled workers were in industries with low levels of union activity, meaning there was less resistance to surveillance, and more information that could be deployed against would-be union activists. In the view of sociologist Paul Attewell, 'far from opening up an age free from drudgery at work, as its admirers prophesied, micro-electronics is said to usher in the age of electronically-sweated labor'.

In the twenty-first century, there was widespread recourse to what was known as Human Resource Information Systems. These involved the data-mining of CV databases, electronic snooping on potential employees' websites, clandestine penetration of intranet systems (a procedure known as 'flipping'), and, to detect blacklisted workers assuming new identities, the use of biometric information such as that yielded by iris scans. As in the past, the chief goal was to ensure the employment of workers who would not be impaired by alcohol or drugs, and who would be honest. But the aim was also to exclude 'professional agitators', the label applied to union organizers and safety campaigners. Safety costs money, and the lack of it makes quick profits—at a potential cost to workers. In 2002, the year after 9/11, 5,500 Americans died in work accidents in the private sector, with 4.7 million injured or falling ill. The US Bureau of Labor Statistics further revealed that 50,000–60,000 workers died annually from occupationally acquired diseases such as asbestosis and miners' black lung. The annual cost to the economy through lost workdays, compensation, and health care was $170 billion. Surveillance may have suppressed labour troubles, gratified controlling employers, and contributed to immediate profits, but it came at a larger cost to society.

Companies wishing to look after their image and interests spied on the blogosphere, where employees could be detected engaging in critical or disrespectful chatter. A Delta Airlines cabin-crew member incurred instant dismissal for posing on her blog 'inappropriate' images of herself in company uniform. Universities began to advise their students not to post risqué images or thoughts on the web, as employers or their agents were trawling the net to obtain such information with the object of not hiring the more imprudent bloggers. There were warnings about the perils of downloading free apps—fail to untick the permissions boxes and you give companies carte blanche to build up a personal profile on you. After a number of disturbing cases, the Electronic Frontier Foundation published guidelines advising net users how better to guard their anonymity.

Although the US government had a history of condemning and legislating against blacklisting, worker surveillance was a cat with nine lives. Corporations and other organizations bent on prying on employees often got away with it. The situation was little different in the United Kingdom. Mark Thomas's drama *Cuckooed* sprang from his experience of being on the construction blacklist—the ICO confirmed the veracity of his claim. *Cuckooed* played to sell-out audiences all over the land in a 2014 tour, but public sympathy was to no avail. No doubt many people felt they were unaffected by the issue. Others saw protestors as freaks, who (in Thomas's words) 'crave the attention to justify their sense of worth, a sort of "I am spied upon, therefore I am"'.[12]

The UK government in London was as ineffective in its response to that kind of surveillance as it was to press intrusion. This had been a smouldering problem for years. Celebrities and members of the UK royal family complained about being spied on by 'paparazzi', photojournalists wielding telescopic lenses. In reaction to these cases, the public showed a wry appreciation that the rich could look after themselves. There was also some sympathy for newspaper pleas that the public had a 'right to know' that, say, a moralistic politician was having an affair with his secretary. However, stories about 'ordinary' people like the Dowler family made the public realize that plain citizens of limited income and with no access to expensive lawyers could also become helpless victims of the nation's more ruthless newspaper proprietors.

On 9 July 2009, *The Guardian* newspaper published the first of its stories about hacking practices at the *News of the World*, the paper that had exploited the Milly Dowler case. Dating back to 1843 and a key part of the media portfolio owned by Australian-American Rupert Murdoch, the *News of the World* was a 'red top' journal that had always specialized in sensational reporting. One of its journalists had already been convicted of phone hacking, and accusations of continuing transgressions were politically sensitive because Murdoch was a supporter of the Conservative Party and because a former *News of the World* editor, Andy Coulson, became the communications director for Tory Prime Minister David Cameron in May 2010.

It turned out that the *News of the World* had hired a number of private detective agencies to tap the telephones of people in whom the paper was interested. Glenn Mulcaire's Nine Consultancy, for example, had signed up for a £92,000 per annum hacking contract in 2004. A number of journalists went on trial for breaking the law. One of them, James Weatherup, a former news editor of the *News of the World* who had been convicted of conspiracy to hack, later said that phone tapping had been 'systematic' at the newspaper.

It subsequently became clear that the *News of the World* was not the only British newspaper engaged in phone hacking. In 2015 the red-top Mirror Group admitted to hacking-based stories— between 2000 and 2006, forty stories in the *Daily Mirror*, forty-nine in the *Sunday Mirror*, and twenty-three in *The People*. A barrister acting for eight Mirror Group victims, including the soccer player Paul Gascoigne whose addiction problems had been mercilessly ventilated, pointed not only to voicemail interception, but also to the extensive use of private detectives and of 'blagging' (theft). A former *Sunday Mirror* journalist, Dan Evans, utilized 'burners', numerous mobile phones used to hack and then thrown into the Thames to dampen the trail. At the peak of his prowess, Evans intercepted the calls of 100 celebrities a day. His editors allegedly pressurized him to invent an 'Enigma' type machine that could crack all pin codes.

Because of the impact of the Milly Dowler scandal but also, perhaps, because of its toxic political connections, the *News of the World* paid a price for its trespasses. Coulson had to resign from the prime minister's team, and later went to prison for conspiracy to intercept voicemails. The costs of litigation mounted, and the Dowler family eventually received £2 million in compensation. Closer to Murdoch's adoptive home, in July 2011 the FBI launched an investigation into allegations that employees of his News Corporation had hacked into the phones of 9/11 victims. The Justice Department never pressed any charges against News Corporation, but Murdoch decided to cut his public relations losses. It was in that month of July that he closed the *News of the World*, a paper that had once had the largest circulation in the English-speaking world and still sold 2.6 million copies weekly.

Prime Minister Cameron's government launched an inquiry into the British press in July 2011, and Brian H. Leveson, a law lord, agreed to chair it. After a series of public hearings, Leveson published his report in November 2012. He recommended the replacement of the old Press Complaints Commission, a toothless in-house body, with a regulatory board headed by a person who would be selected by a panel 'independent of the industry and of Government'. Virtually all newspapers balked at this idea, arguing that it would lead to government interference with the press and endanger free speech. The government did not push against this tide. As in the case of blacklisting, there were thistles in the private domain that the UK government was unwilling to grasp.[13]

11

Snowden

In May 2013, Edward J. Snowden met with three journalists in a Hong Kong hotel. He had stolen some 1.7 million classified documents, and he now began the process of leaking selected items about the NSA and its surveillance activities. The *Washington Post* in America and *The Guardian* in the United Kingdom published excerpts from the documents. Snowden's revelations received sensational coverage both favourable and hostile. In the following year, the *Post* and *Guardian* won a Pulitzer Prize in recognition of their coverage of surveillance's threat to civil liberties in America and Britain. After that, there was talk of Snowden being a candidate for the Nobel Peace prize. In an op-ed for the *New York Times* on 4 June 2015, Snowden claimed as a 'historic victory' the curtailing of 'the mass surveillance of private telephone calls under the Patriot Act'.

The impact of the Snowden story needs to be kept in perspective. The leaker fleshed out his revelations about domestic surveillance by unveiling certain US foreign intelligence practices. However, public opinion reacts mainly to domestic issues, so his revelations began to lose their initial force in his own country, even as they reverberated across the globe. And although Snowden claimed victory and justification in his campaign, US and UK efforts to achieve more open government met with less than universal success.

Yet any story that commands heavy focus in the media for months on end demands scrutiny. Here, there is no better starting point than Edward Snowden himself. Born in 1983 the grandson of a Coast Guard Rear Admiral and FBI official, our protagonist grew up in a community just outside Baltimore, where following his parents' divorce in 2001 he lived with his mother. He dropped out of high school and never attended a university, choosing instead to study the internet and become a computer geek with an anonymous identity. In an online remark at the age of 20, he hinted at his outlook and motivation: 'Great minds do not need a university to make them any more credible: they get what they need and quietly blaze their trails into history.'

At the same age, he enlisted in the Army, intending to fight in the Iraq War. Once in uniform, he became disillusioned with what he saw as the military's killer mindset and then broke both his legs in training, an accident that forced him to quit the Army. He became a Microsoft Certified Systems Engineer and by 2005 was working for the CIA. For that agency, he worked abroad deploying his computer skills, but in Geneva in 2009 became critical of his new employer and began to consider whistle-blowing. He now enlisted with the Dell corporation to work on NSA subcontracts. He was developing a distinctly anti-establishment outlook—stationed in Hawaii in December 2012, he organized a 'crypto party' at the back of a furniture store. Instead of drinking or getting high or making out with the girls (he did have a girlfriend but did not drink), Snowden discussed with his guests methods of encryption—how to keep one's social media activities from the prying eyes of anyone who might want to know about them.

Officially, his job in Hawaii was to search for vulnerabilities in telephone and internet systems so that the NSA could tap into them. Then in March 2013, the consulting firm Booz Allen Hamilton hired Snowden as a systems administrator at the NSA's Threat Operations Center. But he soon asked for medical leave, saying he needed to seek treatment for epilepsy. On 20 May, he departed for Hong Kong carrying four computers that contained digital copies of the secret documents he had collected since 2009. Once in the Chinese territory, he met his journalist contacts and started the process of leaks from his archive of United States secrets. Pursued by the American authorities who wanted to arrest, prosecute, and silence him, he ended up in Russia, whence he continued to issue revelations.

Intelligence officials leak information for a variety of reasons. In the case of Herbert Yardley, whose 1929 book *The American Black Chamber* spilled the beans about US code-breaking, the motive was a personal gripe—the federal government had decided to do away with Yardley's unit and terminate Yardley's federal career. Philip Agee, whose *CIA Diary* in 1976 revealed the identities of serving intelligence officers, explained he was influenced by his conversion to Marxism. When the CIA's Aldrich Ames betrayed US secrets to the Soviet Union and then Russia a few years later, he was driven by greed.

None of these motives applied to Snowden. Instead, he responded to a personal set of principles. He was not a systematic thinker, yet there are scattered clues to his ideological frame of mind. Some of these lead us up blind alleys. Though he once expressed adherence to Buddhism, it does not seem to have played a coherent role in his thinking. George Orwell was similarly a blind alley. Snowden had read *Nineteen Eighty-Four*, but said he was impressed only up to a point. He had worked for Dell and Booz, and might be expected to have picked on Orwell's neglect of the private sector. Instead, he fastened onto the notion that the Englishman was old-fashioned: Orwell's 'technologies now seem unimaginative and quaint. They talked about things like microphones implanted in bushes and cameras in TVs that look back on us. But now we've got webcams that go with us everywhere.' Snowden was too much in love with his own generation to be a full-blooded fan of George Orwell.

On the face of it, political motivation would also seem to be a blind alley. With the leaks process under way, Snowden avoided taking a stance on political issues—he wanted to cultivate friends with a view to enhancing the impact of his revelations and the civil libertarian message he hoped they would convey. In pursuit of apoliticism and also because he simply did not like being categorized and associated with any lumpen mass, he explained to *Guardian* journalists that he was exasperated in being categorized as a conservative libertarian.

Conservative libertarianism, nevertheless, does seem to be the most sensible description of his outlook and ideological motivation. He was an admirer of President Thomas Jefferson, a pioneer philosopher of American libertarianism, even if he did assert federal power to make the Louisiana Purchase from France in 1803. Snowden also had a contemporary philosopher-politician hero. In 2012, he donated $250 to the presidential campaign of the libertarian Congressman Ron Paul (Republican, TX), a long-standing critic of Big Government, and especially federal surveillance.

Snowden expressed admiration for two earlier American whistle-blowers whose actions may have given him courage. The first was Daniel Ellsberg. A former military analyst employed at the RAND corporation, Ellsberg had in 1971 leaked to the *New York Times* and *Washington Post* a collection of secret documents, dubbed the Pentagon Papers, that indicated that President Lyndon B. Johnson had deceived the American people about the reasons for US involvement in the war in Vietnam. President Nixon's notorious 'plumbers' harassed Ellsberg, burglarizing the office of his psychiatrist, and the analyst faced charges under the Espionage Act of 1917 that could have resulted in a 115-year prison sentence. However, Judge Matthew Byrne dismissed the case against him. Ellsberg became a hero of the anti-war campaign of his day, and a significant precursor to those who doubted the authenticity of the Weapons of Mass Destruction *casus belli* of President Bush's war in Iraq.

Snowden also admired US Army Specialist Bradley Manning. After working as an intelligence analyst in Baghdad, Manning had in 2010 leaked almost 750,000 confidential documents to Wikileaks, an online site created by the Australian Julian Assange four years earlier. The documents portrayed US military and diplomatic policy in an unflattering light, for example showing that the imprecision of air strikes in Iraq caused civilian casualties— precisely the kind of trigger-happy behaviour that Snowden had objected to in his own short army career. Indicted under the Espionage Act, Manning paid a heavy price for his indiscretion, receiving a long sentence and spending an extended period in solitary confinement just at the vulnerable time in his life when he was consolidating a gender change, and becoming Chelsea Manning. Snowden declared that 'Manning was a classic whistle-blower. He was inspired by the public good.'[1]

Snowden thought of himself as a whistle-blower driven by principle, just like Ellsberg and Manning. There was, however, a difference between him and those two individuals. Ellsberg and Manning leaked the secrets of foreign and military policy, but Snowden realized it would be more effective to concentrate on *domestic* surveillance, and tried to act in accordance with that perception. Public opinion is more inflammable on domestic matters than on distant foreign problems. In the 1970s, it was the disclosure that the CIA had spied at home that rocked the political establishment, with revelations about foreign assassination plots and other overseas scandals serving only to garnish the main course. In 2013, it was Snowden's leaks about domestic surveillance that ensured he would provoke a national debate in America and beyond. His longer-term impact would rise or fall on the strength of his domestic evidence.

Snowden had this in mind when, in advance of his meeting with journalists in Hong Kong, he thought about the order in which he would make his revelations. Yet he was already promoting a story that was really about foreign intelligence. Well before outing himself as a leaker on 10 June, he had sought to feed the *Washington Post* information on an NSA programme called PRISM. At this early stage the paper had feared legal repercussions, and declined. Snowden now communicated with Glenn Greenwald, an American lawyer and journalist who wrote for *The Guardian* and one of his Hong Kong press triumvirate: 'I don't like how this is developing. I had wanted someone else to do this one story about PRISM so you could concentrate on the broader archive, especially the mass domestic spying, but now I really want you to be the one to report this.'

Introduced in the wake of the FISA Amendment Act of 2008, PRISM was the latest reincarnation of MINARET and Echelon. The 2008 law had exempted companies that turned over their data to the federal government from civil liability, and under the PRISM scheme the NSA exploited the opportunity. Eschewing the 'front door' approach, which would mean media-company clients would know that the government had access and might switch to other providers, the NSA collected its data secretly. The batch of around twenty-five documents that Snowden sent to Greenwald as a taster of what was to come contained a classified PowerPoint presentation, 'PRISM/US-984XN Overview'. Its slides indicated that the NSA was collecting data directly from the servers of Microsoft, Yahoo, Google, Facebook, Paltalk, AOL, Skype, YouTube, and Apple. Google and the rest were daily tools of the American people and the service providers involved were American corporations. Thus at first sight PRISM came across as a domestic programme, though in fact it collected information on foreign targets.

In the event, on 5 June 2013 *The Guardian* launched what would be the first in an avalanche of revelations with a domestic story. It published the text, supplied by Snowden though he had not yet come out into the open, of a FISA court order dated 25 April 2013. It required the telephone company Verizon to hand over to the FBI and NSA 'all call detail records or "telephony metadata" created by Verizon for communications (i) between the United States and abroad; or (ii) wholly within the United States, including local telephone calls'.

The repentant *Washington Post* brought out the PRISM story the next day. Though its relevance to domestic affairs was marginal, a narrative of the disclosures running for more than two years from

June 2013 reveals a continuing determination to emphasize the domestic threat posed by US surveillance. In reality, however, the stories were as often about the clandestine observation of foreigners. Take, for example, the timeline offered by the Electronic Frontier Foundation (EFF) under the heading 'NSA Domestic Spying'. Presented in its class action case *Jewel v National Security* on behalf of AT & T customers alleging their lines had been hacked, the EFF timeline drew on reports in *The Guardian* and by other recipients of Snowden leaks such as Germany's weekly news magazine *Der Spiegel*. In spite of the 'domestic spying' heading, it flagged items such as 'NSA Targeting the Bahamas' Entire Mobile Network', and 'NSA and GCHQ Hacked into German Companies in Attempt to Map Entire Internet'.[2]

On 22 August 2013, *The Guardian* announced that in the eleven weeks since its first Snowden revelations it had published over 300 stories 'on the surveillance state and the political fallout'. Here again, the implied emphasis was on governments that engaged in mass espionage against their own citizens. Some of the early stories were indeed about domestic activities. The German press revealed details of GCHQ's Tempora programme that collected data from the fibre-optic cables of BT, Verizon, Vodafone, Viatel, and other companies. *The Guardian* took up the story and revealed that the NSA reimbursed some of the costs to GCHQ, 'at least' £300 million over the last three years. The suggestion was that US and UK surveillance were inseparable, that each country could spy on its own citizens using its partner as a surrogate, and that the old 'UKUSA' partnership had become 'USUK', with no comment necessary on the pronunciation.

A review of the reports that appeared in *The Guardian* and elsewhere shows that in reality Snowden's revelations were largely international in character. A spate of stories in late June and early July indicated that the NSA spied on the United Nations and on its allies, including Brazil, the European Union, and several individual European countries. Chancellor Angela Merkel of Germany and President François Hollande of France demanded to know why the United States was bugging their embassies and parliaments. On Monday 1 July *The Guardian* opened its front-page story with the observation that 'Transatlantic relations plunged at the weekend.'

But of course the United States and Britain had never been alone in spying on their allies. Furthermore, *The Observer* had the previous day identified a damaging vein of hypocrisy when it reported remarks by NSA veteran Wayne Madsen, who mocked the 'sanctimonious outcry' of European politicians who 'feigned shock' at the Snowden revelations when they knew full well that their own countries supplied the NSA with data in exchange for 'sanitized intelligence' that helped them protect the security of their own nations.

Official overseas indignation made no concession to such nice-ties, and reached boiling point with the revelation that the NSA had eavesdropped on the cell phone calls of two women who happened to be the most powerful political figures in Europe and South America respectively, Angela Merkel of Germany and Dilma Rousseff, President of Brazil. Both women expressed strenuous indignation. There was talk of an end to EU–US coop-eration. Rousseff said there was 'no basis for a relationship' with a country that undermined privacy and sovereignty, and can-celled a visit to the USA—the Brazilian-American chill lasted for two years.

Merkel and Rouseff were angry, but also political. Having in mind the surveillance record of the Gestapo and (in her native

East Germany) the Stasi, Merkel knew that her fellow Germans were sensitive on the subject, and would want their leader to react firmly (when in 2015 it emerged that her secret service the BND had spied on Airbus and the European Commission on behalf of the NSA, her poll ratings plunged). There was also speculation in *The Observer* and *Financial Times* that Merkel was making a fuss because she wanted Germany, Europe's economic powerhouse, to receive the same preferential intelligence treatment from the United States as members of the 'Anglo-Saxon' Five Eyes club (comprising the USA, the United Kingdom, Australia, Canada, and New Zealand).

Rousseff, too, had to be sensitive to opinion in her country. In 2008, the São Paulo weekly magazine *Veja* had revealed that the Brazilian Intelligence Agency, ABIN, was tapping the telephones of senior politicians and judges. ABIN's director lost his job and there was a demand for closer intelligence oversight. So even if the pragmatic side of Rousseff favoured good relations with the United States, she had to satisfy Brazilian sentiment by rebuffing President Obama over the perceived excesses of his NSA.[3]

In 2014, the media revealers returned to the domestic hunt. Britain's *Guardian* resumed its American muckraking campaign. In January it cooperated with the United Kingdom's Channel 4 News to reveal, through its New York correspondent James Ball and with input by Snowden, that the NSA was collecting close to 200 million text messages daily. Dishfire was the project's name, and GCHQ contributed to it. The two agencies ran a non-targeted and unwarranted sweep, collecting everything from bank transactions to missed-call alerts, and making no distinction between known suspects and the general public. A sub-project called Prefer automatically analysed the resulting metadata.

Commenting on the official defence that Dishfire did not target individuals, *New Yorker* journalist Amy Davison mused 'the phrase "not targeted" means "surveilled without the paperwork", or, in plain English, "targeted"'.

Other domestic-focused stories dotted the 2014 calendar. In July, for example, Glenn Greenwald published a breakdown of the NSA's intercepts in the years 2002–8 and concluded that the agency was mounting special surveillance of Muslims, including Rutgers University's Hooshang Amitahmadi, who directed the Council on American-Islamic Relations, a civil rights organization. A spokesman for the Council claimed that Americans were now being targeted for their 'faith as well as their political activism'. Reminiscent as it was of ethnic profiling abuses and complaints about racist police arrests for 'driving/walking/breathing while black', the story had inflammatory potential.[4]

Foreign reports continued to appear as part of the Snowden show, though sometimes they were just regular spy stories dressed up with the fashionable 'surveillance' label. In the summer of 2014, the American journalist James Bamford travelled to Russia on behalf of *Wired* magazine to visit Snowden at his new home in Moscow. He obtained documents indicating that the NSA had cooperated with Israeli intelligence to keep tabs on Palestinian politicians. Snowden realized that the American general public responded to foreign intelligence scandals with a collective yawn, and that stories about them put a dampener on the impact of his domestic campaign. So he tried to put a domestic spin on the NSA–Israeli leak, telling Bamford that it reminded him of how J. Edgar Hoover's FBI had spied on activists in the 1960s. They 'tried to use Martin Luther King's infidelity to talk him into killing himself…Why are we getting involved in this again?'

In November, yet another front-page headline in *The Guardian* opened up yet another new front, revealing that the UK intelligence services were listening in to the confidential exchanges between persons charged with terrorist offences and their lawyers. Snowden was not the source of the story, but by this time the outing of intelligence practices had become a rite of passage for liberal journalists. Going into 2015, the stories were still front-page news. However, by now they were getting repetitive. A *New York Times* story headed 'AT&T Helped US Spy on Internet on a Vast Scale' once again drew on Snowden's trove of documents but would have been news only to returning space travellers. The time had arrived to look back at the Snowden campaign and assess its effectiveness.

To begin with our recurring theme, Snowden failed to scrutinize the private sector. The Snowden revelations were, nevertheless, a wake-up call for private firms. Their links to GCHQ and the NSA having been exposed, they had to make at least a convincing show of resisting the advances of the surveillance state. To their discomfiture, they discovered that in some cases the NSA was tapping their clients' communications without their consent. Basking in the comfort zone of private enterprise self-worship, they had been caught unawares and were now furious, in the words of Canadian scholar Reg Whitaker, that 'NSA geeks had simply been smarter than their own'. Thus, goaded by the Snowden revelations, the private message carriers were once again a potential political counterweight to those advancing the reach of the surveillance state.

Booz-type subcontractors were also unhappy, because in a different way the Snowden revelations potentially threatened their livelihood too. Stewart Baker, formerly assistant secretary for policy at the Department of Homeland Security, wondered what would now happen to the private contractor system. He speculated that the Snowden affair would 'produce some soul-searching about how many contractors the intelligence community has and what they have access to, and how much vetting is done on the employees'. The libertarian Snowden had lacked the inclination to address the problem of private contractors, but he was still a challenge to their complacency.[5]

Snowden was just as silent when it came to assessing the actual harm done by government surveillance. There were doubts about the extent of the damage. Historically, there had been serious abuses. For example, in the cases of MI6 in 1920s Britain and the FBI in 1930s America, information deriving from domestic surveillance had been used and abused for political purposes. More recent examples of political abuse also came to light. In October 2015, the whistle-blower Peter Frances rekindled old anxieties when he revealed that the UK Special Branch had kept secret files on ten Labour MPs, including Jeremy Corbyn, who was the current leader of the party (and therefore of the official opposition to the Conservative government). But these files, if more recent, were still historical. Evidence on contemporary infractions was either hard to come by, or did not exist. The leading intelligence authority Loch K. Johnson wrote in February 2015, 'No evidence has emerged thus far that [the NSA's] metadata program has been misused for political purposes.' Former GCHQ director Sir David Omand noted that Snowden had 'not exposed any British wrongdoing'. Proof of current political misuse was not Snowden's aim. Instead, his revelations reflected concern over principle and *potential* abuse.

Still, with advances in technology putting every citizen within range of the prying eyes and ears of the state, that potential for abuse was enormous. The debate over surveillance was significant in that its outcome would help determine the degree of privacy in Western democracies for decades to come. The outcome of that debate hinged, in large measure, on the reception of Snowden's revelations. An important factor that undermined the force of those revelations was the personal enmity directed at Edward Snowden. It was one thing to criticize the NSA—the journalist James Bamford, a former NSA employee who became a stalwart of US journalism, was respected for his critiques. It was quite another to abscond and criticize. Former president Harry Truman had in 1960 demanded the death penalty for Bernon Mitchell and William Martin, NSA employees who had defected to the Soviet Union. As other precedents indicated, the prospects were not bright for Snowden. Philip Agee, who had named CIA agents in the 1970s, ended up a permanent exile. Bradley/Chelsea Manning received a thirty-five-year prison sentence. The Australian Julian Assange had also paid a price. His WikiLeaks enterprise had been a vehicle for releasing secret documents into the public domain. Hounded by the Americans and by the Swedish authorities who wanted him for alleged sexual offences, he took refuge in the Ecuadorian embassy in London where (like Snowden in Moscow) he remained a virtual prisoner. To flee is to invite censure, and Snowden ran the risk of that.

There was hostile speculation about Snowden's motives, with rumours that he suffered from a personality disorder, that he was covertly working for the Russians, that both Russia and China had laid their hands on the whole body of his stolen files, and that agents in the field had had to be withdrawn because of his revelations. But the verdict of some senior politicians was simpler. Congressman John Boehner (Republican, OH), Speaker of the

House of Representatives, and a critic of the 'weakness' of President Obama's foreign policy, denounced Snowden as a 'traitor'. Across the political divide and in the other chamber, Diane Feinstein (Democrat, CA), chair of the Senate Select Committee on Intelligence, agreed—Snowden had committed 'an act of treason'.[6]

A profound gulf separated officialdom from the Snowden camp. To protect national security, the Snowdenites thought it sufficient to watch only those actually suspected of terrorist or other offences, but officialdom insisted that America and its allies could not afford to abandon the vacuum-cleaner-style collection of all evidence. Champions of the official view were convinced that Snowden had compromised the national security of the United States and Britain. General Keith B. Alexander, NSA director 2005–14, asserted that the Snowden leaks imposed 'the greatest damage to our combined nations' intelligence systems that we have ever suffered'.

Snowden's detractors pointed out that he had gone beyond his self-defined objective of exposing the extent of domestic surveillance in the United States. Why, they asked, had he divulged classified information about foreign intelligence? The NSA quitter released, for example, 58,000 documents about British intelligence. This did not endear him to Sir David Omand. The British intelligence guru accused Snowden of gratuitous spillages, and found fault with him for trusting the press to publish only that information that was of no use to a potential enemy—since when were journalists qualified to make those judgements? Omand also ventured into the field of semantics. He advanced a special definition of surveillance—it meant spying on individuals, not the collection of metadata, so Snowden was barking up the wrong tree.[7]

Snowden annoyed his critics in both America and Britain by advocating greater encryption. He saw this as an aid to privacy, and as a protection against all-pervasive state intrusion. He disseminated 'how-to' encryption instructions, and private firms made the technology available. His critics maintained that this made it easier for terrorists, criminals, foreign powers, child pornography vendors, and others to hide their activities. Furthermore, when he revealed the activities of US official hackers—for example, the NSA had cracked the codes of Huawei, the Chinese telecom company—it meant, according to his critics, that rival powers could recalibrate their encryption, locking out the United States from information that could help protect the nation.

Snowden's critics weakened the impact of his message, yet they wielded a double-edged sword, for so many of them were self-evidently defending their own turf. According to the United Kingdom's Ditchley Foundation, the 'hostile reaction of the British and US governments to the Snowden disclosures of mass surveillance served only to heighten public suspicion of the work of the intelligence agencies'. Perhaps this was a factor affecting opinion; another such factor was the work of Snowden's supporters.

Those supporters took a vehement, collective stand. To the American Civil Liberties Union, Edward Snowden was a patriot. To the scholar William Scheuerman, Snowden's civil disobedience invited comparisons with Henry Thoreau, Mahatma Gandhi, and Martin Luther King. Frederick Schwarz, chief counsel for the Church inquiry in the 1970s, compared Snowden with Benjamin Franklin, who had 'helped fuel the American revolution by leaking' details of repressive British policies. An editorial in *The Guardian* under the headline 'A Whistleblower, not a Spy' demanded a fair trial for Snowden, like the one that had exonerated Daniel

Ellsberg. The *New York Times* took a similar view in its editorial 'Edward Snowden, Whistle-blower': 'he has done his country a great service'.[8]

Militants for the right to free speech rallied to Snowden's side. PEN, an organization devoted to free expression that had enjoyed the support of literary figures like Langston Hughes, Robert Frost, and Susan Sontag, reported on the basis of its commissioned poll of 520 American authors that only 12 per cent of them supported the government's collection of telephone and internet data. It reported a feeling amongst authors that federal surveillance was having a chilling effect on free speech—around a quarter of its sample group admitted to self-censorship of some kind. The NSA apostate did seem to enjoy the support of literary America.

Snowden's defenders argued not only that surveillance was harmful, but also that Snowden's disclosures had done no harm. Admiral Michael S. Rogers, Keith B. Alexander's successor as NSA Director, may have been bluffing America's potential enemies when he said the Snowden leaks had not caused the sky to fall. But from a different perspective there were those who argued that the leaks did no harm because the surveillance programme had been futile. In 2009 a report by the combined inspectors general of the intelligence community had highlighted the faith of senior intelligence community leaders in the usefulness of bulk data collection, but the report had also raised doubts about the process—'FBI agents, CIA analysts and managers, and other officials had difficulty evaluating [its] precise contribution.' To the delight of critics, redacted and then slightly less redacted versions of this report became available before and during the Snowden debate. Another study released in January 2014 by the non-partisan think tank New America Foundation examined the information that led to the arrest of 225 al-Qaeda and other terrorists in the United States in the years since 9/11. Telephone tapping had played a role in only 1.8 per cent of the cases examined, while NSA surveillance of non-US citizens had been a meaningful factor in a mere 4.4 per cent of the anti-terrorism cases examined.[9]

Communications corporations (as distinct from those that contracted to federal defence agencies) showed a tendency to vote with their feet in favour of Snowden. Their cooperation with government surveillance had been partial, reluctant, and predicated on the understanding that they would not be caught in the act. Now that this misfortune had occurred, some of them wanted to quit. Yahoo planned to move its operations out of the United Kingdom to Ireland, where, its managers felt, there would be a more secure legal framework. IBM spent a billion dollars on overseas data centres so that it could assure its customers of their privacy. According to the *New York Times*, continental European and South American companies began to profit at the expense of their UK and US counterparts, fuelling the resentment of Anglo-American corporations. All this amounted to pressure on the US and UK governments to respect client privacy rights.

Although Snowden never detailed the intelligence communities' impact on politics, he did set out to influence politics himself. In an era when intelligence oversight committees in the United States and especially the United Kingdom struggled to assert their authority, his whistle-blowing introduced an element of what Reg Whitaker has called 'guerrilla accountability'. At a time when America's authors worried about surveillance causing self-censorship, Snowden made a big enough noise to avert the danger of another silent generation. Robert Jervis, a professor of international security at Columbia University, agreed with

Snowden's claim to have influenced policy: 'Once Congress understood what the government was doing, it declared that we had drawn the balance between security and civil liberties wrong; the president, who had sponsored the old policy, agreed.' It had become axiomatic to heed Snowden, while denying that one was doing so.[10]

12

Policy and Reform in the Obama–Cameron Era

For those living in the United Kingdom, America can sometimes be an inspiration. The US intelligence reform impulse of the 1970s gave a lift to British libertarians, and UK reformers saw cause for emulation once again in the policies of the Obama administration. Implementation was another matter. Snowden saw the United Kingdom as 'worse than the US'. In June 2015, in an article headed 'America curbs state snooping—Britain gives the green light', former *Times* editor Sir Simon Jenkins faulted the UK government for its inaction. A few days later Eric King of Privacy International pointed to what he saw as GCHQ's uninhibited collection of bulk data and asked, 'How can it be that the US is so much further ahead on this issue?'[1]

As such comments suggest, the histories of intelligence reform in the two countries were linked. This was because of emulation and exchanges of views, and also because reformers in the United Kingdom and USA faced similar beasts. The NSA and GCHQ cooperated and were similar, and in the twenty-first century faced the same technological challenge: enhanced encryption. In both America and Britain the policy-makers to whom the code-breakers answered faced the same conundrum: was enhanced private device encryption an obstacle to foreign intrusion and cyber-attacks or an impediment to government surveillance in pursuit of national security? In each country, it appears, the code-breaking agencies were no longer able to do what they had long been paid to do, break codes (though a little gremlin pipes up as I write those words: 'They would say that, wouldn't they?'). Instead, the NSA and GCHQ focused on 'traffic analysis'—but were still accused of reading innocent citizens' mail.

The US and UK situations were not, however, identical. As Jenkins and King averred, Britain did lag behind America in the matter of reforming government intelligence. In the matter of private surveillance, on the other hand, the United Kingdom was more alert than its transatlantic partner to the dangers posed. Yet when it came to serious reform, Westminster failed to implement any universal solution.

Reform can have two meanings: curbing the excesses of surveillance or making it more efficient. Much of the policy discussion in the United Kingdom was about how to strengthen the surveillance state. In part, this may have been a reaction to the Snowden leaks. In part, it reflected a fear that the intelligence and law enforcement world was 'going dark' because of ever more sophisticated encryption and the flight of telecoms companies beyond UK jurisdiction. At the same time, the surveillance-efficiency discourse was a response to continuing terrorist events, and particularly to the fear that such events might happen at home. In May 2013, a pair of Muslim converts attacked British soldier Lee Rigby in broad daylight outside the Royal Artillery

Barracks, Woolwich, London. They hacked him to death with knives and a cleaver not for personal reasons, but to make a statement on behalf of their fundamentalist cause. It was a prominent media event, and the Tories dominant in the coalition government of the day argued that the assassination justified what their party manifesto called for, greater government powers to intercept internet messages.

These Conservatives were probably in step with public opinion, which, on this issue, remained conservative with a small 'c' regardless of the revelations by Snowden and others. In a TNS poll conducted early in 2014, by which time Snowden had delivered his main revelations, 71 per cent of the responders thought that the government should 'prioritise reducing the threat posed by terrorists and serious criminals even if this erodes peoples' right to privacy'. Some 64 per cent of those polled backed the idea that UK intelligence agencies should be able to monitor the communications of all citizens, not just likely suspects.[2]

Opinion in the intelligence community carried weight on the issue. It was not in every respect what the pro-surveillance lobby might have expected. Sir Richard Dearlove had spent a teenage year at the Kent preparatory school in Connecticut and remained on its board of governors after retiring from the directorship of MI6—he was as much a member of the Anglo-American establishment as any proponent of the NSA–GCHQ bond. But because of what he termed 'the lack of trust in politicians' he came out in favour of The Guardian's proposal for a citizens' body to scrutinize GCHQ and the other UK intelligence agencies. He also told a security think tank in March 2015 that Islamic terrorism should be denied its iconic status and was much less of a threat to national security than a resurgent Russia.

Most governments will, when confronted by a tricky problem, commission a report in the knowledge that such action kicks the issue into the long grass, but also in the hope that some solutions will emerge. In 2014, the Data Retention and Investigatory Powers Act required the Independent Reviewer of Terrorism Legislation, who at the time was David Anderson, QC, to perform the task. The Act had restored snoopers' rights with certain safeguards such as a twelve-month limit on the retention of data. When Anderson reported in June 2015, his findings were encouraging to the Tories in some respects. For example he endorsed meta-data collection and 'data-sharing among like-minded democratic nations', but he also (like Dearlove) put the terrorist threat in perspective, and recommended that the issuance of warrants for interception, both individual and bulk, should be subject to judicial approval.

It was a move in the direction of America's FISA courts and, though by different means, added weight to Dearlove's and *The Guardian*'s recommendation of independent scrutiny. The suggestion, though, was unacceptable to the nation's most experienced intelligence mandarin (by now retired), Sir David Omand. *The Guardian* reported Home Secretary Theresa May to be in agreement with Omand's view that it would be 'unconscionable for a judge to authorise a very sensitive intelligence operation where the political risk, if it went wrong, fell on the home secretary...who...wouldn't have approved it'. Omand, May, and the government's draft legislation did envisage judicial approval of search warrants, but with judges adjudicating on correctness of procedure only, and after the event rather than being involved in decision-making. May and Omand were not alone in asking whether judges were qualified and prepared to play a greater role.

In policy-making circles, the pendulum seemed to be swinging away from George Orwell and Edward Snowden.[3]

In America, the surveillance dispute was not the leading issue of the Obama years (2009–17), when people were more worried about health care, economic recession, Iraq, Syria, and immigration. It was nevertheless prominent enough to demand attention. Acting sooner than his British counterpart, Obama had established his Review Group on Intelligence and Communications Technologies on 27 August 2013. Reporting in December, the Review Group recommended the private storage of metadata, the information to be accessed by intelligence agencies only on the authority of a court order. The Group took it for granted that the collection of metadata should continue.

The stage was now set for a debate between the defenders and critics of mass spying. Intelligence leaders told tales of plots foiled by means of surveillance. The FBI said that it had thwarted an attempt to bomb the New York Stock Exchange. NSA director Keith Alexander revealed that his agency had helped to frustrate more than fifty terrorist attacks since 9/11. The details of such stories had to be kept secret and disbelievers wondered about the evidence. Such scepticism infuriated some. 'It is times like these', House Intelligence Committee chairman Mike Rogers (Republican, MI) complained, 'where our enemies within become almost as damaging as our enemies on the outside.'[4]

The Obama administration found itself defending the right of the federal government to monitor device traffic. Its critics mounted a challenge in the courts. Decisions under the FISA provisions were issued in secret, though a number of them were released because of the exigencies of the surveillance debate in the Obama years. Cases that arose from plaintiff suits were public from the start. However, in *ACLU v Clapper* (26 February 2013), the US Supreme Court decided that a challenge to the constitutionality of the metadata programme was unlikely to succeed. From a plaintiff's point of view, the problem was that one had to prove that one was under surveillance in order for one's case to be considered, but as surveillance practices were kept tightly under wraps, such proof was impossible to obtain. In the following year, a Congressional Research Service review of cases concluded that the federal courts had reached no conclusion on 'the merits of any constitutional challenges to [metadata] collection activities'.[5]

A different type of challenge occurred on the local level. It took its cue from one of the government's own initiatives. The State Department and US Agency for International Development had paid resistance groups in Tunisia and Cuba to set up 'mesh' systems, local communications networks free of the officially sanctioned webs in the nations concerned. In 2014, there was talk of mesh systems being set up in Brooklyn and Detroit—to serve the needs of local people, but also to safeguard against federal snooping.

On the national level, libertarian resistance to federal snooping existed on the right as well as on the left of the political spectrum. Indeed its most prominent proponent was Rand Paul. Like his father Ron Paul (who in February 2014 launched a petition seeking clemency for Edward Snowden), Rand Paul was a physician-turned-Republican politician who declared allegiance to the Tea Party movement and tried for his party's nomination in the 2015–16 presidential campaign. In the Senate he represented Kentucky, a border state. Though the twenty-first-century South was in general more security minded than libertarian, his outlook was consistent with an older southern tradition, characterized by opposition to overweening federal government—and to intrusive secret service.

Rand Paul turned up in March 2014 to address the students in the University of California, Berkeley, traditionally a hotbed of left-radicalism. Dressed down for the occasion but still wearing cowboy boots, he declared it 'ironic' that Obama, the nation's first African-American president, should be allowing NSA policies reminiscent of 'J. Edgar Hoover's illegal spying on Martin Luther King'. Perhaps inventing a bogeyman, he championed students' rights to conduct cell phone conversations without being over-heard. He maintained that the nation's intelligence leaders were 'drunk with power'. Like other critics of US surveillance policy, he failed to identify any current political surveillance, and he admit-ted that Obama was no Hoover, but he insisted that 'power must be restrained because no one knows who will next hold that power'. In addition to articulating a conservative critique, Paul was a thorn in the side of the governing establishment. In May 2015 he conducted a ten-and-a-half-hour filibuster against the renewal of surveillance clauses in the Patriot Act, and ran an effective blocking campaign in the Senate.[6]

Events do change the tenor of political discourse. One of these happened when Senator Diane Feinstein (Democrat, CA) fell out with the CIA. In her capacity as chair of the Senate Intelligence Committee (SIC), 'DiFi' had been pushing an investigation into the CIA's policy of detaining terrorist suspects in Guantánamo Bay, and subjecting them to extreme interrogation. 'Waterboarding', one of the techniques involved, was a form of torture according to its critics. In light of her liberal stance on this and other issues, some of Feinstein's admirers were dismayed when the 80-year-old senator condemned Snowden as a traitor. But soon afterwards, an event occurred that prompted Feinstein to revert to perceived type. The CIA spied on the computers of those of her committee's staff members who had been involved in the investigation of the agency's interrogation practices, and got caught in the act. DiFi went on the warpath.[7]

CIA director James Clapper at first denied charges that he had spied on the Senate and intimidated SIC staff members, and said that to guard national security secrets it was vital for the CIA to find out how the documents fell into unauthorized hands. However, in July 2014 the CIA Inspector General completed a report confirming that to break into the SIC's computers the agency had used false identities in violation of the law and of the separation of powers doctrine of the US Constitution. Clapper's job was on the line. He admitted his agency had erred and apologized. The affair had little to do with the NSA's surveillance practices, but, as President Theodore Roosevelt had discovered more than a century earlier, spying on the Senate incurs political costs, and the event helped to shift opinion.

Obama equivocated on the subject of surveillance. The *New York Times* reminded its readers that in 2007, the future president had demanded 'no more illegal wiretapping of American citizens' and 'no more national security letters to spy on citizens who are not suspected of a crime'. In office, however, he seemed to be a different creature, and Snowden was not alone in doubting the president's commitment to privacy. In December 2013, the *New Yorker*'s Washington correspondent Ryan Lizza recalled how Obama, when a candidate for the Senate in 2003, had called the Patriot Act 'shoddy and dangerous', but concluded that any expectation that Obama in office would curtail surveillance was 'misguided'. White House correspondent Peter Baker reported that once in office Obama realized the seriousness of the terrorist threat, and trusted himself to use surveillance data with greater responsibility than his predecessor in office, President Bush. He titled his article 'Obama's Path from Critic to Overseer of Spying'. According to this perception, Obama had lowered the flag of anti-surveillance and raised the standard of an intrusive state, a blow to the libertarian cause reminiscent of President Wilson's abandonment of the anti-war cause in 1917.[8]

In the event, however, President Obama used his executive powers to curb excessive surveillance. On 17 January 2014, he delivered a defining policy statement on surveillance. He said that intelligence had always contributed to American security and 'our freedoms', but revealed that he had 'maintained a healthy skepticism toward our surveillance programs after I became President'. He was not 'going to dwell on Mr Snowden's actions' but went on to announce a programme of reform, to be implemented that day through a Presidential Policy Directive on Signals Intelligence Activities. The directive itself went to the heart of the matter. The president promised restraint in the collection and dissemination of data, and declared, 'Privacy and civil liberties shall be integral considerations in the planning of U.S. signals intelligence activities. The United States shall not collect signals intelligence for the purpose of suppressing or burdening criticism or dissent.'

In March 2014, with the Patriot Act coming up for renewal under the sunset clause, the president repeated his willingness to see a curtailment of what became known as the '215 program', named after Section 215 of the Act, which allowed analysis of links between telephone calls with the purpose of tracking down terrorists. With the approval of Congress, he endorsed his Review Group's recommendation that the NSA would end its programme of mass collection and storage of telephone calls. The communications companies would store the data instead, giving access when required to do so by the FISA courts. There might also be a limitation to 'hops', the pursuit of callers' contacts through several telephone calls to see where they led.

In June 2014, the Obama administration rolled out an additional reform. It signalled its commitment to greater transparency by issuing data on the number of individuals targeted for special attention under FISA orders. The Office of the Director of National Intelligence estimated that around 91,000 persons had been thus targeted in the calendar year 2013. The figure may have reassured Americans aware that as their nation now contained at least 340 million people, it meant that only one in 3,736 persons were being watched. Additionally, 19,000 National Security Letters had been issued in that year. Critics wondered how many had been targeted on the basis of erroneous information, and whether the information gained had been of any use whatsoever. But the release of the information was a reform in itself.[9]

Another of Obama's reforms fell into the category of improving security efficiency. Here, in spite of the fabled party-political partisanship of the time, he was in tune with the Republican-dominated Congress. Senator John S. McCain (Republican, AZ), the defeated GOP presidential candidate of 2008, in February 2014 demanded a senatorial select committee to investigate not surveillance, but the leaks that had led to disclosures about surveillance. On this point, the gulf between this veteran Republican conservative and the Democratic administration was more apparent than pronounced. The executive was concerned that the 4.5 million personnel in government and industry who had security clearance might not have been properly vetted. Obama's Department of Defense therefore accelerated its 'Continuous Evaluation' programme aimed at profiling employees with access to secrets and forestalling leaks—the target was to cover 1 million persons by 2017. In the interest of security, the aim was to have fewer people knowing a smaller number of secrets, with the consequent potential for fewer Snowden-style revelations.

In the opposite vein, a Quaker Congressman tried to give force to the thoughts of those who saw Snowden and others like him as self-sacrificing patriots. In June 2014, Representative Rush D. Holt (Democrat, NJ) offered an amendment to the Defense Appropriations bill to 'carve out $2 million within the $504 million intelligence community management account and allocate it to the intelligence community whistleblowing and source protection directorate'. He had no success, but in that month the House proposed a USA Freedom bill that would offer privacy protection, and passed by a vote of 293 to 123 an amendment to the Defense Appropriations bill aimed at closing the 'back door' surveillance of international emails and telephone calls that involved American citizens.

Another event now occurred that shaped debate and the options open to policy-makers in the White House and Congress. This was the Republican gain in the 2014 mid-term elections. The Republicans emerged with nine additional seats in the Senate, giving them control there for the first time since 2006. They also increased their majority in the House, where their ascendency was the greatest since 1928.

There was some evidence of Republican queasiness over surveillance in general. Gallup pollsters had found in 2013 that Republicans tended to support surveillance when there was a Republican president but oppose it under the Democrats. Gallup reported in 2015 that 65 per cent of Republicans saw the US government as an 'immediate threat', compared with 32 per cent of Democrats; one *Washington Post* journalist saw this as the culmination of a decade-long trend associated with fears of domestic spying.

But the Republican win in 2014 was not a mandate for curbing surveillance. In the 2014 campaign, election issues such as income inequality, Obamacare, and immigration were still prominent, and had overshadowed the surveillance controversy. Many Republicans stressed the importance of national security, and Republican support for Rand Paul was weak. In 2014, a Pew Research survey of 10,000 respondents found that only 12 per cent of Republicans supported Paul's libertarianism. A *New York Times* opinion poll on the eve of the 2014 mid-terms found that 44 per cent of Republicans thought the existing bulk collection policy was good, and a further 26 per cent wanted it strengthened. The message from the polls was, then, ambivalent. There was no need for the incoming Republican chair of the SIC, Richard M. Burr (Republican, NC), to imitate DiFi and attack the intelligence establishment, and he endorsed renewal of the surveillance provisions of the Patriot Act.[10]

Two weeks after the 4 November mid-terms, the newly ascendant Republicans in the Senate heeded their party's tradition of upholding national security and blocked a move to modify the Patriot Act and revive the summer's reform initiatives. However, with both parties divided, a contentious debate followed. It resulted in compromise when Congress passed the USA Freedom Act in June 2015. The Act reinstated the again-expiring Patriot Act and reaffirmed the federal government's investigative authorities under the Foreign Intelligence Surveillance Act of 1978. But it modified Section 215 by introducing the concept of a 'specific collection term'. Data searches now had to focus on named individuals, addresses, accounts, or devices. Mass sweeps of states or zip codes or internet service providers were supposed to cease.

The courts, however, continued to uphold the constitutionality of surveillance. In August 2015, the three judges on the US Court of Appeals for the District of Columbia Circuit splintered in their opinions in the case *Obama v Klayman*, but still upheld the government's position over the collection of telephone metadata, on the procedural ground that the plaintiff, Amnesty International, lacked legal standing, not having been able to prove actual injury caused by illegal actions.[11]

The Obama administration held to its policy of a balanced course, defending the need for surveillance but with civil liberties safeguards. Arguably, though, the stiffest challenge it faced was technological. In October 2015, it finally yielded in its dispute with Silicon Valley over the counter-encryption of digital devices like iPhones. Security officials wanted a 'back door' to allow them to decrypt messages sent by communications devices, the better to track down criminals and terrorists. But the government's experts now advised that such encryption keys to Google, Microsoft, and Apple devices would do more than offend and alienate consumers and commercial clients. The creation of the counter-encryption pathways would be an open invitation to the cyber-hackers from rival powers like China, and from the worlds of crime and terrorism. In a 2016 law case, Apple chief executive Tim Cook made the further point that if his firm helped the FBI break iPhone passcodes, foreign governments would pressurize his firm to do likewise, a 'chilling' prospect.

Snowden had aimed at government practices, and US politicians who debated surveillance did the same. Outside Congress and the White House, however, there was concern about the private sector. In May 2014, David E. Sanger, the *New York Times*'s Washington correspondent, had wondered what the various reforms would portend for Silicon Valley: 'The question is whether restrictions placed on the NSA...will spill over to regulation of the private sector'.

There was awareness, too, of the impact of the private sector on privacy. Commercial raids on citizens' privately held data received some attention. An Associated Press poll in the spring of 2014 found that 58 per cent of people were 'deeply worried' about being subjected to surveillance while spending online, a slightly higher percentage than those who fretted about NSA intrusions. Tackling private intrusions remained, however, beyond the accepted political remit. President Obama pushed to restore workers' rights, but made no mention of the databases that underpinned blacklisting.[12]

There was greater awareness of the latter issue in British debate. However, on government surveillance, UK officials professed less liberal attitudes than some of their counterparts in the United States. The coalition government that the Conservatives and Liberal Democrats had formed in 2010 did recognize a need for new legislation. Technical advances had rendered the Regulation of Investigatory Powers Act (RIPA) of 2000 obsolete—for example, in Britain as in America digital device encryption posed an unanticipated range of challenges. And though government ministers may have been loath to admit it, from 2013 on there was a need to respond to Snowden's revelations.

The European Court of Justice in Luxembourg intervened in a way that added to the urgency of the debate. The background to its intervention was that the European Union had issued a Data Retention Directive in 2006 following terrorist attacks in the USA,

Spain, and the United Kingdom, and the British Labour government had implemented it in 2009. The directive allowed for the retention of metadata for up to two years. But in April 2014 the Luxembourg court ruled that the directive was too sweeping, and too invasive of citizens' privacy.

In a further ruling in October 2015, the European Court addressed the public–private issue and overturned the Safe Harbour agreement of 2000. In spite of the Echelon controversy, the European Union had agreed back then that social media and commercial data that Europeans entrusted to US communications companies was in 'safe' custody, with no governmental invasions of privacy. Unimpressed, and inspired by the Snowden revelations, Maximillian Schrems, a 27-year-old Austrian law graduate, launched a legal suit charging that his account with the Irish-based European subsidiary of Facebook imperilled the privacy of his data. Some saw Schrems as a latter-day Luddite, and the High Court of Ireland ruled against him. However, the libertarian group Digital Rights Ireland supported Schrems, and, in a challenge to the hegemony of American communications firms, the Luxembourg court overturned the Irish court's verdict. Potentially, this was a boon to the European cloud industry, a blow to its American competitors, and a challenge to the cosy GCHQ–NSA relationship. It also imperilled the viability of 4,500 American companies which used Safe Harbour principles for transatlantic data transfers.

Conservatives in the United Kingdom's coalition pursued a contrasting agenda with a statist emphasis. They wanted a new law with updated empowerment, for example allowing the police to track every website that people had visited. They were conscious of those in their own ranks who were Eurosceptics, wanted no interference from EU courts, and demanded British exemption from the European Convention on Human Rights. The Liberal Democrats dragged their feet on all this, and Labour in opposition demanded a US-style 'sunset clause'.

Prime Minister David Cameron (2010–16) offered emergency legislation that appeased all parties. The Data Retention and Investigatory Powers Act of July 2014 renewed the data-retention facility, and fixed a 'sunset' date of 31 December 2016. This was the law that provided for the Independent Reviewer of Terrorist Legislation, the aforementioned David Anderson, to prepare a report. Meanwhile, Parliament's cross-party Intelligence and Security Committee worked on its own report. This was ready in March 2015. It underlined the point that current legislation was a mess and that the intelligence services might misconstrue it as a *carte blanche*. There was a need for greater clarity regarding surveillance principles and guidelines, but not for an overall restriction of government powers. The committee did not endorse the idea that judges, rather than politicians, should be empowered to issue surveillance warrants.

The Conservatives promised that after the general election due in May 2015 they would introduce new legislation. Critics agitated against a 'snoopers' charter', and another obstacle lay in the way of surveillance enhancement: on 23 March 2015, the Investigatory Powers Tribunal declared that GCHQ had been acting illegally. Set up under RIPA in 2000, the tribunal was an independent judicial body with the duty of investigating complaints against the intelligence services, but it had never before issued such an adverse verdict. Now, it judged that for several years GCHQ had utilized private communications passed on by the NSA and had done so in breach of the privacy provisions of the European Convention on Human Rights. The *New York Times* pronounced on the issue in an editorial headed 'Britain's Surveillance State'. The paper observed that 'Britons have generally been more accepting of intrusive government than Americans'. It noted disapprovingly that all nine parliamentary Intelligence and Security Committee members were Cameron nominees, and that the prime minister was pushing for 'even greater surveillance powers'.

Scotland's *Daily Record and Sunday Mail* offered criticism from a difference perspective. It ran a story, based on leaked documents, indicating that GCHQ may have reinterpreted the Wilson doctrine that banned the surveillance of Members of the Westminster Parliament. Apparently this ban would not apply to members of the European and Scottish Parliaments or of the Welsh Assembly. Wales's *Western Mail* editorialized: 'This is disappointing considering it is now two years since the Edward Snowden revelations emerged.'

As in the case of the United States, the electorate intervened. The Conservatives won the general election of 7 May 2015 with an outright majority of four MPs. This was not quite a mandate for a surveillance state. The economy and not surveillance had been the major election issue. The main parties in opposition to the new Conservative government, the Labour Party and the Scottish National Party, favoured restraint in surveillance matters, and some Conservatives agreed with them. Nevertheless, the electorate had chosen a government that stood for surveillance enhancement, and opinion polls suggested there was only minority opposition to that stance. When the Anderson report appeared in the summer of 2015, the government signalled that it would respond sympathetically, but it gave no sign that it would offer firm checks on the Home Secretary's authority to issue warrants, or introduce parliamentary oversight comparable with the Senate and House intelligence committees in the United States.

In spite of supportive public opinion and its election victory, the Conservative government saw reasons to advance cautiously with its Investigatory Powers bill. Its Commons majority was slim, its traditional Lords majority no longer existed, there was opposition in the press, and the issue remained complex. In November 2015, the government therefore announced a modified bundle of proposals. Future police access to browsing histories would be targeted, not general. There would be no ban on net encryption, and no UK storage of digital data of American derivation. The Wilson doctrine, though now discovered to have had a shaky legal basis, would be partially restored: Westminster MPs and journalists would be protected from surveillance. There would be a 'double lock' sign-off on surveillance warrants, with the Home Secretary issuing the warrant and a judge then adjudicating on its lawfulness and proportionality.

The usual withering commentary ensued. Liberty's Shami Chakrabarti denounced the 'traditional Home Office dance first to ask for the most outrageous, even impractical powers, so that the smallest so-called "concessions" seem more reasonable'. The government's attempt to depoliticize the search-warrant system failed to convince the critics. Surely the judges would be engaged in no more than procedural rubber-stamping? There was a rejoinder here—at times of national emergency, how qualified would the judges be to perform a bigger role? In March 2016 the Home Office unveiled a new 299-page draft charter, hailing it as 'world-leading legislation'. *The Guardian* warned against such 'soothing whispers'. But in November in the shadow of Brexit, the 2016 Investigatory Powers bill quietly became law.[13]

The campaign within the United Kingdom for more effective surveillance extended beyond the traditional intelligence agencies. In July 2014, the director of the National Crime Agency, a kind of fledgling British FBI, demanded more access to communications data. More controversially, covert policing was a factor in public debate—there were 1,200 undercover police officers in the United Kingdom. Historical miscarriages of justice still resonated, one in particular. In 1993, a racist white gang had murdered a young black man named Stephen Lawrence as he innocently waited at a London bus stop. Because of inadequate and allegedly corrupt police procedures no one paid for the crime until a jury convicted two men in 2012. In the intervening years there were charges of institutional police racism, and a campaign for justice. In an illegal act of self-preservation, the Metropolitan Police ('the Met') spied on the campaigners and on the bereaved Lawrence family, only to be caught in the act. A poll conducted in 2013 indicated that the affair diminished the police in the eyes of more than a third of Londoners. Significantly, however, 85 per cent said they still trusted the Met as a whole. As ever, there was underlying public support for surveillance.

Undercover policemen penetrated protest and political action groups that had nothing to do with terrorism. They posed as radicals in order gain credence, and sometimes engaged in intimate relations with group members. On 24 October 2014, *The Guardian* ran two surveillance stories on its front page. One was about MI5 keeping tabs on Marxist historians like Eric Hobsbawm, and the other was how an undercover cop had fathered a son with a protestor—in an out-of-court settlement, the Met had to pay the mother £425,000 in compensation. Responding in the spring of 2015 to the Lawrence and other cases, the Home Secretary set up an inquiry into undercover policing under the former Lord Justice of Appeal, Sir Christopher Pitchford. Its remit was to examine political surveillance and spying on members of the public since 1968. Pitchford promised exemption from prosecution to police officers who testified before it, but there was no suggestion that the extent of undercover police surveillance would in any way be diminished.

The UK government's approach to both national and local surveillance reflected public opinion. It was not just the public's reverence (if qualified) for the Met. In 2014, an Ipsos MORI poll indicated that only 16 per cent of UK citizens disapproved of security agencies' monitoring of students' web searches as they researched sensitive topics at their universities. The TNS poll cited earlier concluded that fewer than half of its sample were 'concerned that British intelligence agencies are monitoring their online activities'.

However, the same poll indicated that 'more than half are concerned by commercial companies doing so'. To a greater degree than in the United States, the UK government demonstrated a potential willingness to respond to such concerns about the private sector.[14] That willingness was, however, put to the test and found wanting in the cases of media control and attempts to curb labour espionage and blacklisting. As we saw in Chapter 10, revelations about transgressions by the *News of the World* and other newspapers resulted in high-level resignations and an official inquiry headed by Lord Leveson, yet the government remained unresponsive to the need for thoroughgoing reform. In December 2015, the Crown Prosecution Service ceased its pursuit of criminal investigations against the Murdoch and Mirror groups of newspapers.

The push to end blacklisting in the labour market and the private data-gathering that underpinned it was another distinctively British move. The push began in Westminster with the Labour government of Prime Minister Gordon Brown (2007–10), then after the formation of the coalition government continued in Wales and Scotland. Just before Cameron's coalition took power, the Employment Relations Act (Blacklists) Regulations 2010 came into effect. The Act made it illegal to compile, use, sell, or supply blacklists. However, anti-union employers were accomplished in the art of evasion. The House of Commons Scottish Affairs Committee noted in a 2013 report on blacklisting how the employers acted in secrecy.

Scotland and Wales had for some years had their own revived parliaments, and were advancing independent initiatives. The Welsh government in December 2012 issued a Procurement Advice Note, giving advice on the potential blacklisting of blacklisters in the construction industry. It urged local authorities to offer firms the option of 'self-cleaning' but stated that in principle they were free to deny public contracts to firms with a record of discriminating against workers via the Consulting Association or by other means. Welsh Finance Minister Jane Hutt commented two years later that her note was 'certainly influencing behaviours in the construction industry' and that 'we have not had any new cases of Blacklisting in Wales highlighted to us'.

In Scotland, the government issued 'guidance' notes discouraging the issuance of public contracts to blacklisting companies, but there was widespread disregard for the advice. At a meeting in the Scottish Parliament in 2016, trade unionists bitterly complained that industry was saturated with informers who fingered activists who were then blacklisted. The governing Scottish

ILLUSTRATION 8. Anti-blacklist demonstration outside the Scottish Parliament, 2015. Blacklisted Dundee electrician Stuart Merchant holds a Support Group banner and speaks to Neil Findlay, MSP, to his right.

National Party had defeated an attempt by Labour MSP Neil Findlay to give statutory force to the prohibition of blacklisting. (See Illustration 8.)

Eight construction companies including Balfour Beattie and Sir Robert McAlpine in the meantime launched a time-limited Construction Workers Compensation Scheme, offering payments of between £4,000 and £100,000 to workers who could prove they had been blacklisted (600 workers had received compensation by April 2016). They were 'sorry that information was held about individuals' resulting in 'hardship'. Unions afforded the scheme a frosty reception and there were complaints that plaintiffs were being bought off, but the existence of the scheme did signify a recognition that worker surveillance was a problem, and was bad for public relations in the private sector.[15]

Once elected in their own right in 2015, the Conservatives decided to put an end to all this. As part of a general crackdown on the labour movement, they promised to allow employers to employ strikebreaking agency staff. This potentially opened the door to the revival of surveillance practices associated with the Economic League and its successor the Consulting Association.

Perhaps because they did not sanctify private business to quite the same extent as Americans, the British had shown a greater disposition to take a broad view of the problems of surveillance. There was some recognition that while state surveillance carried potential dangers, private surveillance by commerce, by the press, and by employers constituted a more immediate threat to UK citizens' privacy and welfare. But in practice only modest reform was achieved. In America there had been more practical success, but it was limited to the public sphere, and furthermore it stemmed from executive promises and initiatives with relatively little congressional backing—and thus suffered from the danger of impermanence. In the meantime, communications companies were taking refuge in advanced encryption, a development that potentially threatened nations' security, but at the same time restored a measure of privacy that governments had been unable to protect.

Conclusion

The evidence reviewed in this book suggests that, in terms of harm done to people on a daily basis, private surveillance outperforms its public counterpart. Consumer profiling programmes generate cold calls and discriminatory insurance premiums. They enable focused advertising that amounts to mind control. Factory regimes that spy on restrooms are another unsavoury aspect of private surveillance. Corporate blacklists are an even more dangerous product of the same phenomenon. They have historically resulted in the dismissal of safety campaigners and ruined the lives of union activists and their families.

Media and political attention nevertheless focuses on *public* surveillance. There is a consistent anti-statist preoccupation here that runs through Orwell, the Church investigation, and Snowden. Private surveillance has received less attention for a number of reasons. The media are privately owned, and less disposed to criticize private than public transgressions—especially their own malpractices, such as hacking. More generally in American society and to an extent in the UK, too, there is a respect for private ownership that falls short of sanctification yet contrasts with the reflex hostility sometimes directed at the state. Furthermore, some of the benefits of private surveillance, such as that conducted by firms assessing creditworthiness, are self-evident.

Anti-statist ideology is a further factor that motivates some to believe that Big Government surveillance is worse than its Big Business cousin. Another is the middle-class citizen's devotion to privacy—one's own space, one's detached house, separate bedroom, study, the inner sanctum of one's car, one's encrypted cell phone—all these things can be invaded by private eyes and that does cause widespread resentment. But in politics this leads to the popular equation of privacy with private property in opposition to state control. Additionally, memories of governmental abuse of surveillance persist on both sides of the Atlantic. None of this means that a majority are against NSA or GCHQ surveillance—the opposite is emphatically the case. But it does mean that the critics focus on government far more than on private abuses.

The fears of governmental digital surveillance are in some ways overblown. The surveillance branches of the US and UK intelligence communities have in recent years behaved relatively well, to the best of our knowledge. However, public recollections of how things have gone wrong in the past, especially episodes of political surveillance such as those connected with McCarthyism, are understandably strong enough to fuel a drive for safeguards against potential abuse of power by the surveillance state. Perhaps at the same time there is a tendency for the word 'surveillance' to evoke memories of the whole history of intelligence scandals, even if many of these involved foreign escapades.

So there have been calls on both sides of the Atlantic, heeded more promptly in the USA than in the UK, for measures to restrain government surveillance. The constitutional separation of powers has given US reformers an advantage—the president (unlike the British prime minister) cannot appoint members of legislative oversight committees and in this way 'fix' potential opposition to his surveillance policy. Institutionalization has nevertheless been a problem with the House and Senate Intelligence Committees. This means that some of the more striking reforms—Attorney General Levi's in 1976 and President Obama's in 2014—have come from the executive, making them vulnerable to the vagaries of political change and legislative challenge.

Each country has aimed at judicial responsibility in the issuing of search warrants, in each case with mixed success. There have been calls, irresolutely acted upon, for measures to protect the welfare of responsible whistle-blowers who expose cases of inappropriate use of surveillance powers. In the same spirit, there has been agitation for an end to over-classification and limits on unnecessary secrecy—the better to safeguard important secrets, and to prevent cover-ups of illegitimate surveillance. Whitehall and the White House agree on this, but progress has been sluggish.

Other factors have played a role in restraining the 'surveillance state'. One has been the untiring efforts of those devoted to the defence of liberty. Another has been resistance by the communications industry, an instance of the private sector playing a benevolent role even if it is triggered by the profit motive, the desire to retain clients by safeguarding the privacy of their messages. A final factor arises from the latter. The sophisticated encryption of digital messages now means that the code-breakers can no longer be relied on to break codes. They resort to the metadata analysis of signals traffic rather than reading messages, doing so not just out of respect for privacy, but also because it is more practical. Present-day private firms have communications channels that are 'dumb pipes'—even they cannot read what goes through them, once they have sold their encryption keys. This is an intoxicating message for the defenders of privacy, and a sobering one for those defending national security.

The story of surveillance is a parable in two senses. One is that where governments possess surveillance powers they will, eventually, abuse them—suggesting a need to be alert to potential problems and to address them pre-emptively through such means as credible legislative and judicial oversight. The second is that while some private companies help to protect us against an over-intrusive state, others exploit the techniques of surveillance in an abusive manner themselves, a situation that requires further political attention and regulatory redress.

APPENDIX

Defining Surveillance

Chapter 1 defined surveillance as 'spying on a mass scale'. This appendix is an opportunity to record the thinking of a range of experts on the subject of definition, and to elaborate on my own approach.

To a team headed by American sociologist James B. Rule, surveillance was 'any systematic attention to a person's life aimed at exerting influence over it'. Rule and his colleagues had in mind surveillance via what in 1983 were the most commonly used US identification documents: social security cards, driver's licences, credit cards, birth certificates, passports, and bank books. Later in the 1980s the Canadian David Flaherty, a leading authority on the history of privacy, published a book on that subject in which he said that 'references to "surveillance" in this volume primarily denote supervision, observation, or oversight of individual behavior through the use of personal data rather than through such mediums as a camera or a private detective'.

The Ontario-based Scottish sociologist David Lyon offered the following definition in his book *Surveillance after September 11*: 'Surveillance, as understood here, refers to routine ways in which focused attention is paid to personal details by organizations that want to influence, manage, or control certain persons or population groups.' Purpose and function were, then, key for Lyon as they were for Rule. Idle scrutiny (if such exists) did not in their view amount to surveillance.

It is also worth pausing to reflect on Lyon's qualifying clause, 'as understood here', a phrase that compares with Flaherty's 'in this volume'. Each scholar must beg for toleration of his or her quest for a definition that fits the purpose of the study he or she has in hand; otherwise, there is a danger of descent into an arid discussion of what one means by surveillance and what constitutes a definition.[1]

Students of the 'surveillance state' might be tempted to look askance at the discussion of the private in this book, and at the implied inclusion of the private in my definition of surveillance. But if (as I hope) there is some novelty in the style of my coverage of the issue, it can hardly be called a new departure. The sociologist Robert Hunter, famous for his book *Poverty* (1904) and later as a golf-course designer in California, in 1914 published a book, *Violence and the Labor Movement*, that rejected the view of French syndicalist Georges Sorel that the chief evils of surveillance sprang from the corruptions of democratic states, and pointed instead to the role of private detectives in America. In the 1980s, Rule implicitly acknowledged the role of private eyes when he said he did not propose to discuss them. David Lyon chose as the subtitle of his prophetic work *The Electronic Eye* (1994) not 'the rise of the surveillance state' but 'the rise of surveillance *society*', and included a chapter on 'The Transparent Worker'. Such examples can be multiplied and, taken collectively, constitute a defence by precedent of my inclusion of the private.[2]

A view exists within British intelligence that the media have used a definition of surveillance that is too wide. According to this view, a more disciplined definition would indicate that 'mass surveillance' is not taking place at all. Sir David Omand articulated this opinion in 2014 in his contribution to a special forum on the Snowden case. The forum focused on state, not private surveillance. Omand argued that only GCHQ's computers had 'bulk access' and that 'mass surveillance implies observers, human beings who are monitoring the population', something that did not happen in the United Kingdom. The following year, Parliament's Intelligence and Security Committee gave that definition its stamp of official approval, saying that surveillance occurred only when human eyes fell upon the data, an argument that *The Guardian*'s Alan Travis described as 'elegant'.[3] Like others before them, defenders of the UK government's collection policies chose a definition that fitted their purposes, in this case making the interesting assumption (in common with the James Bond movie *Spectre*) that 'surveillance' had become a dirty word, one to be rejected. However, as Omand hinted in his allusion to the press, public usage involved a broader definition.

In common with Omand but in a different way, this book, too, narrows the definition of surveillance. It is perfectly legitimate and is in fact time-honoured practice to use the word in relation to microcosmic, individual activity, as in: Mrs Ahmed had seen disturbing signs and decided to place her daughter Leila under nocturnal surveillance. The microcosmic simply is not the subject of this book so it uses surveillance in the more collective sense, as in: the Caliphate decided to place all young girls under secret-service surveillance. Thus, while the phrase 'mass surveillance' may make sense in other people's discourses, the word 'mass' would be redundant according to the definition relied upon in the foregoing pages.

NOTES

Introduction

1. Whitaker, 'Surveillance State', 8.
2. Mark Blunden and Nina Lakhani, 'Orwell's Big Brother Eyes Up his Doorstep', *Islington Tribune*, 6 April 2007; Le Carré, *Delicate Truth*, 252, 278, 281.
3. *The Guardian*, 18 November 2014.

Chapter 1

1. *Henry V*, II, ii, 5–6; Dulles, *Craft of Intelligence*, 71; Mao quoted in Aldrich, GCHQ, 4.
2. Flaherty, *Privacy in Colonial New England*, 83; Adams, *History of the First Administration of Thomas Jefferson*, 79; Sparrow, 'Alien Office', 362.
3. Lyon, *Electronic Eye*, 24.
4. Quotations from Madison, 'Evolution', 169, 180.
5. According to Bev Oates in *The Guardian*, 13 December 2014.
6. Warren and Brandeis, 'Privacy', 195.
7. Parenti, *Soft Cage*, 132.
8. Sulllivan quoted in the *New York Times*, 21 June 2014.
9. Burleson to W. G. McAdoo, 15 January 1918 and F. B. MacKinnon to Burleson enclosing resolution sent to the president, 1 July 1919, in folder 'Correspondence, January 1913–December 1919', Box 2B184, Burleson Papers, Briscoe Center for American History, University of Texas at Austin; Winslow quoted in Kahn, *Reader of Gentlemen's Mail*, 51.
10. Olmsted, *Right Out of California*, 156.
11. Home Office etc. combined memorandum of 15 April 1917 quoted in Millman, *Managing Dissent*, 179.
12. Organization for Economic Cooperation and Development findings reported under a front-page headline in *The Guardian*, 9 December 2014.

13. Orwell, *Nineteen Eighty-Four*, 311.

14. Atwood, *Handmaid's Tale*, 137, 147.

15. Armand Mattelart and Christian Parenti see 9/11 as the turning point, but Athan Theoharis views it as no more than an accelerator: Mattelart, *Globalization of Surveillance*, 1; Parenti, *Soft Cage*, 199–200; Theoharis, *Abuse of Power*, xi–xii.

16. Office of the Director of National Intelligence, *Statistical Transparency Report Regarding use of National Security Authorities, Annual Statistics for Calendar Year 2013*, declassified by Director of National Intelligence James R. Clapper, 23 June 2014, 2; *New York Times*, 27 October and 15 November 2014.

17. Puyvelde, 'Sécurité', 25.

Chapter 2

1. Pinkerton, *General Principles*, 5–7; Pinkerton, *Strikers, Communists, Tramps, and Detectives* (New York: G. W. Carelton, 1878), quoted in Gutman, 'Five Letters', 388–91; Auerbach, *Labor and Liberty*, 99 n. 7, 112.

2. Gowen quoted in Lukas, *Big Trouble*, 178; Hammet quoted in Riffenburgh, *Pinkerton's Great Detective*, 245.

3. O'Neil in *Western Clarion*, 25 January 1906, quoted in *Idaho Daily Statesman*, 28 June 2006, clipping in William H. Borah Papers, Library of Congress, Washington, DC; W. D. Haywood, *A Detective* (n.d.), Joseph Labadie Collection, University of Michigan Library, Ann Arbor; Roosevelt quoted in Pringle, *Theodore Roosevelt*, 452; Buttons quoted in Grover, *Debaters and Dynamiters*, 80.

4. 5 USC 3108, 3 March 1893.

5. Bonaparte testimony, 'Hearings before the subcommittee of the House Committee on Appropriations for Deficiency Appropriations for 1908 and prior years on Urgent Deficiency Bill', 202–3, FBI website; Roosevelt quoted in Noakes, 'Enforcing Domestic Tranquility', 80; *Wall Street Journal*, 22 December 1908; Congressmen's concerns mentioned (critically) in *Pittsburg Leader*, n.d., clipping in Scrapbooks, Vol. 14 (1908), Box 261, Papers of Charles Joseph Bonaparte, Library of Congress, Washington, DC; Sherley quoted in Lowenthal, *Federal Bureau of Investigation*, 8.

6. US Senate, *Violations of Free Speech and the Rights of Labor* (full title of the La Follette Committee report), 76 Cong., 1 sess. (1939), Report no. 6, Part VI, *Labor Policies of Employers' Associations. The National Association of Manufacturers*, 12.

7. Report on detective agencies by Daniel O'Regan mentioned in Inis Weed, 'The Industrial Causes of Violence', 4 parts (n.d.), part III, 1, in US Commission on Industrial Relations materials, National Archives, Washington, DC; Spielman, *Stool Pigeon*, 16; Howard, *Labor Spy*, 1; Huberman, *Spy Racket*, 6, 7, 193.

8. Burns, *The Masked War*.

9. Burns quoted in Belknap, 'Uncooperative Federalism', 27; F. W. Cohen of Pennsylvania Steel to Walter Drew of National Erectors' Association, 26 October 1910, Walter Drew Papers, University of Michigan, Ann Arbor; Burns to Charles McCarthy (former research director, US Commission on Industrial Relations), 16 February 1916, Papers of Charles McCarthy, State Historical Society, Madison, Wisconsin (SHSW); S. A. Doyle to Gompers, 3 April 1911 and M. Boyle to AFL, 3 May 1911, both in Samuel Gompers Correspondence in AFL Papers, SHSW.

10. Chandler, *Lady in the Lake*, 10; Ryan, 'Explosion of Family History', 190; Manhattan Yellow Pages (1979), 987–90, and Los Angeles Yellow Pages (1976), 1088–92.

Chapter 3

1. Genealogical information on Tom Watkins kindly supplied by the researcher Pat Storey. Other elements of the Tom Watkins story come from the author's conversation with his grandfather and with other members of his family.

2. McIvor and Paterson, 'Combating the Left', 139; Walling, 'Can Labor Unions Be Destroyed?', *World's Work*, 8 (May 2004), 4757.

3. Talbert, *Negative Intelligence*, 20.

4. Olmsted, *Right Out of California*, 154; Ned Bell memorandum, 1 May 1919, enclosed with Bell to Leland Harrison, 2 May 1919, Box II 102, Leland Harrison Papers, Manuscript Collections, Library of Congress.

5. Olmsted, *Right Out of California*, 156; Cherny, 'Anticommunist Networks', 28; memorandum, 'The Van Deman Files—Description and Use', Office of the Assistant Chief of Staff, G2, 18 August 1958, and memorandum, 'Van Deman Historical Files', supplied by the Army's Assistant Chief of Staff for Intelligence to US Senate investigators, 16 February 1971, in *US Army Surveillance of Dissidents, 1965–1972: Records of the ACSI Task Force* (digitized microfiche, ProQuest).

6. Goodall, *Loyalty and Liberty*, 106; Amann, 'Dog in the Nighttime', 567.

7. Buchan, *Thirty-Nine Steps*, 230; Walter Hines Page quoted in Olmsted, 'Right Across the Atlantic'.

8. James, *Eyes of the Navy*, 177.

9. Bennett, *Zinoviev Letter*, 91–2.

10. Childs quoted in Porter, *Plots and Paranoia*, 165.

11. Hughes, *Spies at Work*, 14, 30, 45, 63.

12. 'Table 1: Local Economic Leagues and their activities, September 1923–December 1926', in McIvor, 'Crusade for Capitalism', 637.

13. Andrew, *Defence of the Realm*, 125.

14. McIvor and Paterson, 'Combating the Left', 149.

15. Huberman, *Labor Spy Racket*, 9; McIvor, 'Crusade for Capitalism', 648–9, 654 n. 55.

Chapter 4

1. Grand Jury indictment, US District Court for the Southern District of New York, 1, 7, under cover of Special Agent J. Sears to Director FBI, 9 July 1938, 1206800-0-065-HQ-748-Section 14 Serial 661 and Report of Special Agent Leon G. Turrou, 13 March 1938, 57, 1206800-0-065-HQ-748-Section 4 Serial 141 (both in FBI records obtained under the author's FOIA request); *New York Times*, 1 December 1938.

2. Turrou, *Nazi Spy*, 19; Julian Starr, 'Spy Suspects Are All German', *New York Sun*, 26 May 1938; word-search for 'Rumrich' and 'spy' in the ProQuest digital version of the *New York Times*; word-search for 'espionage' in the ProQuest digital version of the *Congressional Record*.

3. Theoharis, *Spying on Americans*, 66.

4. President Roosevelt's Executive Order of 6 September 1939 and Attorney General Murphy quoted in the *New York Times*, 7 September and 1 October 1939, all in United States Senate, *Supplementary Detailed Staff Reports on Intelligence Activities and the Rights of Americans*, Book 3, *Final Report of the Select Committee to Study Governmental Operations with Respect to Intelligence Activities*, 94 Cong., 2 sess., 1976, 404–5.

5. Dr Henry Hitt Crane, 'Foreword', Civil Rights Federation, *The Facts Concerning the FBI Raids in Detroit* (pamphlet, 1940), Joseph Labadie Collection, University of Michigan, Ann Arbor.

6. D. M. Ladd, Memo for Director, 5 January 1932, FBI 62-26422-1; Clyde Tolson and Edward A. Tamm, Memo for Director, 7 May 1940, FBI 62-12114-25C, enclosing 'Attitude of Director of FBI toward Wire Tapping' (documents supplied by kind courtesy of Douglas M. Charles: DMC).

7. Senators Norris and Wheeler quoted in *The Philadelphia Inquirer*, 31 May 1940.

8. Quotation from Charles, *Hoover and Anti-Interventionists*, 144.

9. Hoover to Early, 3 February 1942, quoted in Charles, *Hoover and Anti-Interventionists*, 104.

10. 'Summary of Information, Robert E. Wood, Brigadier General, Retired', 27 February 1942, FBI 100-55659-3 (DMC).

11. Theoharis, *Spying on Americans*; Ladd quoted in Schrecker, *Many Are the Crimes*, 107.

12. Jeffreys-Jones, *FBI*, 11; Andrew, *Defence of the Realm*, 220.

Chapter 5

1. Author's conversations with Jim Compton stretching back to the 1960s with details confirmed in a telephone oral history interview, 4 March 2015.

2. Schrecker, *Age of McCarthyism*, 25; Schrecker, *No Ivory Tower*.

3. Barth, *Loyalty of Free Men*, 147.

4. Donovan to Forrestal, 14 August 1947, Box 73, Forrestal Papers, Seeley G. Mudd Manuscript Library, Princeton University.

5. Kahn, *Reader of Gentlemen's Mail*, 58.

6. Rovere, *McCarthy*, 9–40.

7. Medsger, *Burglary*, 352; McCarran quoted in Fred Cook, 'The FBI: The Final Judgment', *The Nation*, 18 October 1958, reproduced in Kreitner, *Surveillance Nation*, 40.

8. Smith, *Declaration of Conscience*, 17–18, 107; leaflets in folder 'Elections, 1948/"Smear Charges" and Reply' and text of author's oral history interview with Senator Smith, 29 July 1991, both in Margaret Chase Smith Papers, Smith Library, Skowhegan, Maine.

9. American Federation of State, County, and Municipal Employees (AFSCME) court claim quoted in Lisa Buchmeier, 'Wisconsin Labor Wars Continue in Court', *Courthouse News Service*, 31 March 2014: http://www.courthousenews.com/2014/03/31/66591.htm (accessed 18 April 2016); Milwaukee *Journal Sentinel*, 13 March, 14 September 2014.

Chapter 6

1. *Hansard*, 29 March 1950, vol. 166, paras. 607–61; extract from Orwell's diary entry for 20 June 1940 quoted in Smith, *British Writers*, vii; Potter, 'British McCarthyism', 146; Stewart, 'Report on the Security Service' (27 November 1945), partly reproduced as an appendix to Lomas, 'Defence of the Realm', 814; *Manchester Guardian*, quoted in Goodman, 'British Government and Challenge of McCarthyism', 65.

2. *Hansard*, 29 March 1950, vol. 166, paras. 607–61, and press quotations from Potter, 'British McCarthyism', 144–6.

3. *The Guardian* and *Daily Telegraph* headlines quoted in Wilford, *CIA, British Left*, 60–1.

4. Eden, *Facing the Dictators*, 242; Hankey quoted in Rose, *Vansittart*, 210; Jefferson quotation of 1810 reproduced in H. J. Laski, *The Germans—Are They Human? A Reply to Sir Robert Vansittart*, pamphlet (London: Victor Gollancz for The Left Book Club, 1941), 5.

5. W. O. H. Garman, *What Is Wrong with the Federal Council?* (New York, 1948); John T. Flynn, 'Bishop [Garfield Bromley] Oxnam Listed as Member of Communist Front Organizations', *Knoxville Journal* article reprinted in *Christian Beacon*, 23 March 1950; list of UK socialist clergy/ministers, and other associated materials in VNST II/1/46, The Papers

of Lord Vansittart of Denham, Churchill Archives Centre, Churchill College, Cambridge.

6. Rolleston typescript, 14 May 1950, and Craigavon and Rolleston questions underlined in pencil in text of Jacob lecture, 'The BBC in Peace and War', *Journal of the United Service Institution*, 94 (August 1949), 388, both in VNST II/1/45.

7. Smithers quoted in Sanchia Berg, 'Was There a Communist Witch-Hunt at the BBC?', *BBC online Magazine*, 21 January 2016; Potter, 'British McCarthyism', 149.

8. 'True Spies', BBC 2 documentary, 27 October 2002, summarized at https://www.wsws.org/en/articles/2002/12/spie-d10.html (accessed 11 February 2016); Andrew, *Defence of the Realm*, 559; Hollingsworth and Norton-Taylor, *Blacklist*, 2–3; Hollingsworth and Tremayne, *Economic League: Silent McCarthyism*.

9. Campbell and Connor, *On the Record*, 288–9.

10. *Blacklisting in Employment: Interim Report: Ninth Report of Session 2012–13: Report, together with Formal Minutes* (London: House of Commons, Scottish Affairs Committee, 2013), summary; *Blacklisting in Employment: Addressing the Crimes of the Past; Moving Towards Best Practice: Sixth Report of Session 2013–14: Report, together with Formal Minutes, Oral and Written Evidence* (London: House of Commons, Scottish Affairs Committee, 2014), 7.

Chapter 7

1. Forsyth's thoughts quoted in Medsger, *Burglary*, 42; Mitchell quotation in Theoharis, *FBI Reference Guide*, 126.

2. Gallup poll cited in Theoharis, *FBI Reference Guide*, 126; Schwartz, 'Intelligence Oversight', 31.

3. Thomas Charles Huston, 'Domestic Intelligence', memorandum for CIA director Richard Helms, 23 July 1970, DDRS-200778-i1-3. The censorship marks are less obvious in the published version: *Hearings before the Select Committee to Study Governmental Operations with Respect to Intelligence Activities* [henceforth Church hearings], 94 Cong., 1 sess., Vol. 2, *Huston Plan*, 23, 24, and 25 September 1975, 199.

4. Ervin, 'Announcement on Hearings on Computers, Data Banks, and the Bill of Rights', 3 February 1971, and Eastland to Secretary of Defense Melvin Laird, 1 March 1971, accessed electronically through ProQuest's *US Army Surveillance of Dissidents, 1965–1972: Records of the US Army's Assistant Chief of Staff for Intelligence Task Force*.

5. Theoharis, *FBI and American Democracy*, 120; Donner, *Age of Surveillance*, 179; *The Menace of Communism in the United States Today* enclosed with Hoover to Dillon Anderson, Special Assistant to the President, 29 July 1955, quoted in *Intelligence Activities and the Rights of Americans*, Book II, *Final Report of the Select Committee to Study Governmental Operations with Respect to Intelligence Agencies* (26 April 1976), 66 n. 271; Belmont memo to L. V. Boardman titled 'CP, USA—Counterinsurgency Program' (28 August 1956), in Church hearings, 94 Cong., 1 sess., Vol. 6, *Federal Bureau of Investigation* (1976), 372.

6. Director FBI to SAC (Special Agent in Charge) New York, Chicago, Detroit, Los Angeles, and Newark, memorandum titled 'Socialist Workers Party "Internal Security"—SWP Disruption Program', 12 October 1961, in Church hearings, 94 Cong., 1 sess., Vol. 6, *Federal Bureau of Investigation* (1976), 377.

7. Washington, *Other Blacklist*, 4, 23; Drabble, 'Ensure Domestic Tranquility', 328.

8. Clark to Hoover, 14 September 1967, quoted in Scott, *Reining in the State*, 44.

9. 'Charter for Sensitive Sigint Operation Minaret' (1 July 1969), in Church hearings, 94 Cong., 1 sess., Vol. 5, *The National Security Agency and Fourth Amendment Rights* (1975), 150.

10. Quotations from Dallek, *Flawed Giant*, 490, and Jeffreys-Jones, *Peace Now!*, 64; Charles, *Hoover's War on Gays*, 27.

Chapter 8

1. *New York Times*, 22 December 1974; Letter, Colby to President, 24 December 1974 and memorandum of conversation in the Oval Office, 3 January 1975, being Documents 19 and 22 respectively, *FRUS*,

1917–1972, Vol. XXXVIII, Pt 2, *Organization and Management of Foreign Policy; Public Diplomacy*, 1973–1976 (2015).

2. Rockefeller quoted in Colby, *Honorable Men*, 16; numbers collated from *Editorials on File*, 1970, 1975 (New York: Facts on File).

3. Church Committee voting profile based on ADA data in Johnson, *Season of Inquiry*, 18.

4. *Hearings before the Select Committee to Study Governmental Operations with respect to Intelligence Activities*, 94 Cong., 1 sess., Vol. 4, *Mail Opening*, 21, 22, and 24 October 1975, 5, 87.

5. Church quoted in Johnson, *Season of Inquiry*, 57; Pike quoted in Olmsted, *Challenging the Secret Government*, 142; *Foreign and Military Intelligence*, Book I, *Final Report of the Select Committee to Study Governmental Operations with Respect to Intelligence Agencies* (26 April 1976), 427.

6. *Report to the President by the Commission on CIA Activities within the United States* (New York: Manor Books, 1975), 42, 81, 242–6; *CIA: The Pike Report* (Nottingham: Spokesman Books, 1977), 14, 17, 65, 99; *Intelligence Activities and the Rights of Americans*, Book II, *Final Report of the Select Committee to Study Governmental Operations with Respect to Intelligence Agencies* (26 April 1976), 6, 299, 339.

7. Johnson, *Season of Inquiry*, Chapter 10: 'Orwellian Nightmares', 111–29; Olmsted, *Challenging the Secret Government*, 2; *Foreign and Military Intelligence*, Book I, *Final Report of the Select Committee to Study Governmental Operations with Respect to Intelligence Agencies* (26 April 1976), 16, 211–14.

8. Memorandum of conversation, Oval Office, 13 October 1975, DDRS-315044-i1-7; Arnold, *Secrecy in the Sunshine Era*, 2; Levi quoted in Jeffreys-Jones, *FBI*, 192; Scott, *Reining in the State*, 6.

9. Kissinger quoted in Arnold, *Secrecy in the Sunshine Era*, 1–2; Hersh quoted in Olmsted, *Challenging the Secret Government*, 85; *Washington Post* quoted in Jeffreys-Jones, *FBI*, 195; *San Francisco Chronicle*, 17 November 2002; former Senate Intelligence Committee staff director John Blake's comment on Goldwater quoted in Smist, *Congress Oversees*, 97–8; Goldwater quoted in *Time*, 23 April 1984, 6; Goldwater testimony, 'The Role of Intelligence in the Foreign Policy Process', *Hearings before the Subcommittee on International Security and Scientific Affairs of the Committee*

on Foreign Affairs, House, 96 Cong., 2 sess. (28 January, 8, 11, and 20 February 1980), 171.

10. Campbell and Hosenball, 'The Eavesdroppers', *Time Out*, 21–27 May 1976, 8; Churchill quoted in Campbell, *Unsinkable Aircraft Carrier*, 11.

11. Author's interview with Duncan Campbell, Edinburgh, 2 August 2010; *Data Protection Act 1984*, section 2, 22; Campbell, *On the Record*, 11, 274.

12. Blair, *Journey*, 127.

Chapter 9

1. FBI special agents quoted in *The 9/11 Report: Final Report of the National Commission on Terrorist Attacks upon the United States* (New York: Norton, 2004), 273, 275.

2. National Highway Traffic Safety Administration: http://www-fars. nhtsa.dot.gov/Main/index.aspx (accessed 8 June 2015); David Sterman report compiled for the New America foundation, 'Deadly Attacks since 9/11' (June 2015): http://securitydata.newamerica.net/extremists/ deadly-attacks.html (accessed 23 November 2015).

3. Seymour M. Hersh, 'The Intelligence Gap', *The New Yorker*, 6 December 1999, 58; FISA court report on FBI malpractices in 2001–2 and on the need for relaxing the 'wall', released by the US Congress and quoted in the *New York Times*, 23 August 2002.

4. *The Observer*, 2 December 2001; law enforcement official and Ibish quoted in the *New York Times*, 5 October 2002; FBI official quoted in the *Washington Times*, 4 November 2002.

5. *New York Times*, 27 October 2014.

6. NSA documents leaked by Edward Snowden and reported in the *New York Times*, 15 August 2015; Klein quoted in Bamford, *Shadow Factory*, 189–90; Jeffreys-Jones, *FBI*, 236; Keefe, *Chatter*, xiv; *Washington Post* graphics published on 29 August 2013: http://www.washingtonpost. com/wp-srv/special/national/black-budget/ (accessed 18 February 2016); 'Table 1: Intelligence Spending, Fiscal Years 2007–2016' in Miles, *Intelligence Spending*, 8.

7. Dissenting views of Congressman John Conyers (D-MI) and 16 others, 'Electronic Surveillance Modernization Act', *House Report*, 109 Cong., 2 sess. (25 September 2006), 177.

8. Gonzales quoted in the *Los Angeles Times*, 8 February 2006; Williams, 'This Dangerous Patriot's Game', *The Observer*, 2 December 2001; Sandy Star, 'Intelligence Tests', *Spiked*, 19 June 2002; Mosley quoted in the *Observer Review*, 18 August 2002; Bamford, 'Washington Bends the Rules', *New York Times*, 27 August 2002.

9. Inspectors General, 'Unclassified Report on the President's Surveillance Program' (10 July 2009), 38: http://fas.org/irp/eprint/psp.pdf (accessed 11 June 2015).

10. Accuracy of this version of events confirmed by the Dubliner in question: email, Derek Peare to author, 16 June 2015.

11. *The Guardian*, 26 March and 1 June 2015; Aldrich, *GCHQ*, 543–4.

Chapter 10

1. *An Inquiry into the Culture, Practices, and Ethics of the Press: Report* (London: Stationary Office, 2012, henceforth Leveson Report), 4 vols., II, 542–3, 546.

2. Kerr's testimony quoted in *Blacklisting in Employment: Interim Report 2012–13* (London: HMSO for Scottish Affairs Committee, 2013), 7 ff and cited in *Blacklisting in Employment: Addressing the Crimes of the Past; Moving towards Best Practice*, Sixth Report of Session 2013–14 (London: HMSO for Scottish Affairs Committee, 2014), Ev 30, 52, 115, 117. Stephen Ratcliffe, Director of the UK Contractors Group, testified to the last-cited committee that only a minority of his members had used the Consulting Association (at 27).

3. Peter MacLennan, 'Crossrail Response—Unite Drops Claims of Blacklisting on Crossrail Project', 3 September 2013: http://www.crossrail.co.uk/news/articles/crossrail-response-unite-drops-claims-of-blacklisting-on-crossrail-project# (accessed on 16 April 2016).

4. MindSafety report titled 'Cultural Overview—Crossrail Project' and Crossrail spokesman quoted in *The Observer*, 27 April 2014; Whitaker, 'Surveillance State', 5.

5. Le Carré, *A Delicate Truth*, 21, 252, 281; figures from Puyvelde, 'Sécurité', 25, and from a chapter in Damien Van Puyvelde's forthcoming book kindly shown to the author.

6. Shane Harris, 'Palantir Technologies Spots Patterns to Solve Crimes and Track Terrorists', *Wired*, 31 July 2012; Baker quoted in Ewing and Romm, 'Snowden Leak', 2.

7. Anderson, *A Question of Trust*, 195; Obama quoted in the *New York Times*, 11 March 2016.

8. *Blacklisting in Employment: Interim Report 2012–13*, 14, and *Blacklisting in Employment*, 2013–14, 24.

9. *Blacklisting in Employment: Interim Report 2012–13*, 29–30, and *Blacklisting in Employment*, 2013–14, testimony by Cartmail and Jim McGovern (MP for Dundee West), Evidence 1, 6; Morris and Kennedy quotations from *Blacklist*, a film directed by Lucy Parker and produced by City Projects, 2015; accident figures in Smith, *Blacklisted*, 70; RIPA quoted in Ball, 'Workplace Surveillance', 92.

10. 'Surveillance, Sweated Labour and the British Way of Business', *The Guardian*, 11 December 2015.

11. 'Pressures in Today's Workplace', *House Report*, 96 Cong., 2 sess. (December 1980), 21, 22, 27–8; quotation from AFL-CIO Action Center press release, 'The Media Reform Campaign', 3 March 2005: http://www.aflcio.org/About/Exec-Council/EC-Statements/The-Media-Reform-Campaign (accessed on 3 July 2015).

12. Data from Larry Armstrong, 'Someone to Watch over You', *Business Week*, 10 July 2000, 189–90, and Ball, 'Workplace Surveillance', 88, 91; Attewell, 'Big Brother', 87; accident statistics in Hatch, 'Worker Safety, the Issues', 447; Mark Thomas flier for *Cuckooed* distributed at the Traverse Theatre, Edinburgh, 8 August 2014.

13. Weatherup quoted in *The Guardian*, 27 May 2015; Josh Halliday, 'Phone Hacking on "Industrial Scale" at Mirror', lead story in *The Guardian*, 4 March 2015; Leveson Report, IV, 1803.

Chapter 11

1. Snowden quotations from Alan Rusbridger and Ewen MacAskill, 'Edward Snowden in Exile', *Guardian Weekend*, 19 July 2014, 19, and *New York Times*, 15 June 2013.

2. Snowden quoted in Greenwald, *No Place to Hide*, 18; Robert Vinson, Judge, United States Foreign Intelligence Surveillance Court, 'In re Application of the Federal Bureau of Investigation…', 25 April 2013, and National Security Agency, 'PRISM/US-984XN Overview', April 2013, both reproduced in Fidler, *Snowden Reader*, 93–4, 97–9; Electronic Frontier Foundation, 'NSA Spying on Americans: Timeline of NSA Domestic Spying': https://www.eff.org/nsa-spying/timeline (accessed 27 August 2015).

3. *The Guardian*, 22 August 2013; *The Observer*, 30 June and 3 November 2013; Rousseff statement to United Nations General Assembly, 24 September 2013, in Fidler, *Snowden Reader*, 158; *Financial Times*, 14–15 December 2013; poll cited in *The Guardian*, 7 May 2015.

4. *The Guardian*, 16 January 2014; Amy Davison, 'Dishfire and What Obama Couldn't Say about the NSA', *New Yorker*, 16 January 2014; Gadair Abbas, staff attorney for the Council on American-Islamic Relations, quoted in the *New York Times*, 9 July 2014.

5. Snowden quoted in James Bamford, 'Israel's NSA Scandal', *New York Times*, 16 September 2014; *The Guardian*, 7 November 2014; *New York Times*, 15 August 2015; Whitaker, 'Surveillance State', 3; Baker quoted in Ewing and Romm, 'Edward Snowden Leak Exposes Cracks in Contractor System', 2.

6. Johnson, 'Introduction', in Johnson, 'H-Diplo/ISSF Forum', no pagination; Omand, contribution to Johnson (ed.), '*INS* Forum', 806; Feinstein quoted in the *New York Times*, 1 July 2013; Boehner quoted in Glenn Hastedt, contribution to Johnson (ed.), '*INS* Forum', 798.

7. Alexander quoted in Loch K. Johnson introduction and Omand contribution, both in Johnson (ed.), '*INS* Forum', 794, 805–6.

8. Paraphrase of the finding of an international conference of former intelligence officials and others held under the auspices of the Ditchley Foundation, *The Guardian*, 15 June 2015; Scheuerman, 'Taking Snowden Seriously', 71; Schwartz, *Democracy in the Dark*, 150; editorial, *The Guardian*, 25 July 2013; editorial, *New York Times*, 2 January 2014.

9. PEN America, *Chilling Effects: NSA Surveillance Drives US Writers to Self-Censor* (New York, 12 November 2013, accessed online from the

University of Texas, Austin, Library), 3; *Report on the President's Surveillance Program*, Volume 1 (Washington, DC, 10 July 2009: Report no. 2009-0013-A), 69; Bailey Cahall and others, *Do NSA's Bulk Surveillance Programs Stop Terrorists?* (Washington, DC: New America Foundation [since renamed New America], 2014, accessed via the Homeland Security Digital Library, online at the University of Texas, Austin, Library), summary of findings.

10. *New York Times*, 21 March 2014; Whitaker, 'Guerrilla Accountability', 215; Jarvis, contribution to Johnson (ed.), '*INS* Forum', 800.

Chapter 12

1. Snowden quoted in Fidler, *Snowden Reader*, 200; Jenkins, 'America Curbs', *The Guardian*, 4 June 2015; King quoted in Owen Boycott, 'GCHQ Continues to Use Data Techniques Outlawed in US, Say Campaigners', *The Guardian*, 8 June 2015.

2. January 2014 survey conducted by the research agency TNS: http://www.tnsglobal.com/uk/press-release/public-opinion-monitor-britons-give-safeguarding-security-higher-priority-protecting-p (accessed on 14 September 2015).

3. Dearlove quoted in *The Guardian*, 18 March 2015; author's interview with Dearlove, 13 July 2011; David Anderson, *A Question of Trust: Report of the Investigatory Powers Review* (London: HMSO, 2015), 289; Omand quoted in *The Guardian*, 12 June 2015.

4. Rogers quoted in the *New York Times*, 18 June 2013.

5. Edward C. Liu and others, *Overview of Constitutional Challenges to NSA Collection Activities and Recent Developments* (Washington, DC: Congressional Research Service, 1 April 2014), prefatory summary.

6. Rand Paul quoted in the *New York Times*, 19 March 2014.

7. Quotation from the *New York Times*, 1 July 2013.

8. Obama speech of August 2007 quoted in the *New York Times*, 15 January 2014; quoting Obama's speech of 2003, Ryan Lizza, 'State of Deception: Why Won't the President Rein in the Intelligence Community?', *New Yorker*, 16 December 2013, 54, 57; Baker in the *New York Times*, 15 January 2014.

9. Obama's address of 17 January 2014 reproduced in Fidler, *Snowden Reader*, 319–30; Presidential Policy Directive PPD-28, 'Signals Intelligence Activities', 17 January 2014; Office of the Director of National Intelligence, *Statistical Transparency Report Regarding use of National Security Authorities: Annual Statistics for Calendar Year 2013* (declassified 23 June 2014), 2, 5; Steven Aftergood, 'ODNI Declassifies Data on Frequency of Surveillance', *Secrecy News*, 30 June 2014.

10. Holt speech in *Congressional Record*, Vol. 160, No. 95 (Wednesday, 18 June 2014), H5466; Gallup poll released on 12 June 2013 and reproduced in the *New York Times*, 12 May 2015; Frank Newport, 'Half in US Continue to Say Gov't Is an Immediate Threat' (Gallup Report, 21 September 2015): http://www.gallup.com/poll/185720/half-continue-say-gov-immediate-threat.aspx (accessed 29 January 2016); Chris Cillizza in the *Washington Post*, 2 October 2015; Pew Research poll reported in the *New York Times*, 8 April 2015; September 2014 *New York Times* poll reproduced in the same paper, 8 April 2015.

11. Legal Sidebar: 'What Does the Latest Court Ruling on NSA Telephone Metadata Program Mean?', 3 September 2015: http://www.fas.org/sgp/crs/intel/telmet.pdf (accessed on 11 December 2016).

12. Tim Cook quoted in *The Guardian*, 18 February 2016; Sanger in the *New York Times*, 2 May 2014; Associated Press poll cited in *Consumer Reports Magazine*, July (online, May) 2014.

13. Weiss, *US-EU Data Privacy*, 6; Editorial, *New York Times*, 23 March 2015; Jack Crone, 'Is GCHQ Spying on Nicola Sturgeon?', *Mail* online, 25 July 2015; *Western Mail*, 25 July 2015; ComRes poll reported by the BBC, 4 July 2013: http://www.bbc.co.uk/news/uk-england-london-23165983 (accessed 28 September 2015); Chakrabarti quoted in *The Observer*, 1 November 2015; Home Office quoted in *The Guardian*, 1 March, and editorial in same paper, 2 March, 2016.

14. Ipsos MORI PRISMS Survey (undertaken for the Centre for Research into Information, Surveillance and Privacy [CRISP], outcomes copy of August 2014 kindly supplied by CRISP director Charles Raab of the University of Edinburgh), Q. B11, page 49; January 2014 survey conducted by the research agency TNS, cited in note 2.

15. *Blacklisting in the Construction Industry: Policy Advice Note for the Public Sector in Wales* (Cardiff: Welsh Government, 2013), 6; Jane Hutt letter to author, 5 January 2016; remarks by Neil Findlay, Lucy Parker (director of the film *Blacklist*), and various blacklisted workers and union leaders, Campaign Opposing Police Surveillance (COPS) meeting, Scottish Parliament, 10 February 2016, attended by the author; Construction Workers Compensation Scheme statement quoted in BBC News report, 4 July 2014; *The Guardian*, 30 April 2016.

Appendix

1. Rule and others, 'Documentary Identification', 223; Flaherty, *Protecting Privacy*, xiv; Lyon, *Surveillance*, 5.
2. Hunter, *Violence*, 229–30; Sorel, *Reflections*, 77, 112, 127, 186; Lyon, *Electronic Eye*, 119 ff (emphasis added).
3. Omand in Johnson (ed.), 'INS Forum', 806; Travis in *The Guardian*, 13 March 2015.

BIBLIOGRAPHY

Adams, Henry. *History of the United States of America during the First Administration of Thomas Jefferson*, 9 vols. (Cambridge: Cambridge University Press, 2011 [1891]), vol. 1.

Addison, Paul. *The Road to 1945: British Politics and the Second World War*, rev. edn (London: Pimlico, 1994).

Aid, Matthew M. *The Secret Sentry: The Untold History of the National Security Agency* (New York: Bloomsbury Press, 2010).

Alderman, Geoffrey. 'The National Free Labour Association: A Case-Study of Strike-Breaking in the Late Nineteenth and Early Twentieth Centuries', *International Review of Social History*, 21 (December 1976), 309–36.

Aldridge, Richard J. *GCHQ: The Uncensored Story of Britain's Most Secret Intelligence Agency* (London: Harper, 2010).

Amann, Peter H. 'A "Dog in the Nighttime" Problem: American Fascism in the 1930s', *The History Teacher*, 19 (August 1986), 559–84.

Andrew, Christopher. *Secret Service: The Making of the British Intelligence Community* (London: Heinemann, 1985).

Andrew, Christopher. *The Defence of the Realm: The Authorized History of MI5* (London: Allen Lane, 2009).

Arnesen, Eric (ed). *Encyclopedia of U.S. Labor and Working-Class History* (New York: Routledge, 2007).

Arnold, Jason Ross. *Secrecy in the Sunshine Era: The Promise and Failures of U.S. Open Government Laws* (Lawrence: University Press of Kansas, 2014).

Assange, Julian. *Julian Assange: The Unauthorised Autobiography* (Edinburgh: Canongate, 2011).

Attewell, Paul. 'Big Brother and the Sweatshop: Computer Surveillance in the Automated Office', *Sociological Theory*, 5 (Spring 1987), 87–100.

Atwood, Margaret. *The Handmaid's Tale* (London: Vintage, 1996 [1985]).

Auerbach, Jerold S. *Labor and Liberty: The La Follette Committee and the New Deal* (Indianapolis: Bobbs-Merrill, 1966).

Ball, Kirstie. 'Workplace Surveillance: An Overview', *Labor History*, 51/1 (2010), 87–106.

Bamford, James. *The Puzzle Palace: A Report on America's Most Secret Agency* (Harmondsworth: Penguin, 1983 [1982]).

Bamford, James. *The Shadow Factory: The Ultra-Secret NSA from 9/11 to the Eavesdropping on America* (New York: Anchor, 2009).

Barth, Alan. *The Loyalty of Free Men* (London: Gollancz, 1951).

Batvinis, Raymond J. *Hoover's Secret War against Axis Spies: FBI Counterespionage during World War II* (Lawrence: University Press of Kansas, 2014).

Belknap, Michal R. 'Uncooperative Federalism: The Failure of the Bureau of Investigation's Intergovernmental Attack on Radicalism', *Publius*, 12 (Spring 1982), 25–47.

Bennett, Gillian. *'A Most Extraordinary and Mysterious Business': The Zinoviev Letter of 1924* (London: Foreign and Commonwealth Office, 1999).

Blair, Tony. *A Journey* (London: Hutchinson, 2010).

Bruce, Gary. *The Firm: The Inside Story of the Stasi* (Oxford: Oxford University Press, 2010).

Bruley, Sue. *The Women and Men of 1926: A Gender and Social History of the General Strike and Miners' Lockout in South Wales* (Cardiff: University of Wales Press, 2010).

Bruley, Sue. 'The General Strike and Miners' Lockout of 1926 in South Wales: Oral Testimony and Public Representations', *Welsh History Review*, 26 (December 2012), 271–96.

Buchan, John. *The Thirty-Nine Steps* (New York: Doran, 1915).

Burge, Alun. 'In Search of Harry Blount: Scabbing between the Wars in One South Wales Community', *Llafur*, 6/3 (1994), 58–69.

Butler, Rupert. *The Gestapo: A History of Hitler's Secret Police 1933–45* (Barnsley: Leo Cooper, 2004).

Campbell, Duncan. *The Unsinkable Aircraft Carrier: American Military Power in Britain* (London: Paladin, 1986).

Campbell, Duncan and Steve Connor. *On the Record: Surveillance, Computers and Privacy, the Inside Story* (London: Joseph, 1986).

Chamberlain, Phil. 'The Construction Industry Blacklist: How the Economic League Lived On', *Lobster*, 58 (Winter 2009/10), 42–56.

Chandler, Raymond. *The Lady in the Lake* (Harmondsworth: Penguin, 1971 [1943]).

Charles, Douglas M. 'Communist and Homosexual: The FBI, Harry Hay, and the Secret Side of the Lavender Scare, 1943–1961', *American Communist History*, 11/1 (2012), 101–24.

Charles, Douglas M. *Hoover's War on Gays: Exposing the FBI's 'Sex Deviates' Program* (Lawrence: University of Kansas Press, 2015).

Cherny, Robert. 'Anticommunist Networks and Labor: The Pacific Coast in the 1930s', in Shelton Stromquist (ed.). *Labor's Cold War: Local Politics in a Global Context* (Urbana: University of Illinois Press, 2008), 17–48.

Chesterman, Simon. *One Nation under Surveillance: A New Social Contract to Defend Freedom without Sacrificing Liberty* (Oxford: Oxford University Press, 2011).

Colby, William. *Honorable Men: My Life in the CIA* (London: Hutchinson, 1978).

Cooper, Rae and Greg Patmore. 'Private Detectives, Blacklists and Company Unions: Anti-Union Employer Strategy and Australian Labour History', *Labour History*, Issue 97 (November 2009), 1–11.

Corera, Gordon. *Intercept: The Secret History of Computers and Spies* (London: Weidenfeld and Nicolson, 2015).

Crick, Bernard R. *George Orwell, A Life* (London: Secker & Warburg, 1980).

Dallek, Robert. *Flawed Giant: Lyndon Johnson and his Times, 1961–1973* (New York: Oxford University Press, 1998).

Davies, Nick. *Hack Attack: How the Truth Caught Up with Rupert Murdoch* (London: Chatto & Windus, 2014).

Deery, Phillip. 'Confronting the Cominform: George Orwell and the Cold War Offensive of the Information Research Department, 1948–50', *Labour History*, Issue 73 (November 1997), 219–25.

Denniston, Alistair. 'The Government Code and Cypher School between the Wars', in Robin Denniston, *Thirty Secret Years: A.G. Denniston's Work in Signals Intelligence 1914–1944* (Clifton-upon-Teme, Worcs.: Polperro Heritage Press, 2007), 92–115.

Donner, Frank J. *The Age of Surveillance: The Aims and Methods of America's Political Intelligence System* (New York: Alfred A. Knopf, 1980).

Doyle, Arthur Conan. *The Valley of Fear* (London, 1915).

Drabble, John. 'To Ensure Domestic Tranquility: The FBI, COINTELPRO-WHITE HATE and Political Discourse, 1964–1971', *Journal of American Studies*, 38/2 (2004), 297–328.

Dulles, Allen. *The Craft of Intelligence* (New York: Harper and Row, 1963).

Dunn & Bradstreet Corporation Records, 1831–1990: A Finding Aid (Boston: Harvard Business School, 2010).

Eden, Anthony. *Memoirs: Facing the Dictators* (Boston: Houghton Mifflin, 1962).

Ewing, Philip and Tony Romm. 'Edward Snowden Leak Exposes Cracks in Contractor System', *Politico* (9 June 2013), 1–3.

Fidler, David P. (ed.). *The Snowden Reader* (Bloomington: Indiana University Press, 2015).

Flaherty, David H. *Privacy in New England* (Charlottesville: University Press of Virginia, 1972).

Flaherty, David H. *Protecting Privacy in Surveillance Societies: The Federal Republic of Germany, Sweden, France, Canada, and the United States* (Chapel Hill: University of North Carolina Press, 1989).

Foucault, Michel. *Discipline and Punish: The Birth of the Prison* (New York: Vintage, 1995).

Goldman, Aaron. 'Germans and Nazis: The Controversy over "Vansittartism" in Britain during the Second World War', *Journal of Contemporary History*, 14 (January 1979), 155–91.

Goldstein, Robert Justin. *American Blacklist: The Attorney General's List of Subversive Organizations* (Lawrence: University Press of Kansas, 2008).

Goodall, Alex. *Loyalty and Liberty: American Countersubversion from World War I to the McCarthy Era* (Urbana: University of Illinois Press, 2013).

Goodman, Giora. 'The British Government and the Challenge of McCarthyism in the Early Cold War', *Journal of Cold War Studies*, 12 (Winter 2009–10), 62–97.

Greenwald, Glenn. *No Place to Hide: Edward Snowden, the NSA, and the U.S. Surveillance State* (New York: Metropolitan/Henry Holt, 2014).

Gregory, Anthony. *American Surveillance: Intelligence, Privacy, and the Fourth Amendment* (Madison: University of Wisconsin Press and the Independent Institute, 2016).

Grover, David H. *Debaters and Dynamiters: The Story of the Haywood Trial* (Corvallis: Oregon State University Press, 1964).

Gutman, Herbert G. 'Five Letters of Immigrant Workers from Scotland to the United States', *Labor History*, 9 (Fall 1968), 388–91.

Hager, Nicky. *Secret Power* (Nelson, NZ: Craig Potton, 1996).

Harding, Luke. *The Snowden Files: The Inside Story of the World's Most Wanted Man* (London: Guardian, 2014).

Harper, Daniel. 'Blacklists', in Eric Arnesen (ed.), *Encyclopedia of US Labor and Working-Class History* (New York: Routledge, 2007), 162–5.

Harris, Shane. *The Watchers: The Rise of America's Surveillance State* (New York: Penguin, 2010).

Hatch, David. 'Worker Safety, the Issues', *Congressional Quarterly Researcher*, 14/19 (21 May 2004), 447–63.

Hayden, Sterling. *Wanderer* (London: Longmans, Green, 1964).

Heale, Michael J. *McCarthy's Americans: Red Scare Politics in State and Nation, 1935–1965* (Basingstoke: Macmillan, 1998).

Hennessy, Peter and Gail Brownfeld. 'Britain's Cold War Security Purge: The Origins of Positive Vetting', *The Historical Journal*, 25 (December 1982), 965–74.

Hightower, Jim. 'Citizen Snowden: Why He Matters', *Lowdown*, 16 (February/March 2014), 1–6.

Hinton, James. *The Mass Observers: A History, 1937–1949* (Oxford: Oxford University Press, 2013).

Hogan, Michael J. *A Cross of Iron: Harry S. Truman and the Origins of the National Security State, 1945–1954* (Cambridge: Cambridge University Press, 1998).

Hollingsworth, Mark and Richard Norton-Taylor. *Blacklist: The Inside Story of Political Vetting* (London: Hogarth, 1988).

Hollingsworth, Mark and Charles Tremayne. *The Economic League: The Silent McCarthyism* (London: National Council for Civil Liberties, 1989).

Howard, Sidney C. *The Labor Spy* (New York: Republic Publishing Company, 1924).

Howells, Kim. 'Victimisation, Accidents and Disease', in David Smith (ed.), *A People and a Proletariat: Essays in the History of Wales, 1780–1980* (London: Pluto, 1980), 181–98.

Huberman, Leo. *The Labor Spy Racket* (New York: Modern Age Books, 1937).

Hughes, Michael. *Spies at Work: The Rise and Fall of the Economic League* (Bradford: 1 in 12, 1995).

Hunter, Robert. *Violence and the Labor Movement* (New York: Macmillan, 1914).

Javers, Eamon. *Broker, Trader, Lawyer, Spy: The Secret World of Corporate Espionage* (New York: HarperCollins, 2010).

Jeffreys-Jones, Rhodri. *Violence and Reform in American History* (New York: New Viewpoints, 1978).

Jeffreys-Jones, Rhodri. 'The Defictionalization of American Private Detection', *Journal of American Studies*, 17 (August, 1983), 265–74.

Jeffreys-Jones, Rhodri. *The CIA and American Democracy* (New Haven: Yale University Press, 1989).

Jeffreys-Jones, Rhodri. *Peace Now! American Society and the Ending of the Vietnam War* (New Haven: Yale University Press, 1999).

Jeffreys-Jones, Rhodri. *The FBI: A History* (New Haven: Yale University Press, 2007).

Jeffreys-Jones, Rhodri. *The American Left: Its Impact on Politics and Society since 1900* (Edinburgh: Edinburgh University Press, 2013).

Jeffreys-Jones, Rhodri. 'Jessie Jordan: A Rejected Scot who Spied for Germany and Hastened America's Flight from Neutrality', *The Historian*, 76 (Winter 2014), 766–83.

Johnson, Loch K. *A Season of Inquiry: The Senate Intelligence Investigation* (Lexington: University Press of Kentucky, 1985).

Johnson, Loch K. 'James Angleton and the Church Committee', *Journal of Cold War Studies*, 15 (Fall 2013), 128–48.

Johnson, Loch K. (ed). 'An *INS* Special Forum: Implications of the Snowden Leaks', *Intelligence and National Security*, 29 (December 2014), 793–810.

Johnson, Loch K. 'H-Diplo/ISSF Forum on Loch K. Johnson and others, "An *INS* Special Forum [above]"', *H-Diplo/ISSF Forum*, 4 (2015): http://issforum.org/ISSF/PDF/ISSF-Forum-4.pdf.

Johnston, Thomas. *The History of the Working Classes in Scotland* (Glasgow: Forward Publishing, 1920).

Joler, Vladan. 'The Price You Pay for Using Free Apps', *Wired* (August 2015), 21–2.

Kahn, David. *The Reader of Gentlemen's Mail: Herbert O. Yardley and the Birth of American Codebreaking* (New Haven: Yale University Press, 2004).

Keefe, Patrick Radden. *Chatter: Uncovering the Echelon Surveillance Network and the Secret World of Global Eavesdropping* (New York: Random House, 2006).

Kenny, Kevin. *Making Sense of the Molly Maguires* (Oxford: Oxford University Press, 1998).

Knightley, Phillip. *The Second Oldest Profession: The Spy as Bureaucrat, Patriot, Fantasist and Whore* (London: Andre Deutsch, 1986).

Kreitner, Richard (ed.). *Surveillance Nation: Critical Reflections on Privacy and its Threats* (New York: The Nation, 2014).

Ladurie, Emmanuel Le Roy. *Montaillou, village occitan de 1294 à 1324* (Paris: Gallimard, 1975).

Landau, Susan. *Surveillance or Security? The Risks Posed by New Wiretapping Technologies* (Cambridge, MA: MIT Press, 2010).

Le Carré, John. *A Delicate Truth* (London: Penguin, 2014).

Leigh, David and Luke Harding. *WikiLeaks* (London: Guardian, 2013).

Lomas, Daniel W. B. '"…the Defence of the Realm and Nothing Else": Sir Findlater Stewart, Labour Ministers and the Security Service', *Intelligence and National Security*, 30 (December 2015), 793–816.

Lowenthal, Max. *The Federal Bureau of Investigation* (New York: Sloane, 1950).

Lukas, J. Anthony. *Big Trouble* (New York: Simon & Schuster, 1997).

Lyon, David. *The Electronic Eye: The Rise of Surveillance Society* (Oxford: Polity Press, 1994).

Lyon, David. *Surveillance after September 11* (Cambridge: Polity, 2003).

Lyon, David. *Surveillance Studies: An Overview* (Cambridge: Polity, 2007).

Lyon, David. 'Surveillance and the Eye of God', *Studies in Christian Ethics*, 27 (February 2014), 21–32.

MacDonnell, Francis. *Insidious Foes: The Axis Fifth Column and the American Home Front* (New York: Oxford University Press, 1995).

McIvor, Arthur. '"A Crusade for Capitalism": The Economic League, 1919–39', *Journal of Contemporary History*, 23 (October 1988), 631–55.

McIvor, Arthur and Hugh Patterson. 'Combatting the Left: Victimization and Anti-Labour Activities on Clydeside, 1900–1922', in Robert Duncan and Arthur McIvor (eds.), *Militant Workers: Labour and Class Conflict on the Clyde, 1900–1950* (Edinburgh: John Donald, 1992), 106–28.

Madison, James H. 'The Evolution of Commercial Credit Reporting Agencies in Nineteenth-Century America', *Business History Review*, 48 (Summer 1974), 164–86.

Mahl, Thomas E. *British Covert Operations in the United States, 1939–44* (Washington, DC: Brassey's, 1998).

Manget, Fred F. 'Intelligence and the Rise of Judicial Intervention', in Loch K. Johnson (ed.), *Handbook of Intelligence Studies* (London: Routledge, 2007), 329–42.

Mangold, Tom. *Cold Warrior: James Jesus Angleton: The CIA's Master Spy Hunter* (London: Simon and Schuster, 1991).

Mattelart, Armand. *The Globalization of Surveillance: The Origin of the Securitarian Order* (Cambridge: Polity, 2010).

Medsger, Betty. *The Burglary: The Discovery of J. Edgar Hoover's Secret FBI* (New York: Vintage, 2014).

Miles, Anne D. *Intelligence Spending: In Brief* (Washington, DC: Congressional Research Service, 2016).

Millman, Brock. *Managing Domestic Dissent in First World War Britain* (London: Frank Cass, 2000).

Moran, Christopher. 'Turning against the CIA: Whistleblowers during the "Time of Troubles"', *History*, 100 (April 2015), 251–74.

Morgan, Kenneth O. *Rebirth of a Nation: Wales 1880–1980* (Oxford: Clarendon Press, 1981).

Morgan, Ted. *Reds: McCarthyism in Twentieth-Century America* (New York: Random House, 2003).

Murphy, Walter F. *Wiretapping on Trial: A Case Study in the Judicial Process* (New York: Random House, 1966).

Naftali, Timothy. *Blind Spot: The Secret History of American Counterterrorism* (New York: Basic, 2005).

Noakes, John A. 'Enforcing Domestic Tranquility: State Building and the Origins of the (Federal) Bureau of Investigation, 1908–1929' (University of Pennsylvania PhD, 1993).

Olmsted, Kathryn. *Challenging the Secret Government: The Post-Watergate Investigations of the CIA and FBI* (Chapel Hill: University of North Carolina Press, 1996).

Olmsted, Kathryn. 'Right across the Atlantic: British and American Anticommunism between the Wars', paper at the University of Edinburgh, 15 May 2014.

Olmsted, Kathryn. *Right out of California: The 1930s and the Big Business Roots of Modern Conservatism* (New York: The New Press, 2015).

Orwell, George. *Nineteen-Eighty Four* (London: Secker & Warburg, 1949).

Parenti, Christian. *The Soft Cage: Surveillance in America from Slavery to the War on Terror* (New York: Basic, 2003).

Parssinen, T. M. and I. J. Prothero. 'The London Tailor's Strike of 1834 and the Collapse of the Grand National Consolidated Trades' Union: A Police Spy's Report', *International Review of Social History*, 22 (April 1977), 65–107.

Pattison, Derek and Brian Bamford. *Boys on the Blacklist*, 2nd edn (Rochdale, Lancs.: Tameside TUC, 2014).

Pinkerton, Allan. *General Principles of Pinkerton's National Detective Agency* (Chicago: Fergus, 1873).

Porter, Bernard. *Plots and Paranoia: A History of Political Espionage in Britain 1790–1988* (London: Routledge, 1992 [1989]).

Potter, Karen. 'British McCarthyism', in Rhodri Jeffreys-Jones and Andrew Lownie (eds.), *North American Spies: New Revisionist Essays* (Edinburgh: Edinburgh University Press, 1991), 143–57.

Preston, Andrew. 'Monsters Everywhere: A Genealogy of National Security', *Diplomatic History*, 38 (June 2014), 477–500.

Pringle, Henry F. *Theodore Roosevelt* (London: Jonathan Cape, 1934).

Puyvelde, Damien Van. 'Quelle leçons tirer de la privitisation du renseignement aux États-Unis?' *Revue internationale et stratégique*, 87 (2012/13), 42–52.

Puyvelde, Damien Van. 'Sécurité de l'information et partenariats public-privé dans le renseignement americain', *Sécurité & stratégie*, 17 (October 2014), 25–30.

Renshaw, Patrick. *The General Strike* (London: Eyre Methuen, 1975).

Riffenburgh, Beau. *Pinkerton's Great Detective: The Amazing Life and Times of James McParland* (New York: Viking, 2013).

Rimington, Stella. *Open Secret: The Autobiography of the Former Director-General of MI5* (London: Hutchinson, 2001).

Rose, Norman. *Vansittart: Study of a Diplomat* (London: Heineman, 1978).

Rovere, Richard H. *Senator Joe McCarthy* (London: Methuen, 1959).

Rule, James B. and others. 'Documentary Identification and Mass Surveillance in the United States', *Social Problems*, 31 (December 1983), 222–34.

Ryan, Mary P. 'The Explosion of Family History', *Reviews in American History*, 10 (December 1982), 181–95.

Salper, Roberta. 'U.S. Government Surveillance and the Women's Liberation Movement, 1968–1973: A Case Study', *Feminist Studies*, 34 (Fall 2008), 431–55.

Scheuerman, William E. 'Taking Snowden Seriously: Civil Disobedience for an Age of Total Surveillance', in David P. Fidler (ed.), *The Snowden Reader* (Bloomington: Indiana University Press, 2015), 70–87.

Schneider, Bruce. *Data and Goliath: The Hidden Battles to Collect your Data and Control your World* (New York: Norton, 2015).

Schrecker, Ellen. *No Ivory Tower: McCarthyism and the Universities* (New York: Oxford University Press, 1986).

Schrecker, Ellen. *Many Are the Crimes: McCarthyism in America* (Boston: Little, Brown, 1998).

Schrecker, Ellen (ed.). *The Age of McCarthyism: A Brief History with Documents* (Boston: Bedford/St. Martin's, 2002).

Schwartz, Jr, Frederick A. O. 'Intelligence Oversight: The Church Committee', in Loch K. Johnson (ed.), *Strategic Intelligence*, 5 vols. (Westport, CT: Praeger, 2007), vol. 5, 19–45.

Schwartz, Jr, Frederick A. O. *Democracy in the Dark: The Seduction of Government Secrecy* (New York: The New Press, 2015).

Scott, Katherine A. *Reining in the State: Civil Society and Congress in the Vietnam and Watergate Eras* (Lawrence: University Press of Kansas, 2013).

Shpayer-Makov, Haia. *The Ascent of the Detective: Police Sleuths in Victorian and Edwardian England* (Oxford: Oxford University Press, 2011).

Sielman, Jean E. *The Stool Pigeon and the Open Shop Movement* (Minneapolis: American Publishing Company, 1923).

Smist, Frank J. *Congress Oversees the United States Intelligence Community, 1947–1987* (Knoxville: University of Tennessee Press, 1990).

Smith, Dave and Phil Chamberlain. *Blacklisted: The Secret War between Big Business and Union Activists* (Oxford: New International Publications, 2015).

Smith, James. *British Writers and MI5 Surveillance, 1930–1960* (Cambridge: Cambridge University Press, 2013).

Sorel, Georges. *Reflections on Violence*, trans. T. E. Hulme (New York: Free Press, 1950 [1908]).

Sparrow, Elizabeth. 'The Alien Office, 1792–1806', *The Historical Journal*, 33 (June 1990), 361–84.

Stansky, Peter and William Abrahams. *Orwell: The Transformation* (London: Constable, 1979).

Talbert, Jr, Roy. *Negative Intelligence: The Army and the American Left, 1917–1941* (Jackson: University Press of Mississippi, 1991).

Theoharis, Athan. *Spying on Americans: Political Surveillance from Hoover to the Huston Plan* (Philadelphia: Temple University Press, 1978).

Theoharis, Athan. *The Truman Presidency and the Origins of the Imperial Presidency and the National Security State* (Stanfordville, NY: Earl E. Coleman Enterprises, 1979).

Theoharis, Athan. *The FBI and American Democracy: A Brief Critical History* (Lawrence: University Press of Kansas, 2004).

Theoharis, Athan. *Abuse of Power: How Cold War Surveillance and Secrecy Policy Shaped the Response to 9/11* (Philadelphia: Temple University Press, 2011).

Thompson, E. P. *The Making of the English Working Class* (Harmondsworth: Penguin, 1968).

Torpey, John. *The Invention of the Passport: Surveillance, Citizenship and the State* (Cambridge: Cambridge University Press, 2000).

Turrou, Leon G. *The Nazi Spy Conspiracy in America* (London: George G. Harrap, 1939).

Warren, Samuel D. and Louis D. Brandeis. 'The Right to Privacy', *Harvard Law Review*, 4 (15 December 1890), 193–220.

Washington, Mary Helen. *The Other Blacklist: The African American Literary and Cultural Left of the 1950s* (New York: Columbia University Press, 2014).

Weiss, Martin A. and Kristin Archik. *US–EU Data Privacy: From Safe Harbor to Privacy Shield* (Washington, DC: Congressional Research Service, 2016).

Whitaker, Reg. 'The Failure of Official Accountability and the Rise of Guerilla Accountability', in Michael Geist (ed.), *Law, Privacy and Surveillance in Canada in the Post-Snowden Era* (Ottawa: Ottawa University Press, 2015), 205–24.

Whitaker, Reg. 'The Surveillance State', in Leo Panitch and Greg Albo (eds.), *Socialist Register 2016: The Politics of the Right* (Powys, Wales: Merlin Press, 2015), 347–73.

Wilford, Hugh. *The CIA, the British Left and the Cold War: Calling the Tune?* (London: Frank Cass, 2003).

Willis, Resa. *FDR and Lucy: Lovers and Friends* (New York: Routledge, 2004).

Winkler, Allan M. *The Politics of Propaganda: The Office of War Information, 1942–1945* (New Haven: Yale University Press, 1978).

Wright, Peter. *Spycatcher: The Candid Autobiography of a Senior Intelligence Officer* (New York: Viking Penguin, 1987).

ILLUSTRATION CREDITS

2.   Courtesy of the Library of Congress.

3.   US National Archives photo no. 111-SC-155490.

4.   Cartoon by David Low. The British Cartoon Archive, http://www. cartoons.ac.uk, © Solo Syndication and *The Mail on Sunday*.

5.   © The author.

6.   Cartoon by J.W. Taylor © Punch Limited.

7.   Cartoon by Steve Breen. By permission of Steve Breen and Creators Syndicate, Inc.

8.   © Neil Findlay.

INDEX